TOWARD A NUCLEAR PEACE

The Future of Nuclear Weapons

Edited by

Michael J. Mazarr

and

Alexander T. Lennon

St. Martin's Press
New York
in association with
the Center for Strategic and International Studies

First published in the United States of America 1994

Printed in the United States of America
Design by Acme Art, Inc.

ISBN 0-312-10404-9

Library of Congress Cataloging-in-Publication Data

Toward a nuclear peace : the future of nuclear weapons / edited by
    Michael J. Mazarr and Alexander T. Lennon.
        p. cm.
    Includes bibliographical references.
    ISBN 0-312-10404-9
    1. Nuclear arms control—United States. 2. Nuclear arms control
—Soviet Union. I. Mazarr, Michael J., 1965- . II. Lennon,
Alexander T.   III. Center for Strategic and International Studies
(Washington, D.C.)
JX1974.7.T678 1994
327.1'74—dc20   93-28019
                                                                 CIP

CONTENTS

Part II: European Nuclear Forces

Part I

United States Nuclear Policy
by Nuclear Strategy Study Group

1

The Future of Arms Control

In June 1992, U.S. president George Bush and Russian president Boris Yeltsin met in Washington for their first major summit. The two leaders, chiefs of state from formerly bitter adversaries now meeting as friends, announced a number of major initiatives. Most profound, in many ways, was their accord on nuclear arms control: by roughly the year 2000, Bush and Yeltsin agreed, Russia and the United States would cut their strategic nuclear arsenals to a level of not more than 3,500 warheads, less than a third of their peak during the cold war. Many observers immediately hailed the agreement as the most important symbol to date of the cold war's passing and a positive step toward lasting U.S.-Russian friendship.

Perhaps unintentionally, however, START II (as the initiative has become known) achieved something else as well. It exhausted the consensus, in the United States and elsewhere, on the future of arms control. Most arms control specialists in the United States, as well as officials in Europe and other regions with a stake in U.S.-Russian relations, had agreed that reductions to roughly 3,000 warheads on each side were a good idea. (Table 1.1, "National U.S. and Russian Strategic Forces Under START II," displays force totals under the accord.) Most U.S. analysts also concurred that banning land-based intercontinental ballistic missiles (ICBMs) with more than one warhead, another central element of START II, would improve strategic stability.

Once one began talking about reductions below 3,000 warheads, however—or about complementary arms control measures like a Comprehensive Test Ban Treaty, a pledge of no first use of nuclear weapons, or a ban on tactical nuclear weapons—that consensus broke down. The U.S. Air Force, backed by an influential outside report prepared at the Defense

Department's request, argued that U.S. world responsibilities demanded the indefinite maintenance of a nuclear arsenal close to 3,000 warheads in size, supported by continued nuclear testing and a robust modernization program. Cautious observers questioned the value of further cuts, arguing that smaller nuclear arsenals were not inherently desirable—and might actually be inherently *un*desirable.

In an important sense, therefore, nuclear arms control has reached a crossroads. The end of the cold war and beginning of a new U.S.-Russian relationship made START II, or something very like it, almost inevitable. From that point forward, however, the stewards of U.S. arms control policy will be wading through increasingly tangled intellectual—and political— thickets. Deeper reductions and other, more ambitious, arms control initiatives will magnify the trade-offs, controversies, and risks—as well, perhaps, as the benefits—of the process. This part aims to lay out a coherent path for this difficult period ahead, one that capitalizes on the opportunities offered by the end of the cold war while preserving central U.S. national interests. Our analysis focuses on the medium and long term and discusses what might be achieved within the framework of existing U.S. nuclear policy as well as speculating on some possible nuclear end states.

Our ideas and conclusions will emerge throughout the following chapters, but it may be useful to make one thing clear at the outset: We believe strongly that START II should not be the end of the line in U.S.-Russian arms talks. There will be an inevitable pause, because before the United States and Russia can consider going beyond START II, they must first meet its terms. This in itself will be a difficult enough challenge, one likely to absorb several years of diligent effort. And it is critical that this task be done well and thoughtfully: getting the implementation and verification of START II right is a key prerequisite for subsequent accords.

Nonetheless, progress beyond START II is necessary, justified, and probably inevitable in both numerical and operational arms control. The U.S. government must begin thinking about what interests it has at stake in the arms control process and what accords would meet those interests. In other words, the United States needs a new road map for nuclear arms control.

ONE PREREQUISITE: CONTINUED REFORM IN RUSSIA

A pressing question that immediately arises in connection with any study of arms control has to do with politics in Russia: What does one assume about the end of the cold war? Does one take it for granted that U.S.-Russian

Table 1.1

National U.S. and Russian Strategic Forces Under START II

UNITED STATES	Delivery Vehicles	Warheads
ICBMs (Minuteman III)	500	500
SLBMs (Trident I, 4 warheads)	192	768
(Trident II, 4 warheads)	240	960
Bombers (B-52H with 8-12 ALCM)	93	952
(B-2 with 16 bombs)	20	320
	——	——
TOTALS	**1,045**	**3,500**

RUSSIA	Delivery Vehicles	Warheads
ICBMs (SS-25 in SS-18 silos)	90	90
(Mobile SS-25)	500	500
(SS-19)	105	105
SLBMs (SS-N-18, 3 warheads)	192	576
(SS-N-23, 4 warheads)	112	448
(SS-N-20, 6 warheads)	120	720
Bombers (Bear-H with ALCMs)	60	800
	——	——
TOTALS	**1,179**	**3,239**

hostility is a thing of the past? Or must one design all arms control treaties taking into consideration that Russia's incomplete experiment with democracy could collapse under the weight of economic disorder and social unrest?

Already it is clear that this question is more than a theoretical one. As of this writing, conservatives in Moscow are challenging President Boris Yeltsin, and the survival of a reformist government is in serious question.

This section deals with this issue simply by presuming that a government will remain in power in Russia with which the United States feels able to reach arms control agreements. This presumption could encompass a wide range of circumstances, but at a minimum it assumes that aggressive nationalists do not rise to power and that U.S.-Russian hostility is not reinvoked. It is fruitless to try to insulate the analysis or practice of arms control from a *complete* reversal of reform in Moscow. If Yeltsin's government fell to a truly hard-line regime, political considerations in the United States—and perhaps in Russia as well as elsewhere in the West—would stymie efforts toward more radical arms control.

There are many degrees of reform, however, and many somewhat more cautious versions of a Yeltsin government with which the West could do business. Arms control could survive many peaks and valleys in the reform process, such as the ouster of free-market-oriented Prime Minister Yegor Gaidar in December 1992—and even, possibly, Yeltsin's replacement by friendly, if economically cautious and democratically suspect, conservatives. And in the meanwhile, more ambitious arms control, if fully or even partially implemented *before* a collapse of reform in Russia, would mitigate the effects of such a collapse; chapter 2 makes the case for this argument.

NUCLEAR STRATEGY: A TWO-PHASE APPROACH

For the purposes of our analysis, it will be helpful to think of the future of nuclear strategy as a two-phase process. Two very different questions are at stake today: What further arms control is justified given the present role of nuclear weapons in defending and promoting U.S. national security? And what bolder vision of nuclear arms control might achieve a more fundamental contribution to that security? These two questions represent the short-term and long-term issues facing arms control, and they must be considered separately. Each subsequent chapter will approach its subject at least partly through the intellectual prism of this distinction.

In our analysis of the initial phase, therefore—a period that, for the sake of discussion, we will define as lasting until roughly 2010—we will examine what further steps in nuclear arms control are possible and desirable *without changing any fundamental assumptions* of U.S. nuclear strategy. The analysis will consider both the number of warheads in U.S. and Russian inventories and associated arms control measures such as a test ban treaty and a ban on tactical nuclear weapons. The number of warheads each held by Washington and Moscow would fall to roughly 1,000 or fewer.

Even during this period, and certainly in subsequent periods, the role of other existing and potential nuclear powers will become far more important. The "middle" nuclear powers—China, France, and the United Kingdom—will have to be included in the arms control process, and nonproliferation efforts must continue to keep the nuclear club from growing. These issues are discussed in subsequent chapters.

This part's examination of a second, more distant phase of nuclear arms control, which is largely confined to chapter 7, will consider more basic issues. A time may well come when international politics and U.S. security requirements have evolved to the point where the current assumptions of U.S. nuclear policy no longer hold. At this point it may become necessary for states now possessing nuclear weapons to agree upon some nuclear end state, whether it be nonoperational nuclear forces, international control, or some other arrangement. Chapter 7 will discuss which end states would be most desirable for international and U.S. security. Indeed, clarity as to the nuclear end state may be crucial to stability and success in more immediate arms control.

Distinguishing between these two phases will require determining the cutoff point below which the existing roles and missions of the U.S. nuclear force cannot be sustained. To define such a point, we need a firm understanding of what those roles and missions are. Table 1.2, "Assumptions of Current U.S. Nuclear Policy," attempts to specify the current, major assumptions of U.S. nuclear strategy. Taken together, these assumptions would define the cutoff point; their absence would indicate a shift from the first phase to the second.

In the analysis that follows, chapter 2 lays out the case for further arms control. Chapters 3 through 6 then examine the issues involved in the arms control process during the initial phase of arms control: how many nuclear weapons are required, what their role is in extended and regional deterrence, and what contributions can be made by strategic defenses. Each of these chapters presumes that all nine assumptions noted below continue more or less to hold true. In chapter 7, the study turns to longer-term questions, discarding those assumptions and attempting to conceive some desirable and feasible nuclear end state.

Whether or not one accepts every assumption, it is undeniable that the time has come for a major reexamination of U.S. nuclear strategy and force structure. For forty years, the cold war held the threat of imminent nuclear devastation over world politics, a threat that the United States and its allies turned to their advantage through the strategies of massive retaliation and flexible response. The conditions that brought that threat into being, and

Table 1.2
Assumptions of Current U.S. Nuclear Policy

Assumption 1. The international system remains essentially anarchic, and a case can be made that nuclear weapons play an important role in keeping peace between major powers by rendering war unthinkably destructive.

Assumption 2. A full-scale nuclear retaliation would be capable of causing what is generally understood to be "assured destruction." This might roughly be defined as tens of millions to hundreds of millions of immediate deaths, the annihilation of much civilian and military industry, and the end of advanced society as we know it in some parts of the targeted nation for a period of years.

Assumption 3. A full-scale nuclear retaliation would do enough damage to military installations to fulfill the notion of "military sufficiency"—that is, to do enough damage to an aggressor's military to render that military ineffective. We have already reached the point at which a capability for nuclear warfighting is not integral to U.S. nuclear strategy and Russian forces cannot conduct a disarming first strike.

Assumption 4. United States nuclear forces are capable, in both military and political terms, of extending deterrence to allies; French and British nuclear forces cannot do so, or at least not in any substantial fashion.

Assumption 5. The dominant nuclear balance remains a bipolar one. None of the "middle" nuclear powers has deterrent forces that match those of Russia and the United States. They might come closer, but as a rule of thumb Washington and Moscow will each control roughly as many warheads as all the middle powers combined.

Assumption 6. Nuclear forces held by developing-world proliferators do not provide a guide for force numbers, nuclear strategy, or procurement. Neither the United States nor Russia produces low-yield weapons (sometimes called "mininukes" or "micronukes") designed primarily for deterring—or, if deterrence fails, attacking—regional powers.

Assumption 7. Pressure from advocates of strategic defense continues a slow, gradual trend toward the deployment of defenses against tactical ballistic missiles as well as limited, ground-based strategic defenses. These plans will not include major space-based components for many years. If the United States and Russia cooperate at all on such systems, they do so only in a limited fashion and largely on nonweapons components of the systems.

Assumption 8. Spending on nuclear forces will continue to decline. Budget pressures will add force to arguments about the cost-effectiveness and fiscal sustainability of various force levels.

Assumption 9. Arms reductions have significant effects on the drive for reform and democracy in Russia. Properly designed treaties will help Russia cut its defense budget and dismantle its defense industry while convincing Russian military leaders that the United States is dealing honestly and fairly and not seeking any advantage. Arms treaties that try to maximize short-term gains for the United States—such as the recent Washington summit agreement—can have the opposite effect.

which prompted NATO to make a devil's bargain with it, have now changed. The United States badly needs a better sense of long-term direction in its nuclear policy, a new strategy calculated to address the risk of nuclear war, the accumulated U.S. and Russian nuclear infrastructures, and the growing danger of the proliferation of weapons of mass destruction.

This section suggests one possible strategy to achieve those goals, and we believe our recommendations to be worthwhile. But even more important than any specific proposal is the broader need to encourage a fundamental rethinking of the roles of nuclear weapons in world politics and in U.S. policy. This book aims to begin such a process.

2

The Case for Further Progress

In the wake of START II, new questions are being asked about the future of arms control. Where do we go from here? What new nuclear future do we wish to build for ourselves? Presumably, that future will at some point involve fewer than 6,000 nuclear warheads, and far fewer, we hope. Already many observers have called for much more ambitious long-term disarmament schemes.

It is not self-evident, however, that additional steps should be taken beyond START II. During the cold war, the strongest arguments for arms control were that it would reduce the risk of war and contribute to an overall improvement in U.S.-Soviet relations. With these goals now achieved, some observers see little reason to cut strategic nuclear weapons beyond the levels mandated by the new agreement. It is simply not clear, even to some in the arms control community, why Washington and Moscow should go further, why a balance at 1,000 weapons is intrinsically preferable to one at 3,000, presuming that are both stable and secure—especially now that the risk of war is so low.[1]

Brent Scowcroft betrayed such a skepticism of deep cuts at an October 1988 conference. "We are asked," he said, "to take the value of deep reductions pretty much on faith." Under the right circumstances, reductions in nuclear forces could be valuable, but Scowcroft worried that they could also impair strategic stability, add burdens to verification, and increase incentives to cheat. "My point here," Scowcroft added, "is not to say that we are necessarily wrong [to propose deep cuts], but that the arguments in favor of this course seem singularly unpersuasive. What are the rewards of deep cuts which would lead us to undergo the kinds of risks they may present?"[2]

In this chapter we lay the groundwork for the overall study by arguing that more progress in arms control—reductions to lower numbers of weapons, reductions in alert rates, and controls on the production of nuclear weapons—would indeed offer important rewards. These are reducing the risk of war, limiting damage if war occurs, forestalling proliferation, and reducing cost.

REDUCING THE RISK OF WAR

The one objective of arms control that has probably enjoyed the broadest support is that of enhancing stability and reducing the risk of war. Arms control's wide appeal is attributable to its role in promoting U.S. national security: properly designed arms treaties can reduce the threat of nuclear attack on the United States, partly by enhancing the security of the U.S. deterrent force and partly by reducing mistrust with potential adversaries. Thus, war prevention is among the most common themes in arms control literature.

Today there seems little urgency to this task, with the risk of war so low already. But additional steps in operational and numerical arms control can help make a new cold war less likely. Arms control can also provide a hedge against new international rivalries by enhancing the stability of the nuclear balance and reducing the risk of a "breakout," or rapid buildup, of nuclear weapons.

In the short term, arms control can help prevent accidental war by reducing the threat posed by Russia's unstable nuclear command and control structure. There is a debate as to how much of a concern this ought to be, but few would deny that there is some risk of accidental or unauthorized use. Nuclear weapons could become pawns in dangerous political and military schemes. Deep cuts, reductions in alert rates, and other steps would address this risk directly: smaller and less-active strategic arsenals are easier to control and less likely to fall into unreliable hands. In the right circumstances, such steps might also accelerate the process of denuclearizing Kazakhstan and Ukraine.

More fundamentally, when viewed as part of a broader U.S.-Russian dialogue on nuclear issues, deep reductions in nuclear weapons can give tangible evidence of friendship and thereby help sustain the momentum for peace. If Russia and the United States have truly overcome their mutual hostility and become geopolitical friends and partners, then they certainly cannot justify keeping 6,000 or more nuclear weapons aimed, rhetoric aside, primarily at each other. By slashing their nuclear arsenals, they can serve powerful notice—to each other and the world—that they are serious about their new relationship.

In short, the U.S.-Russian nuclear balance must come to reflect relations between friends rather than between adversaries. If it does not, then deeply held fears and suspicions on both sides may well reemerge, energized by the latent risk of huge nuclear arsenals.

Finally, arms control can provide insurance against a failure of reform in Russia. It can do this in two ways: by making breakout more difficult and by enhancing the stability of the nuclear balance.

Small nuclear forces on a low-alert posture hedge against breakout more effectively than large ones. If, in a move to very small nuclear forces, both sides agree to take most or all nuclear forces off alert and to close down and dismantle virtually all nuclear production sites—for fissile materials, warheads, and delivery vehicles—then a hostile government in Moscow would have to reactivate its existing nuclear arsenal and rebuild its entire nuclear industry to make a new arms race possible. If the two sides eschew operational and numerical cuts much beyond 3,000 warheads, on the other hand, they can keep much of their nuclear infrastructure intact, thus allowing a more rapid breakout in the event of a reversal in Moscow.

Arguments that it would be dangerous to have cut to a level of 1,000 or fewer warheads also presume that smaller balances are inherently less stable, but this need not be the case. In fact, arms control measures beyond the June 1992 Bush-Yeltsin agreement could, if designed wisely, enhance strategic stability. The effect of all arms control, of course, depends on the details, and it is by no means true that smaller force numbers produce a linear increase in stability. Indeed, many have argued that the opposite is true. If designed properly, however, arms control can render the strategic balance more secure by

- *Reducing warheads, not targets.* Reductions could come primarily in warheads deployed on existing systems, rather than the delivery systems themselves. Additional numerical cuts can improve stability by changing the ratios of attacking warheads to defending targets in favor of the defense, thus discouraging first strikes and enhancing strategic stability.[3] Chapter 3 makes a more detailed analysis of the vulnerability issue.

- *Eliminating the hair trigger.* Reductions in the operational tempo of nuclear forces can also make the nuclear balance more secure. If nuclear weapons are configured so as to require hours or days of preparation before being launched, and if that preparation is easily observable, then a first strike becomes almost impossible. Chapter 3 suggests a number of operational arms control measures.

• *Reducing the risk of destabilizing new weapons.* Finally, prohibitions on certain elements of the nuclear weapons production cycle would make it much more difficult for either side to develop or deploy new technologies that could threaten the nuclear balance. Without the ability to obtain fissile material for new bombs, or to test new nuclear weapons or missiles, the militaries of both sides would be out of the nuclear modernization business. Neither would be able to obtain the dangerous weapons, now on the drawing board, that may render mobile or silo-based ICBMs, and perhaps someday even submarines, vulnerable.

DAMAGE LIMITATION

Limiting damage to the United States in the event of war has long been a goal of U.S. nuclear strategy and remains so. For some time, however, seeking damage limitation through counterforce—destroying the enemy's nuclear force before it can be used—has been a losing proposition for the United States. The alternative, of course, is arms reduction. To this point we have been looking at various types of arms control, but here the focus is on numbers: by slashing the number of warheads that could be used in a nuclear war and by promoting escalation control, deep cuts would reduce the damage inflicted by such a war.

Such calculations involve many variables, and casualty and damage estimates are necessarily very rough. But in a nuclear war, smaller arsenals might do less damage and kill fewer people. It is possible to imagine a conflict in which 1,000 weapons would kill more people than 3,000, but, in many circumstances, reducing the number of weapons fired in a war might well reduce the amount of damage done in that war. And when the difference involves tens of millions of human beings and spares whole cities from attack, it is a difference worth considering.

Some have criticized smaller nuclear forces on the grounds that they might actually increase damage by forcing both sides to target mostly cities. This argument is not persuasive. For one thing, smaller nuclear forces are not restricted to targeting cities alone. Chapter 3 lays out a possible targeting scheme focused on conventional military forces and the industries that support them; such an attack would of course do enormous collateral damage to society and would shoot a number of warheads at military industries located in the heart of major cities, but it would not be aimed at civilian populations per se. Moreover, all unclassified reports indicate that U.S. nuclear plans contain many urban-industrial targets and always have. Thus a retaliation from a force of 3,000 warheads might not aim fewer weapons at cities than a smaller arsenal—it would merely have more left over to shoot at other targets.

Yet the advantage gained through pure numerical reductions is hardly linear, and indeed, many would argue that it is hardly noticeable at all in the difference between 3,500 and 1,000 warheads. But additional arms control offers a second route to damage limitation: escalation control—halting the conflict after only a few warheads have been fired for negotiations or a pause in hostilities.

Additional numerical and operational arms agreements would help, not hinder, efforts at escalation control. A state with a large nuclear arsenal may be much more likely to fire more nuclear weapons in an initial strike than one with a minimum deterrent. In either case, if a "demonstration shot" is intended, then the initial attack will be very small. But if the first strike has military significance, then the attacker has reason to fire a larger salvo. With arsenals of 3,000 warheads or more, an initial strike short of an all-out, disarming blow might be as large as several hundred warheads; achieving escalation control after such an attack would be exceedingly difficult. A nation with only 500 or 750 warheads, on the other hand, might be hesitant to shoot more than 30 or 40 in a first salvo, and might shoot far fewer than that. By magnifying the importance of each warhead, deep cuts reduce the ability to conduct large initial attacks and thereby promote escalation control. Operational restraints, such as reduced alert rates and the verification schemes that accompany them, would also promote escalation control.

For these reasons, deeper reductions in nuclear weapons and new operational arms control measures would reduce the destruction that would result if, despite the best efforts of nations, a nuclear war did occur.

REINVIGORATING THE NONPROLIFERATION TREATY

With the collapse of the Soviet Union, efforts to restrain the proliferation of weapons of mass destruction assumed chief importance for many world powers, especially the United States. Yet those concerned with proliferation often forget that the United States is treaty-bound to seek a reduction of its own nuclear arsenal as a corollary to Third World nonproliferation.[4] The U.S. and Soviet failure to do so is often cited by China, India, and other developing states as a reason the Nonproliferation Treaty (NPT) has no legitimacy. By continuing to maintain (and in some cases modernize) large nuclear arsenals, Washington and Moscow send a strong signal about the persisting value of nuclear weapons, a signal that cannot be lost on leaders in the developing world.

With the NPT up for renewal in 1995, the next several years constitute a defining moment in the history of global arms control. All U.S. and Russian decisions during this period will be watched carefully. Major new arms control initiatives can give powerful impetus to the worldwide drive for nonproliferation.[5]

Several lines of analysis support this general point. For one thing, it is clear that several of the linchpin nations in the nonproliferation field pay close attention to the size and operations of U.S. and Russian nuclear forces. China, whose cooperation will be vital in forestalling the spread of nuclear weapons, has real and legitimate concerns about the relative size of U.S. and Russian nuclear stockpiles compared with its own. If dramatic reductions in U.S. and Russian arsenals put Chinese leaders more at ease about their strategic position, then they might be more willing to cease undermining the spirit and enforcement of the NPT.

India has based its own program partly on the supposed threat from Chinese and U.S. arsenals, and the Indian case provides an example of how U.S.-Russian restraint can influence proliferation. Although Delhi has been most concerned with a Chinese threat, there is some connection between the Indian nuclear weapons program and a veiled U.S. nuclear threat: during India's 1971 invasion of Pakistan, the U.S. aircraft carrier *Enterprise* appeared in the Bay of Bengal, a move India interpreted as a nuclear threat. "Although this was untrue," notes Kathleen Bailey, "it did influence the debate over the development of nuclear weapons" in India.[6] Even today, many strategic thinkers in New Delhi assume that U.S. nuclear weapons are pointed their way. They know that China's nuclear arsenal is, and they hope to break Beijing's regional nuclear monopoly. India's pursuit of the bomb was legitimized in part by the earlier U.S. effort: the legitimacy of nuclear weapons "is reinforced by the [U.S.] doctrine of nuclear deterrence," writes one Indian analyst, which "provides a powerful conceptual base and incentive for nuclear proliferation."[7]

Thus, while India has many motives besides central deterrence for acquiring nuclear weapons—to support its military objectives in South Asia, for example, and to reaffirm its position as a major world power—a drastic reduction in U.S. and Chinese arsenals would help remove Indian justifications for nuclear weapons. If such a move did not persuade New Delhi to abandon its existing program, at least it would help forestall the trend in Indian (and Pakistani) thinking that favors open declaration and deployment of nuclear arsenals rather than secretive research and covert assembly of bombs. This is not a trifling concern, for once the weapons are out in the open it may be impossible to get rid of them.

With the collapse of the Soviet Union, the world suddenly acquired three more linchpin states in the nonproliferation arena—the new states of Ukraine, Kazakhstan, and Belarus. Each had nuclear weapons from the former Soviet arsenal on its territory, and each will keep a watchful eye on Russia when deciding whether to agree to complete disarmament. In theory, by the Lisbon Protocol of May 1992, all three nations committed themselves to the provisions of START and, as rapidly as possible, to joining the Nonproliferation Treaty as nuclear-free states. This goal is critical: if any of the three former Soviet republics decided to keep its arsenal, other countries—most notably Germany—might well rethink their position as well, and Russian leaders might be forced to rule out further reductions in their nuclear force.

As of this writing it is unclear whether all three—or, indeed, any of the three—will give up their nuclear weapons. None has demanded complete Russian disarmament as a condition for doing so, and all, especially Ukraine, have so far emphasized their desire for economic, as opposed to strategic, rewards for nonproliferation. Russia's commitment to much deeper reductions in nuclear forces, however, would remove part of the strategic rationale for proliferation and remove a major excuse on these nations' part for failing to join the NPT. And once they have joined the treaty, deep cuts in Russian forces would help keep them there.

Second, even if, as some suggest, the concern expressed by potential proliferators about U.S. and Russian programs is insincere, it would be well worth exposing that concern as such and forcing proliferators to fall back on other arguments. Arms control that deprives proliferators of *excuses* and not *reasons* for proliferation is still valuable; the former are often as much a barrier to nonproliferation as the latter. Nonproliferation efforts in the 1990s and beyond will take on a wide-ranging diplomatic, military, and economic cast. Convincing a state not to go nuclear will require a subtle combination of carrots and sticks—addressing its security concerns, raising the prospect of economic and political sanctions, granting it additional diplomatic respect, and so on. Deep reductions in U.S. and Russian nuclear forces could play an important role in such a tapestry of nonproliferation measures, depriving proliferators of a traditional excuse and perhaps allaying some of their concerns. And if such steps become part of a general shift in world opinion against the utility and cost effectiveness (in the broadest sense) of nuclear weapons, then their effects would be even greater.

Third and finally, elements of a U.S.-Russian deep-cuts treaty could be extended worldwide and used as powerful tools against proliferation. A nuclear test ban, for example, would add a further hurdle for any states hoping to achieve declared nuclear weapons status. Nonnuclear-weapons states have for some time focused on a test ban as the most direct avenue to halt the East-West arms race, and the lack of progress on this issue is particularly galling to those states that signed away their right to possess nuclear weapons in the NPT. If some version of a comprehensive test ban (CTB) is not in place by 1995, the NPT could well collapse.

A CTB could be complemented by other steps: a global ban on the production of fissile materials for nuclear weapons, for example, would deny proliferators the building blocks of weapons, partly by justifying a nuclear inspection regime far more robust than the current International Atomic Energy Agency (IAEA) system, which is not well designed for dealing with uncooperative states. The United States cannot expect the developing world to look favorably on such a proposal until more progress is made in U.S.-Russian arms control.

REDUCING COST

Much smaller nuclear forces would also cost less than existing or planned ones. The cost savings will not be dramatic, because most nuclear modernization has come to a halt and most expensive new nuclear systems will likely remain on the drawing board. Yet deep reductions of several thousand warheads less than START II levels would save several billion dollars per year in operations, maintenance, and other standing costs of the nuclear balance.[8] With the changed nuclear strategy and reduced forces proposed in this study, for example, the planned upgrade of U.S. Minuteman III missiles could be canceled; the de facto termination of the Trident II missile retrofit could be made formal; additional B-52 bombers could be released from service; and the operational tempo, and thus expense, of the remaining forces would be much reduced.

Perhaps more important, additional arms control might make unnecessary a new round of modernization. Within a decade, many of the systems in the U.S. strategic arsenal—even some of the original Ohio-class submarines— will be reaching the end of their service lives. If by that time world nuclear arsenals have declined considerably, those older systems could merely be mustered out of the force as part of continuing arms reductions. If, on the other hand, U.S. strategic forces remain at a level of 3,000 warheads, new systems—and new expenditures—may be required.

THE BENEFITS OF FURTHER REDUCTIONS

On close examination, then, it appears that there are good reasons to continue reducing nuclear forces beyond the 3,000 to 3,500 mandated by the most recent U.S.-Russian agreement. This chapter has not attempted to prove that a balance at lower numerical and operational levels would be sufficient for deterrence—in either a political or military sense, in the U.S.-Russian context or outside it; those topics are addressed in subsequent chapters. The purpose here was merely to suggest that bolder steps in arms control would be valuable if the other criteria for U.S. security were met.

NOTES

1. Charles Glaser has suggested that "once the superpowers resolve their disputes and develop confidence that these problems will remain resolved, there would be essentially no need to disarm." Charles Glaser, *Analyzing Strategic Nuclear Policy* (Princeton, N.J.: Princeton University Press, 1990), pp. 200-201.
2. Quoted in Thomas Wander, Elizabeth J. Kirk, and Eric H. Arnett, eds., *Science and Security: Technology and Arms Control for the 1990s* (Washington, D.C.: American Association for the Advancement of Science, 1989), pp. 79-80.
3. The question then becomes whether the smaller retaliation promised by a 1,000-warhead arsenal is sufficient for deterrence. Chapter 3 addresses this issue.
4. Article VI of the Nonproliferation Treaty of 1970 reads: "Each of the parties to the treaty undertakes to pursue negotiations in good faith on effective measures relating to cessation of the nuclear arms race at an early date and to nuclear disarmament, and on a treaty on general and complete disarmament under strict and effective international control." Cited in Council on Foreign Relations, *Blocking the Spread of Nuclear Weapons: American and European Perspectives* (New York and Belgium: Council on Foreign Relations and Centre for European Policy Studies, 1986), p. 94.
5. Proliferation expert Lewis Dunn has ably summarized the value of deep cuts in the nonproliferation context. Extension of the NPT, he writes, will depend "above all" on "whether the NPT's parties, especially the developing countries (which hold the balance of votes), agree that the nuclear weapons states have met their commitment under Article VI." To achieve this end, he recommends that the

United States and Russia reduce "to an absolute minimum the role of nuclear weapons in their relationship." Such a step would "provide irrefutable evidence" of progress in meeting article VI; "only the most dogmatic officials in developing countries," Dunn concludes, "could deny that the superpower nuclear arms race had, in effect, ended. Long-term NPT extension would be all but assured." Lewis Dunn, "Containing Nuclear Proliferation," *Adelphi Paper,* no. 263 (London: International Institute for Strategic Studies, Winter 1991), pp. 33-35.

6. Kathleen Bailey, *Doomsday Weapons in the Hands of Many: The Arms Control Challenge of the 1990s* (Urbana, Ill.: University of Illinois Press, 1991), p. 19.

7. Jasjit Singh, "Weapons Proliferation in a Disarming World," paper presented at the United Nations Institute on Disarmament, Research Conference of Research Institutes on Asia and the Pacific, March 23-25, 1992, pp. 3, 5.

8. Estimates on cost are taken from FY1992-93 authorization and appropriation reports; from Congressional Budget Office, *The START Treaty and Beyond* (Washington, D.C.: CBO, October 1991), pp. xiv-xvi; and William W. Kaufmann and John D. Steinbruner, *Decisions for Defense: Prospects for a New Order* (Washington, D.C.: The Brookings Institution, 1991).

3

How Much Is Enough?

If, as argued in the previous chapter, the nuclear balance ought to be reduced, then the immediate and timeless question of to what degree it can be reduced—or, as it is more commonly phrased, *how much is enough?*—arises once again. In the post-cold war era, just how many nuclear weapons does the United States require for its security? Is that number compatible with what Russia thinks it needs? Would both figures allow confident reductions below the 3,000 to 3,500 warhead level?

The next three chapters attempt to answer those questions by focusing on the two traditional missions for U.S. nuclear forces: central and extended deterrence. This chapter deals with central deterrence of a major nuclear attack on the United States; chapters 4 and 5 examine the roles nuclear weapons play in reassuring allies and deterring adversaries abroad.

Importantly, all three chapters assume the international context would be that of the initial phase of arms control. In other words, they discuss the minimal nuclear posture compatible with the present basic assumptions of U.S. nuclear strategy—which, in terms of central deterrence, means the minimal force capable of sustaining four of the nine assumptions laid out in chapter 1: namely, assumption 2, that a nuclear retaliation would cause assured destruction; assumption 3, that a retaliation would cause enough damage to military targets to fulfill notions of military sufficiency; assumption 5, that the dominant nuclear balance remains bipolar; and assumption 9, that this force structure cannot cost more than the existing one.

DETERRENCE

The most fundamental assumption of the nuclear age has been that any large-scale nuclear war would be unthinkably horrific for both aggressor and victim. This notion of assured destruction is highly resistant to changes in the size of the nuclear balance, having been generally accepted since the days when nuclear forces were much smaller than they are today. Even 100 or 200 nuclear weapons would flatten a host of major cities on both sides and kill tens of millions or hundreds of millions of people. There is little chance, therefore (absent large-scale deployments of strategic defenses), that reductions to some 1,000 warheads on each side will jeopardize assured destruction.

What such low levels might jeopardize, on the other hand, are traditional measurements of military sufficiency. United States nuclear planners, even of the post-cold war variety, might balk at the notion that a retaliation of a few hundred warheads, and therefore a total U.S. nuclear force of roughly 1,000 weapons—which we will term a "finite deterrence" force[1]—would offer sufficient military effect for deterrence. But if the United States altered its method of nuclear targeting and of determining military sufficiency, such a force would indeed be sufficient.

NUCLEAR STRATEGY AND THE NUMBER OF NUCLEAR WEAPONS

First, it is important to consider something of the nuclear balance's history. Since the 1950s, an enormous amount of time and energy has been devoted to shaping the U.S. nuclear force and justifying its military adequacy. Over the years, changes in the assumptions about what damage needed to be done have alternately accelerated and slowed the U.S. nuclear modernization program.

In November 1988, one year before the fall of the Berlin Wall, the U.S. Strategic Air Command completed the most extensive revision of the U.S. nuclear war plan—the Single Integrated Operational Plan (SIOP)—in a decade. Incorporating more flexible targeting options,[2] reevaluating targeting criteria, and taking advantage of the collapse of the Warsaw Pact and changes in the Soviet arsenal, this process trimmed some 20 percent of strategic targets (2,500 of 12,500) from the late-1980s plan.

Early in 1990, Secretary Dick Cheney continued this momentum by directing a "historic and unprecedented" 18-month review of strategic targeting,[3] one that was "separate and apart from the [routine] annual review."[4] A joint Department of Defense, Joint Chiefs of Staff, and Defense Intelligence Agency working group evaluated "network analysis" and targeting criteria, eliminating much layering and redundancy that had crept into the war plan over the years.[5] The review further reduced the number of warheads called for in various attack options, trimmed leadership and conventional military target sets, and deleted hundreds of targets in Eastern Europe[6]—thus eliminating another 20 percent of the earmarked targets (2,000 of 10,000 targets).

Later, in the wake of the August 1991 coup attempt in Moscow that further weakened hard-liners there and tore at the fabric of the Soviet Union itself, President George Bush directed an "urgent reassessment" of the U.S. nuclear posture.[7] This study resulted in the unilateral U.S. nuclear initiatives of September 27: the United States declared that it would eliminate all ground-based tactical nuclear weapons, consolidate sea-based tactical nuclear weapons at central sites on U.S. territory (destroying half of them), and reduce the inventory of tactical nuclear bombs based overseas. Soviet leader Mikhail Gorbachev responded with comparable Soviet initiatives on October 5. After the collapse of the Soviet Union at the end of the year, President Bush offered a second set of disarmament initiatives in his State of the Union message, canceling more weapons, and called on the new Commonwealth of Independent States to reciprocate, while proposing a scheme for the elimination of all multiple independently targeted reentry vehicle (MIRVed) ICBMs.

Meanwhile, the government continues paring away at the SIOP of October 1991. The removal of additional non-Russian targets, targets whose military function had ended, as well as many targets related to the former Soviet Union's shrinking conventional power projection capabilities, eliminated more than 3,000 of the 8,000 targets remaining in the U.S. war plan. The Department of Defense is now at work on SIOP 93, a routine reevaluation process that will probably eliminate another 40 percent of the Russian targets (2,000 of 4,800). Some 3,000 targets will remain on the lists—not coincidentally, roughly the number of weapons expected to be in the U.S. nuclear force by 2003.

Yet arsenals of 3,000 strategic warheads may finally force fundamental changes in the national targeting guidance. The commander in chief of the Supreme Allied Command, General Lee Butler, stated in 1991, referring to targeting lower than the START force levels, that "we haven't hit that breakpoint yet as we have [already] modified target sets and requirements." A limit of 3,000 warheads, he said, "would require different guidance because you couldn't cover today's target set according to today's weapons rules."[8] Butler was referring to layered targeting of hardened launching silos and underground shelters, currently accounting for almost one-third of the 4,800 targets in the SIOP target list.

While damage criteria has been lessened and target selection reformed with the end of the cold war, U.S. nuclear weapons policy has not yet been reshaped. The primacy of counternuclear targeting, the emphasis on notions of nuclear warfighting, the relationship between targets and the design of the war plan, and the size of the strategic nuclear force relative to the target base all remain largely unchanged.

A COUNTERPOWER TARGETING STRATEGY

What would a more rational post-cold war targeting strategy look like? Under a nuclear balance closer to finite deterrence, the conduct of central deterrence would change radically. No longer could the United States and Russia threaten the devastation offered by thousands of nuclear weapons to help deter war, nor could U.S. or Russian leaders rely on overkill and excess capacity to guarantee a retaliation. This leads many to conclude that a finite deterrent would be insufficient for deterrence.

The problem today is that neither of the two nuclear strategies that have dominated debates for the last forty years—counterforce and countervalue—is feasible or attractive. Given the increasing percentage of nuclear warheads on submarines and mobile missiles, even a nuclear force of 3,500 weapons would have difficulty offering a credible counternuclear punch. Smaller forces would almost certainly be incapable of reliable counterforce targeting—as they should be, in a sense, because counterforce targeting has always threatened to destabilize the nuclear balance by putting one or both side's retaliatory forces at risk. Yet a pure countervalue strategy involving retaliation against civilian targets alone is distasteful and often held to be "morally objectionable"[9]; whether or not that is true, a strategy aimed purely at the Russian people and their cities may not be politically sustainable. Nor are U.S. targeting officials likely to adopt a countervalue-only policy: the legacy of forty years of counterforce targeting argues strongly against such a shift.

What is required, then, is something between counterforce and countervalue, a strategy that aims some retaliation against enemy military targets yet continues to promise severe societal damage. Strategies known as "counterpower" (or "countercombatant," "counternational," or "countermilitary"), which aim a retaliation at conventional military forces, military bases and other facilities, defense industry, and other military-related targets, represent such a doctrine.[10] Counterpower strategies target conventional forces and the war industries that support them, with the corollary that many industrial cities are targeted as well. Nuclear forces are generally left off counterpower target lists, both because counternuclear targeting is increasingly difficult and because leaving them off may help escalation control (holding nuclear forces at risk encourages their early use). For both reasons, this approach requires an invulnerable reserve force capable of the countervalue mission.

Counterpower targeting would offer advantages over both counterforce and countervalue strategies. It would avoid the instability created by counterforce, because in a crisis neither side (or no side, if there are more than two) will fear for the safety of its deterrent force. Counterpower sidesteps the moral problems of countervalue by not explicitly targeting civilians solely for the purpose of causing deaths, and it would provide many targeting options besides suicidal ones. On the whole it is less provocative than counterforce and more flexible and credible than countervalue.

A close analysis of potential target sets, moreover, suggests that a counterpower retaliation of a few hundred warheads would be sufficient for deterrence. Russia, the largest potential target base, will apparently have a military of roughly 1.2 million to 1.5 million personnel, twenty to thirty ground divisions, ten to twenty major airfields facing the West, and between twenty and thirty major naval ports. U.S. Defense Department figures had by 1990 identified roughly forty "key Soviet military production centers," only thirteen of which appear to have been located in the Russian Republic.[11]

Allocating two warheads for each of twenty or so Russian ground force divisions, one warhead each for some sixty stationary air and naval bases, and three warheads to each of something more than thirty major industrial sites (or 100 warheads for Russian defense industry) produces a total retaliatory requirement of roughly 200 warheads. A U.S. second strike of roughly that size would appear capable of destroying most of Russia's deployed conventional forces and military industry and in the process would likely kill tens of millions of people and devastate Russian society. The threat of such damage would be more than sufficient for deterrence, and if that is true for Russia, it will also hold true for lesser military powers capable of being deterred.

In the end, of course, all judgments about the deterrent value of various nuclear arsenals must be subjective. We cannot know for certain that an arsenal of 200 or 500 or 5,000 weapons would make war impossible; war *could* occur regardless of how many nuclear weapons are deployed, although, as we have seen at a certain level of nuclear armament, the likely effects of any major war serve as a powerful disincentive to beginning one. No analysis can "prove" that a given threat of retaliation will deter war.

Nonetheless, it is difficult to escape the impression that a *retaliation* in the range of 200 to 300 warheads would be "enough." The level of social and military destruction it would cause might well have been enough even during the cold war, and it seems generous for the less-rigorous deterrent requirements of the 1990s. Given U.S.-Russian friendship and the changing perceptions of Russian leaders, the prospect of 200 or 300 nuclear weapons striking their cities and defense establishment cannot fail to make a strong impression. A careful analysis of the post-cold war requirements for deterrence, therefore, suggests that a retaliation of several hundred warheads, which would be assured by a nuclear force of roughly 1,000 weapons, would be sufficient.

SUSTAINING THE NUCLEAR MACHINE

With the end of the forty-five year period of nuclear abundance has come a disruption of the cycles of research, development, testing, and production of nuclear weapons, as well as a drastic reduction in the huge amount of resources previously allocated to the nuclear machine.

None of the U.S. military services has any new nuclear weapons in or near production. For the first time since 1958—the year the Polaris missile was test-fired—the U.S. Navy is not developing a new strategic missile; the navy's fiscal 1993 budget makes no mention of any new missiles. The air force was developing a new land-based ICBM—the Midgetman, or Small ICBM (SICBM)—but it has now been canceled. The Department of Energy has virtually halted work on new nuclear weapons, and a comprehensive test ban seems likely. Production of the B-2 bomber will be halted at fifteen to twenty aircraft, and the air force has no new-generation strategic bomber in the works.

The low level of strategic weapons production that remains will end completely by the close of this decade. The last of twenty B-2 bombers will roll off the production line in 1997-98. The last Ohio-class submarine will be delivered in the same years, and the last Trident II missiles will be produced at about the same time. New purchases of the stealthy Advanced Cruise Missile were canceled in 1992, and the last of 400 ACMs will be delivered in 1993. In short, U.S. nuclear modernization is coming to a complete halt. New systems would not be needed again until the current backbone systems in the U.S. nuclear arsenal reached critical age without any replacements at hand. The Minuteman III missile will be around through 2020, but cannot last much longer than that.[12] The first Ohio-class submarine will be twenty years old in the year 2001, even before START II is scheduled to be fully implemented.

Partly for this reason, arguments are already being heard that competent, reasonable stewardship of nuclear weapons demands a high level of activity and modernization.[13] Defense industry officials have warned the air force that cessation of missile procurement "could gut the capacity of American industry to produce ICBMs."[14] Production stoppages reportedly threaten the capacity to produce rocket motors, reentry vehicles, missile electronics and guidance systems, and nuclear-powered vessels. The military and the Department of Energy argue that cessation of nuclear weapons research and development threatens "the preservation of an environment which will continue to attract and retain a quality force of volunteers."[15] A lower level of forces can also highlight new problems in maintaining an operational force, such as having enough missiles (or sufficient testing) for follow-on test and evaluation. United States Air Force officials note that the launch rate for a given level of confidence does not vary with the number of missiles in the field.[16] Finally, retention of "a robust C^3I and strategic warning network" requires major financial investment.[17]

All of this suggests that the question of "how much is enough" may be more complicated that commonly assumed. A force level adequate for deterrence now might not be sufficient to prevent the long-term erosion of the size and quality of the U.S. deterrent, a disastrous outcome at very low levels.

On closer examination, however, the U.S. nuclear infrastructure should be supportable at a level of 1,000 warheads. The simplest issue to resolve may be the nuclear weapons design laboratories. There are simply no new warheads to produce, and at such reduced levels, the entire U.S. nuclear research and perhaps production program could be condensed from the numerous research, test, and production sites now in operation to a single lab, probably a modified Los Alamos National Laboratory. Attracting good candidates to research in the area will indeed be difficult, but it will become more difficult in any case as nuclear weapons fade into the background of world politics. And in no way will this consideration be decisive: the United States ought not to risk the trust of Russia and endanger nonproliferation efforts by retaining a large nuclear infrastructure merely to retain a better pool of nuclear scientists.

Nor would deep reductions exacerbate the challenges of future modernization. The United States has already ceased producing all major delivery vehicles and will not begin production again any time soon even if 3,500 warheads are retained. If U.S. leaders in the next century decide to replace Ohio-class submarines with a new model, or to develop a new ICBM or bomber, reducing from 3,000 to 1,000 or fewer warheads in the meantime will not make that task any harder.

In fact, deep cuts in offensive forces would lessen the modernization burden in at least two ways. In the most basic sense, further reductions would reduce the number of systems we would need to procure. While the unit costs would increase substantially, overall it would cost less to purchase 200 ICBMs than 500, 80 or 120 submarine-launched ballistic missiles (SLBMs) rather than 300 or 400, or 30 to 40 strategic bombers rather than 150 or 200, and future procurement would cause a significant balloon in current low levels of spending. But again, a force of smaller numbers is not precluded by lost research or technological capabilities.

More fundamentally, however, the only opportunity we have to make such additional modernization unnecessary lies in further arms reductions. If a cut to 1,000 or 500 warheads in the year 2010 or 2020 becomes a prelude to even more dramatic reductions, it is possible that the major powers could forgo most nuclear modernization on a nearly permanent basis. Arms control also holds the potential to restrict nuclear forces to single systems—a bomber-only force, for example—and thereby renders purchases of ICBMs and strategic submarines not only unnecessary but also illegal.

Finally, there is the issue of the day-to-day supporting nuclear infrastructure for whatever arsenal retained by the United States, including spare missiles for testing and the like. Again, this is not a persuasive reason to maintain large nuclear arsenals. No new missiles, nuclear warheads, or nuclear materials will be produced, and therefore the need for testing equipment will not now sustain the U.S. nuclear industry. The United States must retain other capabilities, such as command-and-control facilities and maintenance crews, regardless of how many weapons it has. Further reductions therefore pose no additional threat.

NUCLEAR WEAPONS AND PRESTIGE

Nuclear weapons have always been objects of prestige as the five nuclear powers sought to deny nuclear capabilities to others while modernizing and developing their own nuclear forces. During much of the cold war, the five nuclear powers viewed complete nuclear disarmament as a threat to their influence and prestige. Yet with the fall of Gorbachev and the collapse of the Soviet Union, Russia's disarmament policy has undergone an important change. The elimination of nuclear weapons is no longer being pursued as a public or private objective.

The change in Russian disarmament policy is not believed to be merely a case of other priorities overwhelming the Russian agenda. It is a subtle statement of a new reality for the former superpower. The old Soviet Union knew it was the center of the world, and any disarmament stance was part of its political strategy for the global struggle. But with the collapse of the union, nuclear weapons may be the only means by which Russia maintains the same prominence. One can only conclude that Russia will want to retain some nuclear weapons for prestige reasons in the future.

In some ways, the United States has a similar antidisarmament bias. Beyond specific threats, nuclear weapons are being promoted as useful for U.S. status and prestige. "[I]n a world where others have nuclear weapons," Thomas Reed and Michael Wheeler have stated, "the United States cannot exercise leadership unless it also has a nuclear arsenal."[18]

What, then, are the political requirements of a smaller nuclear arsenal to preserve Russian and U.S. political prestige? The Bush administration enunciated three criteria: the United States must have (1) a modern and flexible nuclear force that is (2) at least as large as the Russian arsenal, and (3) as large as all non-Russian nuclear arsenals combined. A force of that size and sophistication would satisfy not only the narrow requirements of deterrence but also broader concerns about power and prestige.

A force of 500 to 1,000 nuclear warheads could fulfill these requirements. A nuclear arsenal at those levels based on current, modern weapons in the U.S. arsenal would satisfy these criteria. If reductions to those levels were accomplished in mutual arms reductions with Russia, the second criterion would be satisfied. And if Britain, China, and France joined negotiations as U.S. and Russian strategic forces dipped closer to their own levels—as London, Beijing, and Paris has each pledged to do—then the arsenals of the medium nuclear powers could be altered to meet the third criterion. Our phase 1 assumption of continued nuclear bipolarity, therefore, would be upheld by U.S. and Russian nuclear forces in the range of 500 to 1,000 warheads, as long as arms negotiations concomitantly reduced the size of the medium nuclear powers' arsenals.

OPERATIONAL STEPS: DISMANTLING THE CONFRONTATION

The growing emphasis on confidence building as opposed to numerical reductions in arms control suggests that the question of "how much is enough" applies to more than just the number of nuclear weapons in U.S. and Russian arsenals. It must also encompass the operational tempo and deployment patterns of those weapons. Regardless of the size of the arsenals, important steps can be taken to reduce the danger they pose—both to the peace and to the future of U.S.-Russian relations—by restricting their ability to be used in a first strike. The following list of ideas is meant to be suggestive, not exhaustive. It seeks to promote one basic principle: the notion that U.S. and Russian nuclear forces are not necessary for deterrence or use on a daily basis.

For *bombers,* many important operational restraints have already been imposed. Both Russia and the United States have taken their bombers off "strip alert," divorcing the aircraft from their nuclear bombs, which are stored separately at the same air base. The U.S. Air Force has announced that it is shifting the peacetime focus of its B-1 fleet to conventional missions,[19] leaving the fifteen to twenty B-2s and several dozen B-52s as the only dedicated nuclear bombers in the U.S. nuclear inventory. In START II, signed in January 1993, the United States granted Russia greater access to its airbases to verify the status of U.S. B-2s.

These developments could be supplemented with one simple but dramatic step: a formal agreement that *no strategic bombers will visit airbases where nuclear weapons are held.* In other words, bombers will be physically separated from their cargos. The locations of bomb stocks could be mutually exchanged, and each side could be allowed to place observers at the other's bomb sites. This arrangement would ensure that strategic bombers could not be used in a nuclear attack except after obtaining and loading their payloads.

Several important agreements have also been made with regard to *ICBMs.* The most important is a structural one: in START II, the two sides have agreed to ban all MIRVed ICBM warheads, which were inherently destabilizing because they institutionalized a warhead-to-target ratio favorable to an attacker. Both sides have also stated that their ICBM fleets are partially or completely off alert, although it is not clear what this means in practical terms.

Two additional measures would further increase the operational stability of the ICBM forces. First, the United States and Russia should *codify their agreement to move almost all ICBMs to a nonalert status.* This will require negotiations between technical specialists about what the notion of an "alert" force actually means and an accord on specific, verifiable measures that will confirm the ICBMs' nonalert status. If such measures existed that would require several hours or days for the ICBM force to be readied for use, and if the measures could be adequately monitored, both sides would know that the other could not employ its ICBMs in a first strike on a day-to-day basis. The verification process might require periodic visits, or even constant monitoring, of each nation's ICBM fields by teams of experts from the other.

Second, *each side should be permitted to install an early-warning system on the missile fields of the other.* Intercontinental ballistic missiles have a long flight time relative to close-in SLBMs in any case, and giving instantaneous warning of their launch would provide additional confidence in the predictability and stability of deterrence. A missile-field early-warning radar would also help deal with accidental launches by giving more rapid and reliable information about their origin and timing. To prevent misuse of the radars, such as their employment in targeting, their transmitting capability could be designed so as not to give pinpoint locations of silos or other militarily useful data.

Reducing the threat posed by strategic missile *submarines* is a trickier business. Submarines pose a dilemma for stability: they rely for their survival on stealth and secrecy, but that very stealth theoretically allows them to creep up undetected to an enemy's coast and launch a sudden, devastating, short-notice attack. Any effort to restrict the operation of submarines must address this basic problem.

Still, if one presumes that the improvement in U.S.-Russian relations has changed deterrence from an actual to a potential task, then placing constraints on submarines appears less worrisome. Therefore we propose that *the daily operations of SSBNs should be restricted to an area several hundred miles away from the shores of other nuclear powers,* a requirement that would be verified by various monitoring techniques. For example, SSBNs could be tagged for identification, and once or more per month each side would be allowed to request a random surfacing and location of one of the other's submarines. A sufficient number of random call-ups could establish a statistical improbability that a significant number of submarines were violating the agreement. Eventually, British, French, and Chinese SSBNs could be included in the same arrangement. This arrangement would not render the submarines vulnerable; each call-up would only allow the location of a single SSBN, and that only for a brief time. But the effect would be to significantly improve confidence on both sides that neither was capable of launching a short-notice surprise attack.

VULNERABILITIES

If a force of 500 or 1,000 warheads were not survivable, however, it might not even produce a retaliation of 100 warheads. At lower levels of weapons, the vulnerability of nuclear forces becomes a much more distinct concern. If designed properly, however, a small nuclear force could be highly survivable;

and the operational restraints discussed above can play a critical role in establishing a secure force.

Under the arrangements proposed here, the conduct of nuclear deterrence—and, with it, the definition of vulnerability—would change dramatically. Most U.S. and Russian nuclear weapons would be unusable on a daily basis and could only be made ready for use through a time-consuming, and very public, process. In the past, survivability depended on both sides' ability to employ a nuclear arsenal rapidly; in the future, it might rely on their inability to do so. We will move from considerations of "crisis stability" or "first-strike stability" to ones of "operational stability."

Military and political leaders in Moscow and Washington, however, are likely to insist on a nuclear balance that remains stable even if the trust underlying such operational measures collapses. And such a balance can be created.

One important aspect of the nuclear balance that remains valid is the invulnerability of strategic missile submarines when at sea. If 300 warheads of a 500-warhead U.S. nuclear arsenal were based on submarines, for example, and two-thirds of them were at sea at any one time, then the United States would have a secure retaliatory force of the size recommended above. The importance of SSBN invulnerability at lower levels argues for complementary arms control measures designed to preserve that condition, such as restrictions on antisubmarine warfare (ASW) weapons and research.

Bombers will remain vulnerable as long as they are off alert. In a crisis, however, or after a period of worsening relations, placing them back on alert would render them highly survivable, especially if both sides continued to respect the restrictions on SSBN deployment areas and thereby reduced the risk of a short-notice attack on bomber bases.

Perhaps the ultimate in strategic stability would be a nuclear balance consisting only of bombers. This proposal, and a similar one to ban all ballistic missiles, is more appropriate to long-term plans for minimal nuclear deterrence and is therefore considered at length in chapter 7. It is possible, though, that even in a finite deterrent, the various nuclear powers might see advantages in such proposals.

Finally there is the question of strategic defenses, which we address in chapter 6. Because of their ability to interfere with the retaliations from small nuclear forces, and also because of their inherent ability to be expanded rapidly, even limited strategic defenses would hold the potential to destabilize the strategic balance. Continued respect for the ABM Treaty is therefore critical to preserving the stability of the nuclear balance at lower levels—even the levels already mandated in START II.

A HOPEFUL GOAL

Taken together, the numerical and operational arms control measures outlined above would dramatically alter the role nuclear weapons play in U.S.-Russian relations and in the defense policies of both nations. The threat of imminent nuclear war would no longer affect the way the two nations thought about or related to one another. Nuclear weapons would be pushed further to the margins of world politics.

NOTES

1. All terms for various levels of deterrence are somewhat arbitrary, but for the purposes of this book, a significant difference exists between finite and minimum deterrence. The former, a nuclear balance totaling more than 1,000 nuclear weapons, assumes a variety of continuing roles and missions for those weapons. Minimum deterrence, on the other hand, which we discuss in chapter 7 as a possible nuclear end state, assumes that the only mission of nuclear forces is direct deterrence of a nuclear attack; nuclear forces designed to support this mission might be only a few dozen, or at most 100 or so, nuclear weapons.
2. Richard Halloran, "U.S. Revises Its War Plan for a New Age," *New York Times,* November 2, 1988, p. A7. According to the *Times* report, Minuteman III computers previously programmed with 100 combinations for each flight of ten missiles, each missile with three warheads capable of being aimed at four different targets, were being increased in capacity to 2,400 combinations. In 1985, the Joint Strategic Target Planning Staff (JSTPS) was reorganized "to improve our ability to replan the SIOP more efficiently," with an emphasis on "flexibility for rapid replanning and new adaptive planning requirements." See the JSTPS "Unclassified History of the Joint Strategic Target Planning Staff," March 1989.
3. Larry Grossman, "SAC's Twin Triads," *Air Force Magazine,* August 1991, p. 56.
4. U.S. Senate, Defense Appropriation Subcommittee, FY1991 Defense Appropriations, hearings transcript, June 12, 1990.
5. Early accounts reported that the new plan would reduce the number of targets by some 1,000; the actual number was closer to 3,000. See R. Jeffrey Smith, "U.S. Expected to Reduce Number of Nuclear Targets," *Washington Post,* April 19, 1991, p. A17.
6. Ibid., p. A9, and R. Jeffrey Smith, "U.S. Trims List of Targets in Soviet Union," *Washington Post,* July 21, 1991, p. A1.
7. Testimony of Secretary of Defense Dick Cheney before the Senate Armed Services Committee on the Strategic Arms Reduction Treaty, July 28, 1992, p. 2.
8. Grossman, "SAC's Twin Triads," p. 56.

9. Ashton Carter, "Emerging Themes in Nuclear Arms Control," *Daedalus* 120, no. 4 (Winter 1991): 241.

10. Counterpower strategies have been examined at length elsewhere. See Jeffrey Richelson, "The Dilemmas of Counterpower Targeting," in Desmond Ball and Richelson, eds., *Strategic Nuclear Targeting* (Ithaca, N.Y.: Cornell University Press, 1985); Bernard Albert, "Constructive Counterpower," *Orbis* 20, no. 3 (Summer 1976); and Bruce Russett, "Assured Destruction of What? A Countercombatant Alternative to Nuclear MADness," *Public Policy* 22, no. 2 (Spring 1974).

11. These figures, and the conclusions outlined below, are outlined at much greater length in Appendix 2, "Military Targets for a Minimum Deterrent: After the Cold War, How Much Is Enough?"

12. See the General Accounting Office, "Strategic Forces: Minuteman Weapon Systems Status and Current Issues," September 1990, pp. 1-2.

13. Testifying before Congress this April, General Butler stated:

> I must note that as we shrink our nuclear arsenal further, operational considerations will assume increasing weight in the process of determining how to reduce weapons levels. For example, the supporting infrastructure for our ICBMs and nuclear-role bombers will increasingly influence the number of warheads assigned to any single delivery system. As the force comes down, crucial judgments will come into play regarding the ability to hedge against technological surprise (to include failure), the cost to maintain a particular weapons system, and the size of the basing structure. In other words, there is a tyranny of small numbers that exacts an increasing price for misjudgment and hasty decision. Some options, once foreclosed, may well prove irretrievable.

Statement of General Lee Butler, commander in chief, Strategic Air Command, to the Senate Appropriations Committee Defense Subcommittee, April 9, 1992, p. 8.

14. Bruce Schoenfeld, "MX Makers Warn Cheney About Cuts," *Defense Week*, March 18, 1991, p. 6.

15. Butler, April 9, 1992, testimony, p. 3.

16. David F. Bond, "Cuts in Production, Testing Raise MX Reliability Concerns," *Aviation Week and Space Technology*, March 25, 1991, p. 42.

17. Butler, April 9, 1992, testimony, p. 6.

18. Thomas Reed and Michael Wheeler, "The Role of Nuclear Weapons in the New World Order," statement before the Senate Armed Services Committee, January 23, 1992, p. 10.

19. In his June 17, 1992, letter to Russian Foreign Minister Andrei Kozyrev, U.S. Secretary of State James Baker formalized this policy and, in the eyes of some, essentially promised that the United States would not use its B-1s in a nuclear role.

4

Deterrence in Europe

For more than forty years, the United States has employed nuclear weapons in support of its NATO commitments. These weapons have served both strategic and political purposes. Strategically, NATO intended its theater nuclear forces (TNF) to deter conventional and nuclear attack on Western Europe and to support battlefield operations in case of war. Politically, the deployment of TNF on the continent symbolized the American commitment to NATO by effectively tying U.S. national survival to the alliance. It also reduced incentives on the part of nonnuclear allies to acquire nuclear weapons of their own. These strategic and political purposes were subsumed under the broader strategy of extended deterrence.

In 1975, in the depths of the cold war, the United States deployed some 7,400 weapons in Western Europe to support these missions. Since that time, the number of U.S. nuclear weapons in Europe has declined steadily—to 6,000 in 1980, 4,600 in the mid-1980s, and less than 1,000 today. Arms control accounts for a small part of these reductions, with the 1987 Intermediate-range Nuclear Forces (INF) Treaty eliminating merely 400 U.S. weapons; the rest have been unilateral, including the decision in 1979 to withdraw 1,000 tactical nuclear weapons as part of the INF deployment decision, the additional cut of 1,400 weapons announced in 1983, and the elimination of all ground-based weapons and a 50 percent cut in air-based weapons announced by President George Bush in September 1991. As a result, only some 700 U.S. air-based bombs remain deployed with U.S. and allied forces in the United Kingdom, Germany, the Netherlands, Belgium, Italy, Greece, and Turkey.

The doctrine governing the use of TNF has also undergone significant changes. From the 1950s supposition that tactical nuclear weapons would be used on a massive scale at the outset of war to the 1960s belief that TNF would support NATO's flexible response options of direct defense, deliberate escalation, and general nuclear response, U.S. nuclear weapons in Europe were until recently central to NATO's political-military strategy. The revolutionary events of 1989-90 changed all that, with NATO proclaiming in July 1990 that nuclear weapons were now "truly weapons of last resort."[1] The alliance's New Strategic Concept, adopted in November 1991, further relegated nuclear weapons to the margins of NATO strategy by stating that the "circumstances in which any use of nuclear weapons might have to be contemplated" are "remote."[2]

Given these fundamental changes in the political context and NATO's perception of nuclear weapons, what role remains for U.S. nuclear weapons in Europe? Are American nuclear deployments on the continent, even at today's vastly reduced level, still necessary?

This chapter addresses these questions. As in chapter 3, this chapter's analysis is limited to developments in and recommendations for phase 1. To move into phase 2 of the future of nuclear strategy, one of two fundamental assumptions would have to change: either great-power war in Europe would have to become virtually impossible and nuclear weapons irrelevant to its deterrence; or the United States would have to cease caring enough to connect its nuclear policy to developments there. We do not foresee either of these developments by the end of the century, and they therefore are not considered at length in this chapter. Chapter 7 takes them up as part of its discussion of nuclear end states.

WHAT ROLE FOR U.S. NUCLEAR WEAPONS IN EUROPE?

The breakup of the Warsaw Pact in 1990 and the dissolution of the Soviet Union the following year had a fundamental impact on nuclear weapons policy in general and the role of theater nuclear forces in particular. Whereas before these revolutionary events the credibility of deterrent threats had stood central, the dissolution of a nuclear weapons state confronted NATO, and indeed the world, with a new potential threat: the instantaneous proliferation of nuclear weapons to new states within the former Soviet Union and to unstable regimes outside it.

Concerns about loose Soviet warheads provided the West, and particularly the United States, with a powerful incentive to consolidate the former Soviet nuclear stockpile under central control (preferably in one country) and to reduce sharply the number of weapons. The result was the initiative announced by President Bush in September 1991. The Bush initiative reflected a fundamental reevaluation of the role of theater nuclear forces. The chief concern guiding U.S. policy in this arena was no longer how these weapons could contribute to deterring a Russian attack; rather, the principal fear had become the prospect of Russian leaders losing control over their nuclear stockpile.

The changing political landscape in Europe has produced a strategic revolution: neither deterrence of conventional attack nor deterrence of nuclear attack any longer requires the presence of large numbers of readily usable nuclear weapons on the European continent. Except for Norway and Turkey, European members of NATO now border on friendly, nonnuclear states. Prospects for a conventional attack—let alone a combined arms or nuclear offensive—have effectively disappeared. What remains is a simmering uncertainty about the future course of the post-Soviet states; but the conventional capability of the former Red Army has been withdrawn to the strategic rear, and its nuclear potential is being consolidated and reduced.

Under these circumstances, what role remains for nuclear weapons in Europe? NATO's newly formulated answer, as presented in its new strategic concept, stresses its continuing political utility, first to ensure "uncertainty in the mind of any aggressor about the nature of the Allies' response to military aggression" and, second, "to provide an essential political and military link between the European and the North American members of the Alliance." The latter includes the traditional role of linking U.S. strategic nuclear forces to the defense of Europe. United States nuclear weapons in Europe also continue to be perceived in Washington and elsewhere as a means to reassure nonnuclear allies, thus reducing any incentives on their part to acquire nuclear weapons. This is the not-so-hidden meaning of the statement that "a credible Alliance nuclear posture and the demonstration of Alliance solidarity and common commitment to war prevention continue to require widespread participation by European Allies involved in collective defense planning in nuclear roles, in peacetime basing of nuclear forces on their territory and in command, control and communication arrangements."[3]

The question remains as to whether any of these roles requires the permanent stationing of U.S. nuclear weapons in Europe as the NATO countries maintain. A review of the security landscape in Europe suggests that *only one role—reassuring America's European allies—argues for the continued stationing of U.S. tactical nuclear weapons in European soil.* But because the residual U.S. nuclear presence is so uncontroversial, the United States should respect that role and resist the temptation to withdraw its nuclear forces unilaterally—while encouraging trends that will, before long, allow multilateral agreement on that step.

Nuclear Weapons as Hedge Against Uncertainty

As long as some allies with armed forces based in Europe possess nuclear arsenals, any aggressor will face some degree of uncertainty concerning whether this capability will be used. This is the essence of what is known as "existential" deterrence: the mere existence of nuclear weapons cannot help affecting the calculus of the aggressor.

Given that the risks of aggression on a scale that would make NATO or the United States contemplate using nuclear weapons has become very small indeed, the uncertainty added by nuclear deployments in Europe may be insignificant. This is particularly so because no potential aggressor can discount the possible use of nuclear weapons based in the United States so long as the United States clearly demonstrates an interest in preserving the security of its NATO allies.

In this context, much more important than the basing of U.S. tactical nuclear weapons in Europe is the broader U.S. military presence there. As long as a substantial number of U.S. troops are based in Europe, a healthy residue of existential deterrence will remain. United States troops establish the risk that any attack on NATO will draw in the United States and, eventually, its nuclear arsenal. Existential deterrence abandons the complexities—and, defenders would claim, the credibility—of finely tuned strategies for theater nuclear escalation. But in the changed strategic environment, with Russia having lost its conventional predominance and its interest in expansion, the existential deterrence provided by the presence of U.S. conventional forces in Europe seems sufficient.

This argument becomes especially compelling when one considers the circular logic supporting U.S. nuclear deployments in Europe. In an important sense, it is almost impossible for the United States to renounce extended deterrence. To do so would require ruling out the use of U.S. nuclear weapons in connection with a war that begins in Europe, and no one can guarantee that the course of such a war would not eventually draw in U.S. strategic nuclear forces. Herein lies the heart of existential deterrence. The question then becomes, must the United States deploy nuclear weapons *in Europe* to reinforce that fact and to support any U.S. promises of nuclear use? Deploying ground-based tactical nuclear weapons near the inter-German border may have done so by making nuclear escalation nearly inevitable, but the current U.S.

arsenal of air-delivered nuclear weapons in Europe, which can be withdrawn to the United States or otherwise moved, does not offer that advantage.

Threatening escalation from Europe-dedicated SSBNs in the Atlantic, or even from nuclear forces in the United States, could therefore serve as a reasonable substitute for the deployment of U.S. tactical nuclear weapons in Europe. It will not be as strong a symbol of commitment or threat of escalation; no one can deny that the physical basing of nuclear bombs in Europe signals a stronger commitment than do pledges to use U.S. strategic forces in European missions. But the question is how severely is the U.S. extended deterrent commitment likely to be tested? And, second, what political and military costs does it have?

In fact, much of the cold war rationale for U.S. nuclear deployments abroad had to do with escalation dominance. The United States initially deployed tactical nuclear weapons in Europe to counteract Soviet conventional superiority. Once Moscow had tactical weapons in Europe too, however, many quickly argued that this was a new reason the United States had to have them there also, because responding to a Soviet tactical nuclear attack with U.S. strategic forces was not viewed as reasonable. Hence the logic that supported the deployment of U.S. Pershing and cruise missiles to Europe in 1983: the Soviets had the SS-20, the Carter and Reagan administrations contended, and without a suitable matching weapon the U.S. escalatory ladder would be missing a rung and would therefore not be credible.

All of this, of course, assumes that the Soviet Union had—and that Russia has—weapons of the category the United States deploys in Europe. Theoretically, a ban on all or most tactical nuclear weapons would eliminate this rationale for U.S. nuclear forces in Europe by establishing a single rung of nuclear escalation, strategic nuclear weapons.

Finally, it is worth considering what "uncertainties" nuclear weapons might be useful in deterring. Absent a re-creation of the former Soviet Union, now impossible without major war, Russia will never regain its conventional predominance in Europe. Its ground, air, and naval units will be at least matched in quantity, and far exceeded in quality, by those of Western Europe's core states: France, Germany, and the United Kingdom. Those countries and other European members of NATO taken together will possess military forces larger than Russia's, and when we add the United States, the Central European nations (the Czech Republic, Hungary, Poland, and Slovakia), and perhaps a handful of former Soviet republics (such as Ukraine and Georgia) to the mix, we find that Russia is heavily outnumbered in the region. No nuclear risk, therefore, is necessary to guard against Russian conventional forces, as was the case during the cold war.

We are left, then, with Russian nuclear forces as the chief reservoir of uncertainty and potential threat to U.S. allies and interests in Europe. Nuclear blackmail has never been a very successful enterprise, however, and it is not clear how Russia might make use of its limited nuclear predominance over Western Europe. So long as Britain and France each has a survivable deterrent, Russia would be risking the destruction of a number of its major cities by threatening nuclear war. Moreover, if, as we have recommended, the United States and Russia follow START II with an accord to reduce their strategic arsenals to 1,000 or fewer warheads, then the French and British deterrents might be more capable, in a political sense, of "deterring uncertainty" more independently. And the residue of existential U.S. extended deterrence, as defined above, would remain in place as a final hedge against Russian nuclear blackmail.

Preserving Political-Military Ties

The second purported role of U.S. nuclear weapons in Europe has been to maintain the political and military link between the two sides of the Atlantic. The time is long past when the specific number of U.S. nuclear weapons in Europe (or U.S. troops, for that matter) was taken as a firm indication of the strength of the American commitment to NATO. Otherwise the 90 percent reduction in nuclear deployments and the 50 to 75 percent cut in U.S. personnel that are now under way would surely have signaled a massive change in the nature of the American commitment. Few, if any, have interpreted the reductions this way.

There is, of course, a difference between reducing nuclear deployments by 90 percent and reducing them to zero. But if this difference is so substantial that in the former case the "essential political and military link" between Western Europe and the United States is sound and secure, while in the latter case the link has been severed, then the ties that bind the United States and Europe are precarious indeed.

The transatlantic partnership has always been and continues to be based on shared political, economic, and cultural interests in addition to military ones. To suggest otherwise is to confuse symbols with substance. American nuclear deployments in Europe have long symbolized the substance of the link between Europe and North America. In the new era we are entering, one where military power no longer predominates as before, it is unclear that nuclear symbols are still appropriate. If what we want is a less nuclear world, then it is folly to insist on the continuing centrality of nuclear symbolism. In short, either the transatlantic link will survive the complete withdrawal of

U.S. nuclear weapons from Europe because of the strength of shared interests or, absent these shared interests, the partnership will dissolve no matter how many or few nuclear weapons remain.

Nor must the United States continue to play its role as the "nuclear-hatted core" of the NATO alliance. At one time it may have been true that U.S. commanders in Europe benefited from having a nuclear capability and the authority to use it. Today, however, nuclear weapons are not relevant to Europe's security problems; if NATO has failed to act in Yugoslavia, it is not because of any shortcoming in the nuclear field. Indeed, the opposite might be closer to the truth—NATO's historical overemphasis on an all-or-nothing, nuclear-based defense of Western Europe has rendered it less capable in dealing with smaller regional crises. What U.S. forces in NATO need to be useful today is not a nuclear trigger but the capability to project power and the political will to play a role in the civil wars and national conflicts that will trouble Europe in the years ahead.

There are also ways of strengthening extended deterrence even if its nuclear component fades into the background. Advanced conventional weapons, long heralded as the agents of a revolution in warfare, now allow the United States to conduct many extended deterrent missions without nuclear strikes. Precision-guided munitions (PGMs), battlefield command-and-control systems like the Airborne Warning and Control System (AWACS) or the Joint Surveillance Target Acquisition and Reconnaissance System (JSTARS), and real-time reconnaissance and battle-damage assessment may well give U.S. and allied forces the capability to crush offensive forces moving through Eastern Europe. Given the experience of the Gulf War, any adversary would have to view such a force as a potent deterrent, with weapons capable of destroying hardened command and supply centers—missions formerly assigned to tactical nuclear weapons.

A large difference remains, of course, in deterrent effect between advanced conventional weapons and nuclear bombs. But NATO today does not face threats of an order that would render that difference worrisome. Advanced conventional weapons have also been shown capable of defeating forces of superior size but inferior technology, a reality perhaps demonstrated by the Persian Gulf War and with relevance for NATO's deterrent missions in Europe.

Reassuring Nonnuclear Allies

This leaves one potential reason for continuing the deployment of U.S. nuclear weapons in Europe: to reassure nonnuclear allies. Such reassurance is important to successful nonproliferation policy; without it, one or more European states may gain added incentives to acquire the nuclear means they still perceive as necessary for their defense.

One way to address this requirement is to reduce the nuclear risk to nonnuclear countries in Europe. The announced reductions in Russian strategic and nonstrategic nuclear forces have gone a long way toward this end. As argued in chapter 3, it is possible and desirable to extend this process even further. A critical component of risk reduction will be persuading Ukraine and Kazakhstan to fulfill their pledges to abandon their considerable nuclear arsenals.

Nonetheless, as long as Russia retains a nuclear capability, and as long as uncertainty about Moscow's economic and political course persists—as surely it will for some time—nonnuclear countries in Europe will face a potential, though very much reduced, nuclear risk. Assuming that we do not want to reverse the decades-old policy of discouraging nuclear proliferation in Europe (and, by extension, elsewhere), some degree of reassurance will remain necessary.

The question is whether this reassurance continues to demand the stationing of U.S. nuclear weapons on European soil. And this question must be asked, not from the perspective of the aggressor, but from that of the ally being protected. This has always been the crux of NATO's nuclear predicament—what may be sufficient to deter an adversary may not be sufficient to reassure an ally. If the European members of NATO subscribed fully to the analysis of the previous two sections, the answer would be clear: given the current threats to Europe, U.S.-based nuclear weapons, conventional forces, and other alternatives to tactical nuclear weapons would pose a credible deterrent in the eyes of NATO leaders.

Most European states, however, would be uncomfortable with an immediate withdrawal of all U.S. tactical nuclear weapons. Decision makers in Bonn, Paris, London, and elsewhere in Europe feel, more powerfully than U.S. officials, the hypothetical threat from the East lurking in the turmoil and growing nationalism of the former Soviet Union. The European Community remains on slippery footing; it is not cohesive enough, for example, to convince German leaders that they themselves, let alone other EC members or East European governments, will act responsibly. And it certainly has not evolved to the point where French and British nuclear forces can begin assuming the burden traditionally borne by U.S. nuclear weapons. For these and other reasons, European governments are clearly not prepared to advocate or acquiesce to a complete U.S. nuclear withdrawal from the Continent.

Much rides on the question of how European governments would react to a unilateral U.S. withdrawal. They might react positively—working further to integrate defense planning in the Western European Union, looking to British and French nuclear forces for reassurance, and in general seeking to replace the lost American guarantees. They might do nothing, counting on a continuation of the current threatless environment. Or they might respond in frustration and disappointment, turning their growing anger and concern against the United States and, increasingly, each other. In the extreme case, a few nations might seek independent nuclear arsenals or at least the hint of them, and coordinated EC defense planning might stall in the face of newly renationalized security planning.

In a nutshell, this is the same question that has bedeviled American strategists since the 1950s: Would a U.S. withdrawal from Europe energize or dash the development of a common European security architecture? The answer today is no more clear than it was then, although the depth of the EC process suggests that the nations of Western Europe are unlikely to threaten one another any time soon.

For the United States, the key policy question is straightforward but far from simple. What interests does it have at stake in Europe that justify a continued security commitment expressed through nuclear deployments? Part of the answer lies in the general value of the U.S. presence in Europe, which helps forestall the rise of an expansionist power there, aids in the creation of a stable European Community receptive to U.S. trade, and augments U.S. economic and political leverage. Europe is today one of the three great centers of commerce and politics; the United States retains important cultural bonds with the nations there; and the lesson of the past century is that major wars in Europe tend to draw in the United States.

It only makes sense for the United States to remain involved in European affairs, and it does this in large part through its military and political commitments to the NATO alliance. And in the eyes of many European governments, some residual nuclear presence constitutes an important element of those commitments.

The U.S. nuclear presence also has value in preventing the worst-case scenario outlined above. If a U.S. nuclear withdrawal sparked recriminations and hostility among the nations of Western Europe; if Germany and perhaps Poland or Hungary began reconsidering their nuclear options; if progress toward a common European security identity collapsed amid these tensions—then U.S. trade and political interests would be severely damaged. Europe would accuse the United States of abandoning it, and the warm transatlantic relations built through forty years of cold war would begin to fade.

Such an outcome is not inevitable if the United States decided unilaterally to remove its nuclear weapons. It may not even be very likely, given the status of and official dedication to pan-European cooperation today. But it remains a risk, and continued nuclear deployments obviate that risk.

In the context of reassuring America's European allies, then, the value of continued residual nuclear deployments, while not overwhelming, seems clear enough. The issue then becomes one of cost: What costs do the United States and NATO assume, politically and militarily, by leaving a few hundred U.S. nuclear weapons in place?

Politically, within Europe, there is little cost to the deployments today. Nuclear weapons are simply not an issue. Antinuclear peace groups have, for the time being at least, lost their energy; opposition parties seldom place much emphasis on U.S. nuclear withdrawal; and the presence of U.S. nuclear weapons is hardly discussed in the press. NATO runs little political risk, therefore, by retaining the weapons—though, as will be argued below, this situation could change.

For the United States, there is one broader cost: the risk that the weapons might actually have to be used. During the cold war, U.S. tactical nuclear weapons in Europe were pointed reminders of a standing American pledge to engage in nuclear war to protect the West. Many doubted the veracity of this promise from the beginning, wondering why the United States would be willing to commit national suicide to prevent something that did not even threaten its territorial integrity. Observers as authoritative as Henry Kissinger warned of the dangers of basing U.S. policy on what, in the end, may have been an unprecedented geopolitical bluff.

Much the same problem attaches to U.S. nuclear weapons in Europe today. Would the United States be willing to fight over those events that might call on it to fulfill its reassuring promises, such as a new Russian threat? What about intermediate crises—a nuclear-armed Ukraine invading a Poland that had become a member of the EC? Clearly these events do not involve U.S. interests to the degree that they do European ones, or to the degree that U.S. interests were threatened during the cold war. Should Washington make implied promises in terms of nuclear escalation it is not prepared to keep?

The best answer is probably the same one arrived at during the cold war: for the time being, it is best simply to live with the uncertainties and potential dilemmas of the U.S. nuclear presence. NATO has already declared that nuclear weapons will be a "last resort," and that and other statements clearly imply that the United States no longer has a responsibility to be prepared to escalate to nuclear use in every crisis or war. Europeans understand that fact;

it is a halfway point to recognizing that a U.S. nuclear presence in Europe is no longer necessary at all. United States policymakers can simply wait, then, and decide in an ad hoc manner when and in what manner they are willing to threaten nuclear escalation.

A continued fudging of the nuclear dilemma poses much less risk than in the cold war, for two reasons. First, the residual U.S. nuclear pledges are much less likely to be tested. The risk of war is low, and even a renewed Russian threat would not have the dimensions of the former Soviet one and hence would not automatically demand a return to the doctrine of massive retaliation. And second, the nature of U.S. nuclear deployments in Europe is less dangerous today. When ground-based tactical weapons were located close to the inter-German border, many believed that a Soviet attack would inevitably and rapidly produce a nuclear war; indeed, NATO cultivated this perception as part of its deterrent strategy. Today, the air-delivered weapons that remain are based far from the potential "front lines" and could be removed rapidly if the United States decided to avoid the risk of escalation. Unlike the situation in the cold war, then, U.S. nuclear deployments in Europe today are unlikely to draw the United States into a nuclear war against its will.

In the long run, as suggested below, the United States should become an advocate of a denuclearized alliance, attempting to persuade its European allies that nuclear weapons are no longer necessary to reassure them. Such a process will specifically address the potential costs of nuclear deployments already mentioned: a NATO that is gradually shedding its nuclear baggage will be less susceptible to political pressure and less likely to pose apocalyptic and wrenching questions for U.S. leaders in times of crisis.

A NEAR-TERM AGENDA

In sum, there is little persuasive about the reasons for American nuclear weapons based in Europe. The immediate threat to European allies has effectively disappeared, and crisis management, not nuclear deterrence, is the alliance's chief task today. European-based nuclear weapons are superfluous for the purpose of confronting a potential future aggressor with the prospect of nuclear use; weapons based in the United States will suffice. While they may depict the essential links between Europe and North America, raising these symbols to a strategic and political orthodoxy as NATO has done is folly if they are likely to be withdrawn some time in the not-too-distant future.

The one role that remains relevant for U.S. nuclear weapons in Europe is that of reassuring U.S. allies. This task is far different from that during the cold war; it is changed, weakened, based on political perceptions rather than military balances. And while, in the long run, the essence of such reassurance must be a strong security commitment that rests on shared interests rather than shared nuclear risks, for the time being the costs of a residual nuclear presence are low, its benefits important.

The United States should not, therefore, immediately move to withdraw its tactical weapons from Europe. Those weapons have not yet become a political liability, and there is no urgency to remove them.

Washington should, however, become an advocate for the denuclearization of the NATO alliance. The United States ought to work with its NATO allies in a gradual process of nuclear withdrawal, perhaps beginning with those tactical weapons reserved for the use of U.S. forces—leaving some 100 weapons dedicated to allied forces. In the past, the United States has argued strongly *for* continued nuclear deployments in Europe, contending that objective military and political factors required such deployments. Those factors no longer exist. And while there is little cost to U.S. nuclear deployments today, that may not always be true.

Our first conclusion, then, is that the United States should gradually *make clear that nuclear weapons are not the basis of the Atlantic Alliance* and declare its willingness, *when European governments request it,* to consider a complete or partial withdrawal of all U.S. nuclear weapons from Europe. Making this clear should be done both privately within NATO councils and later publicly. It would be helpful if official NATO statements dropped their emphasis on continuing missions, even if "last-resort," for nuclear forces; indeed, it would probably be best not to mention nuclear weapons at all.

Second, the United States and Russia should *codify the elimination of ground- and sea-based nonstrategic nuclear weapons in a multilateral treaty that includes an effective regime for on-site monitoring.* The reductions in nonstrategic nuclear forces announced last fall are unilateral undertakings that can be reversed at any time. Given a clear commitment to eliminating large parts of this inventory, there is no reason not to codify this commitment in a legally binding agreement. *Such an agreement should provide for the full elimination of sea-based tactical nuclear weapons,* which would render the Bush-Gorbachev initiative more comprehensive.

A more formal accord would be especially useful to NATO. In the event of a new crisis in Europe, the redeployment of U.S. tactical nuclear weapons that have been withdrawn may prove politically impossible, even if it is allowed by the terms of the existing unilateral commitments. A formal treaty would merely impose on others the same restriction NATO can expect in any case.

Third, *the United States should privately declare to its NATO allies its willingness to consider a total ban on all tactical nuclear weapons.* This would of course presume that Europe had become comfortable with a U.S. nuclear withdrawal and was willing to see the U.S. air-delivered weapons depart. Once that was the case, the way would possibly be clear for the elimination of tactical weapons of all sorts.

For a variety of reasons, a ban on tactical nuclear weapons would benefit U.S. and international security. It would eliminate the threat of direct nuclear proliferation through the dispersion of Russian tactical weapons, further reduce the Russian nuclear threat to Europe and the Far East, and contribute to the goals of arms control outlined in chapter 2. Such a ban would be particularly helpful on the nonproliferation front: it would end plans for using small nuclear weapons in regional conflicts, a threat that engendered a number of developing-world nuclear programs. Some Indian strategists, for example, have remarked that the elimination of Chinese tactical nuclear weapons would do much to put them at ease, because they are less concerned about China's use of its strategic arsenal in a regional conflict.

Such a ban would have to apply broadly to be effective, and it is not at all clear that two key players in the nuclear field—Russia and China—would approve a treaty banning nonstrategic weapons. Nonetheless, within the next decade, both might see the value of a tactical nuclear weapons ban—Russia as it develops solid relations with its neighbors, and China as it deploys a more reliable strategic deterrent. A public U.S. call for such a step might set into motion a productive round of discussions and negotiations that would be useful in themselves in establishing the basis for multilateral nuclear arms control talks.

The problem of definition will face any effort to address a particular category of nuclear weapons. Debates about what is and what is not a "strategic" weapon have raged for years, energized in part by the proximity of U.S. nuclear forces in Europe to the former Soviet Union. We would suggest the following formula: a ban on nonstrategic nuclear forces would prohibit any nuclear delivery vehicles apart from ICBMs, SLBMs, and a select number of air-launched nuclear cruise missiles and gravity bombs to be based within the owner's country. Those last two weapons could be used in a "tactical" or regional configuration, of course, but so could strategic missiles. The goal is not so much to eliminate tactical *missions* so much as tactical *weapons*. Indeed, our analysis suggests that missions persist for U.S. nuclear forces besides strategic deterrence. But retaining an arsenal of small, low-yield, "tactical" weapons to fulfill those missions is both unnecessary and counterproductive.

But again, the United States should not take this step unilaterally. It should declare its willingness to do so and begin consulting with NATO. If the consensus of the NATO allies is that it is too early for either or both of these initiatives, then the United States should not force the issue.

THE LONGER TERM

The preceding analysis has made the case that the presence of U.S. nuclear weapons does little to safeguard the peace today. But the situation in Europe has not finished evolving, and it is possible that new incentives to proliferate could arise later, after the U.S. weapons had been withdrawn. Phase 1 itself lasts nearly twenty years, and during that time Europe could change radically. The evolution of the European Community; the roles and interactions of Germany, France, and Britain; the emergence of possible nuclear threats from Iraq, Algeria, or Libya—any of these developments could have profound implications for the security situation in Europe.

The issue can be put another way. Ten years from now, what might the West wish it had done to reassure Germany so that it had no reason to wonder whether a nuclear capability would increase its security?

Any argument that U.S. nuclear weapons can be withdrawn from Europe must therefore deal with more than the issue of whether such weapons are needed today. It must also consider whether they might regain their usefulness in some future time. Some would argue that the possibility of such a shift makes any withdrawal of U.S. weapons inadvisable.

We do not agree. First, the model for nuclear consultation suggested here presupposes that European members of NATO, including Germany, have asked that U.S. tactical nuclear weapons be withdrawn. If they do so, one can assume that they have reasonably powerful political or military reasons for their action. Perhaps U.S. nuclear weapons will become a more severe political liability; perhaps Germany would feel more secure in the broader scheme of things if all tactical nuclear weapons were banned. The nonnuclear states of Europe would therefore bear primary responsibility for the withdrawal, and this might make it less likely that they would build their own arsenals later.

Moreover, even in the future, it is the overall health of the Western alliance that will determine whether the nonnuclear states feel secure in future crises. If ten or fifteen years hence Germany is confronted with some new enemy, and if the EC has not advanced much and NATO has long since devolved into a hollow shell, German leaders might look to a nuclear arsenal whether or not U.S. nuclear weapons remain on the Continent. The United Stated deployed thousands of those weapons in Europe in the 1950s and 1960s, but could not convince the French that Washington could be relied upon to use them; similarly, if transatlantic cooperation declines in the years ahead, the presence of U.S. weapons in Europe alone would not be sufficient reassurance. A robust U.S.-EC relationship of cooperation and trust, on the other hand, would be likely to reassure Germany about its security regardless of the presence of U.S. weapons.

And if one accepts that the present trend is toward a complete U.S. nuclear withdrawal from Europe, then the task of defining the alliance in nonnuclear terms becomes all the more urgent. By emphasizing NATO's political and nonnuclear military bonds, by energizing the alliance through new missions in support of the United Nations (as in the former Yugoslavia), and by discussing alternatives to the deterrence provided by U.S. nuclear weapons, the United States can ease the way for the withdrawal of those weapons when it occurs.

FINITE DETERRENCE AND EXTENDED DETERRENCE

If U.S. nuclear weapons are removed from Europe, the burden of extending deterrence there will fall, at least initially, largely on U.S. strategic systems. In the longer term, as is argued below, British and French nuclear forces should assume a larger share of nuclear deterrence for Europe, but it may be some years before a Europeanized deterrent becomes credible. In the meantime, nonnuclear allies in Europe will continue to look to the United States for reassurance. The U.S. extended deterrence mission traditionally called for large, counterforce-capable strategic forces, along with thousands of tactical and theater weapons; could a strategic force of 1,000 warheads or fewer now assume that same mission alone?

But assuming that the country to be deterred does not possess appreciably more nuclear weapons than the United States (a most unlikely eventuality), a U.S. finite deterrent could fulfill the requirements of post-cold war extended deterrence without in any way detracting from the ability to deter a direct attack on the United States.

In the new political environment, the nuclear targeting requirements of central and extended deterrence do not differ in any meaningful sense. Both require holding at risk targets on the territory of the aggressor. The one difference is that extended deterrence may require using strategic forces before the U.S. homeland has come under direct nuclear attack, weapons not available for retaliation in case of a direct attack. Any strategic strikes in support of extended deterrence, however, would be strictly limited, involving no more than a few warheads. Thereafter, the aggressor would either desist and negotiate an end to the war or escalate by using his own weapons, thereby reducing his own available inventory as well.

The strategic force requirements for central and extended deterrence are also compatible. In both cases, forces should be highly survivable in case of attack, able to respond rapidly to a launching order, and capable of flexibility in selecting targets. Likely targets will therefore increasingly consist of conventional force projection capabilities and war-sustaining industries—the same targeting strategy outlined for a strategic retaliation in the previous chapter.

In short, as long as the United States retains forces about equal in size to those of a potential adversary, there is no direct conflict between the ability to extend deterrence with strategic forces and the necessity of deterring a direct attack on the U.S. homeland. Any strategic employment in support of extended deterrence will involve only a few weapons, and the targets will be similar to those held at risk for the purpose of central deterrence. An arsenal of 500 to 1,000 warheads would be able comfortably to support both missions.

NEW DILEMMAS: SECURITY PROBLEMS OF EASTERN AND CENTRAL EUROPE

The end of the cold war has, in a way, complicated extended deterrence by potentially forcing NATO to extend it into Eastern and Central Europe. No European government can turn a blind eye to the ethnic conflicts, political instabilities, and interstate wars now brewing from Hungary and Slovakia eastward to the Ukraine and the Caucasus. If there is any region in the world with the potential to bring Russia and the West into a new confrontation, this is it.

The risks to security in Central and Eastern Europe are numerous and varied. Ethnic tensions and mass migrations plague the entire region, from the Silesian nationalism in the Czech Republic to the vicious ethnic warfare in the Caucasus to the tens of thousands of refugees from the Yugoslav war scattered throughout the area. Relations between Hungary and Slovakia, Ukraine and Russia, Poland and Lithuania, and many other states hold the seeds of new Central European conflicts.

From the perspective of this study, the questions raised by these facts are straightforward, but by no means simple. What role are nuclear weapons likely to play in U.S. and NATO policy regarding Eastern Europe? And what implications does that role hold for U.S. nuclear policy?

To date, NATO has been unwilling to extend any formal security guarantees, let alone full or partial alliance membership, to the countries to its east. Russian concerns constitute a major roadblock: Moscow would not look favorably on a NATO security zone that extended through Central Europe, particularly as conservatives gain a larger voice. Sparking new fears and mistrust in Russia would not serve the West well in the years ahead. And NATO purists reject any expansion of the alliance, fearing that its credibility and ability to act will be diluted.

And yet, if a hostile Russia posed a military threat to Central and Eastern Europe, NATO could not sit idle. The West would have clear interests at stake, not least sending a firm signal that aggression would not be tolerated. Insofar as Russia alone does not possess conventional superiority over the West, moreover, NATO might have an interest in preventing the recreation of the former Soviet Union. Once such a threat becomes apparent, NATO security guarantees might be required to keep several European states from seeking nuclear weapons. And as the EC process continues, it is possible that NATO will acquire indirect security guarantees as Central European states join the Community.

It is not entirely clear today, therefore, what NATO's position will be in five or fifteen years regarding security guarantees to the East. If NATO never assumed such burdens, no additional stress would be laid on U.S. extended deterrent pledges, and the ramifications for U.S. nuclear policy would be small. Increasingly, however, it appears that the West may consider more formal expressions of a security interest in Central and Eastern Europe—through security guarantees, EC membership, or more vague statements of concern. If it did so, would this cause problems for U.S. extended deterrent policies? Would 1,000 U.S. warheads be insufficient for such deterrence?

There is every reason to believe that a U.S. finite deterrent arsenal of 1,000 or fewer warheads would support NATO security guarantees to the East, for the same reasons that it would support extended deterrence in general. As mentioned above, the Russian conventional threat is much smaller than the former Soviet threat was, reducing the need for NATO to rely on nuclear deterrence; this is even more true the farther east NATO is defending, since Central and Eastern European states could then be tallied on NATO's side of the ledger. Existential deterrence would continue to loom large: the U.S. strategic arsenal still sits at the top of the escalatory ladder, a fact that no

Russian leader could ignore when considering a strike west. And even—perhaps especially—for conflicts in the East, the targeting requirements of central and extended deterrence would remain complementary, thus reducing the tension between the two.

In short, the possibility of the West becoming more concerned with the security of Eastern and Central Europe is not a reason for retaining a larger nuclear force than would otherwise be the case. To combat proliferation in those areas, *the United States and its NATO allies might be well advised to work out a formula for extending security guarantees to the nations of Central and Eastern Europe.* Ukrainian officials have already demanded some form of such guarantees as a condition for joining the NPT, and in the years ahead many former communist states and republics—from Poland, the Czech Republic, Slovakia, and Hungary to Ukraine, Belarus, Kazakhstan, and even the Baltic states—will want a hedge against Russia's nuclear arsenal.

THE ROLE OF FRENCH AND BRITISH NUCLEAR FORCES

While the United States and Russia have agreed to sharp reductions in their strategic nuclear forces, British and French nuclear modernization plans continue forward, albeit at a somewhat reduced pace. Before the end of the century, the United Kingdom will replace its sixty-four Polaris missiles, each with 2 (or possibly 3) warheads with a similar number of Trident D-5 missiles, capable of carrying 8 warheads, thus possibly increasing its total warhead number almost threefold and its potential target coverage eightfold. France is also continuing the modernization of its *Force Océanique Stratégique,* with each of its four (and possibly six) SSBNs soon carrying sixteen M-4 missiles with 6 warheads each. By the mid-1990s, both countries will therefore have several hundred warheads on submarines.

Other elements of the British and French nuclear force posture face a less certain future. The United Kingdom has decided to eliminate its ground-based nuclear systems (artillery and missile systems) as well as its sea-based tactical nuclear weapons. London has also cut its tactical air-based stockpile in half. Although it continues to be interested in modernizing this component of its deterrent force with a new tactical air-to-surface missile, no decisions have been made. France has decided not to modernize the land-based leg of its strategic deterrent, consisting of eighteen intermediate-range ballistic missiles deployed on the Plateau d'Albion. A decision to modernize the air leg by deploying an extended-range air-to-surface missile, still defined as a nonstrategic weapon, has been in the works for some time, but will likely depend on whether the United Kingdom will agree to joint development of the missile. Finally, Paris decided in June 1992 to halt production of its new short-range missile and to store the thirty Hades missiles that had been built.

The bulk of British and French nuclear forces will therefore remain deployed in submarines, and it is even possible that other elements of their deterrent forces will eventually be eliminated altogether. The several hundred warheads each will deploy represent a formidable deterrent to direct attack on their respective territories, especially considering the planned reductions in Russian forces. This is particularly true insofar as the counterpower or countermilitary targeting strategy discussed in chapter 3 is employed for British and French forces. Most unclassified analyses suggest that both France and Britain have pursued targeting policies that are almost completely countervalue in nature. Both have targeted Soviet cities, believing that their small deterrent forces were insufficient for any other missions.

Most commentators have therefore argued that, with their minimal deterrent forces, France and Britain cannot pursue credible independent deterrence and certainly not the extended variety.[4] But if the advantages of counterpower targeting are taken seriously, many of these objections lose force. Given current French and British SSBN modernization, each of those two countries may have more than enough warheads to achieve the sort of 200-warhead counterpower retaliation described in the previous chapter. In fact, a shift to counterpower might represent more of an evolutionary, rather than dramatic, step for Paris and London. France has already expanded its targeting ambitions once: in 1980, reportedly in response to Soviet civil defense programs, French targeteers began to consider aimpoints beyond Soviet cities. French official declarations made clear Paris's intention to destroy Soviet cities and industry a more "complete" and "credible" targeting policy. The next logical step would seem to be a full counterpower strategy.[5]

Nonetheless, the role of British and French forces beyond deterring a direct attack on national territory is uncertain. Neither Paris nor London has ever explicitly extended its deterrent force to cover the territory of allies, although the British forces are nominally under NATO command and France is committed to consulting Germany should a decision on whether to use nuclear weapons arise. Although it is in principle conceivable that French and British nuclear forces might one day form the nucleus of a highly capable and credible European nuclear deterrent, the political basis for such a development is still a long way off.

At the same time, even without a formal sharing of control and responsibility, the very existence of these forces has contributed at least indirectly to deterrence in Europe. The fact of multiple independent nuclear decision-making centers did confront the Soviet Union with an added degree of uncertainty regarding how NATO would respond to aggression. Moreover, notwithstanding a high likelihood of self-deterrence in case of conflict, Moscow could not completely discount the possibility of nuclear use even before British or French territory was directly affected.

And it is not at all impossible that British and French nuclear forces will play a greater role in European deterrence than they have in the past. Much depends, of course, on the process of European Community integration, and in particular on the Maastricht Treaty's provisions for a common foreign and security policy. If that process broadens and deepens, however, and the nations of Europe come to share their security more fully than ever before, then there is every reason to expect some form of extension of the deterrent effect of British and French nuclear weapons, explicit or not. However it develops, the policies of France and Britain—and, in particular, their cooperation in the nuclear field—will send the most powerful signals about the status of European nuclear cooperation in the years ahead.

Yet Europe's independent nuclear stance could go too far. If fully completed, the French and British nuclear modernization programs will result in a combined sea-based force that would be larger than the U.S. and Russian forces under a finite deterrence regime. Adjustments and reductions in the former are therefore likely to be a prerequisite for achieving the latter.

We draw two primary conclusions from this discussion. First, *Franco-British nuclear cooperation will play a critical role in determining how their arsenals figure in Europe-wide deterrence, and the United States should therefore encourage and support such cooperation.* United States support could take the form of eased restrictions on the sharing of nuclear secrets, provision of key equipment, or other steps.

Second, *the inventory of French and British nuclear forces should be reduced by half.* So long as the United States and Russia agree not to deploy strategically significant missile defenses (i.e., over and above those allowed by the ABM Treaty), Britain and France can meet their deterrent requirements with a force of roughly 200 operational warheads each. While delivery systems need not be reduced, the number of warheads on each missile could be cut from 8 to 4 in the case of the British Trident and from 6 to 3 in the case of the French M-4 missile.

THE FUTURE OF EXTENDED DETERRENCE

If a posture of finite nuclear deterrence is to mean anything, it must mean a commitment to forgo possessing nuclear weapons primarily useful for tactical situations, that is, nonstrategic nuclear forces. The political situation in Europe has changed dramatically—as is evidenced by the historic reductions in U.S. and Russian forces at the strategic level and, particularly, at the nonstrategic level.

The process set in motion by President Bush's initiative should now be extended to its logical conclusion—a legally binding agreement to eliminate all nonstrategic nuclear forces. As U.S. and Russian force levels come down, the United Kingdom and France can no longer escape the reality that their nuclear inventories must be adjusted and reduced.

NOTES

1. "London Declaration on a Transformed North Atlantic Alliance," *NATO Press Communiqué,* S-1(90)36, July 6, 1990, p. 5.
2. "The Alliance's New Strategic Concept," *NATO Press Communiqué,* S-1(91)85, November 7, 1991, p. 15.
3. Ibid.
4. "It is only in the framework of an anticities strategy," one French commentator argued in 1980, "that the desirable level of damage can be guaranteed with the means that remain in proportion to the scientific, industrial, and economic possibilities of France. Any other strategy . . . could not but weaken deterrence." But Lewin, cited in David S. Yost, "French Targeting Policy," in Desmond Ball and Jeffrey Richelson, eds., *Strategic Nuclear Targeting* (Ithaca, N.Y.: Cornell University Press, 1986), p. 143. François Heisbourg refers to "the sort of counter-force options found indispensable to NATO's extended nuclear deterrence" and suggests that, without a significant expansion of current French and British modernization plans, attempts by them to perform extended deterrence would not be credible. François Heisbourg, "The British and French Nuclear Forces: Current Roles and New Challenges," *Survival* 31, no. 4 (July-August 1989): 316.
5. Yost, "French Targeting Policy," p. 133. Indeed, Yost notes (p. 144) Gen. Pierre Gallois's suggestions that France already targets "at least some Soviet soft military targets in the Kola peninsula."

5

Regional Deterrence

The two previous chapters dealt with the cold war obsession of U.S. nuclear planners—the (former) Soviet nuclear and conventional threat. In this chapter, our study turns its attention to the chief concern of post-cold war U.S. military strategy: regional contingencies. Regional challengers outside Europe pose a growing threat to the United States. Some have or may someday have nuclear weapons; others have substantial conventional forces; still others are developing ballistic and cruise missiles of steadily increasing range and accuracy. Several have nationalistic, ideological, or religious motives to undermine U.S. allies and interests.

At issue is the extent to which nuclear weapons can help deter such aggressors, or wars once regional conflicts have begun. The book on this question was opened, not closed, by the Persian Gulf War of 1990-91, in which veiled U.S. threats of nuclear use may have helped deter Iraqi chemical attacks on U.S. allies and forces. With a declining defense budget and a growing need to project power to isolated hot spots around the world, the United States will need to assess carefully the role nuclear weapons will play in its regional contingency plans.

TEMPTING PROLIFERATORS?

Before examining that subject, however, it is necessary to look first at the potential impact of arms control on proliferation. Chapter 2 has already made the case that deep reductions in nuclear arms, as well as operational arms control and other confidence-building measures among all five declared nuclear powers, might help contain nuclear proliferation. Yet some observers contend that it might have the opposite effect, that it might actually tempt nations into proliferating.[1] If U.S. and Russian nuclear arsenals were much smaller, the argument goes, regional powers and other states might suddenly decide that they could afford nuclear parity.

This argument does not stand up to close examination. Those who make it say that deep U.S. and Russian reductions would convey the impression that the acquisition of even a few nuclear warheads would be very important. Yet it has been true for decades that the possession by some rogue state of a few bombs would change the global balance of power in important, and perhaps fundamental, ways. This very belief has already motivated all of the world's efforts to halt proliferation, including the Nonproliferation Treaty itself. A decision by Washington and Moscow to go down to 300 or 500 or 1,000 weapons would be highly unlikely, by itself, to lead proliferators to decide that small arsenals would be more useful.

Moreover, such an effect is empirically false. Many of these states have been diligently seeking nuclear weapons for decades, thus belying the notion that large nuclear arsenals deter proliferation. The deep reductions required to move to small arsenals might not stop proliferation, but it is hard to make the case that they would accelerate it.

Nor is the vast size of U.S. and Russian arsenals a significant factor in keeping potential proliferators from acquiring the bomb today. A host of other issues are involved, not least the immense economic and diplomatic cost of building an overt nuclear arsenal. In particular, the motives driving states *toward* the acquisition of nuclear weapons are in large measure unique to their situation. This fact, as we recognized in chapter 2, mitigates the value of deep cuts as a nonproliferation tool; it also reduces the degree to which such reductions can serve as a new incentive for proliferators to join the NPT.

Finally, the key to measuring a nuclear force is quality rather than quantity. As long as the United States and Russia have a profound *technical* lead in nuclear weapons over any potential proliferators, the quality gap will be so large that this alone, quite apart from the question of numbers, would deter proliferators from thinking they could somehow "match" Washington's and Moscow's arsenals. Even the CIA posits a decade before any more nations get true ICBMs, and that time could be lengthened— perhaps indefinitely—with more rigorous enforcement of the Missile Technology Control Regime (MTCR) and with new sanctions for violators.

Little reason therefore exists to fear that the arms control steps proposed in the preceding chapters would tempt additional nations into considering nuclear weapons programs or into expanding programs already under way.

DETERRING REGIONAL AGGRESSORS

What role then, can nuclear weapons play in supporting U.S. foreign and defense policy in the developing world? Deep cuts might not create new temptations for proliferation, but would they hurt U.S. interests by undermining necessary functions of U.S. nuclear weapons? Of what use are nuclear weapons in a regional context?

This second question gains added importance from the fact that U.S. military strategy is increasingly gaining a regional cast.[2] The days are past when the United States faced a unified global threat. Today, potential threats to U.S. interests come in a variety of regional flavors: a resurgent Iraq, a rapidly rearming Iran, a North Korea some believe to be intently building a nuclear arsenal, and others. Most U.S. military planning is today focusing on regional issues, and most military capabilities are being viewed in terms of the contribution they can make to regional operations. In this context, the most important role for U.S. nuclear weapons in the years ahead may be in supporting U.S. policies of regional deterrence and warfighting.

Nonetheless, we believe it is important for U.S. decision makers to understand that *the presumption must always be against the use of nuclear weapons, for deterrence or combat use, in regional contingency plans.* A strict and hopeful taboo has held since the 1950s: the taboo against the use of nuclear weapons for any but the most grave purposes. United States leaders rejected the nuclear option in Korea and again in Vietnam, and in doing so they helped to keep alive the notion that nuclear weapons are somehow different from other weapons—unique, unthinkably destructive, unsuitable for anything short of all-out war.[3] This prohibition against nuclear use (except in retaliation) safeguards U.S. interests by making it more difficult for potential adversaries to use nuclear weapons against U.S. forces engaged in combat; and it makes additional sense given the U.S. dominance in conventional warfare.

Keeping nuclear weapons out of regional contingency plans is also important from a nonproliferation perspective. Recently enunciated U.S. plans to target "every reasonable adversary" would have, as recognized by former U.S. SALT negotiators Ralph Earle and John Rhinelander, "a disastrous impact on our nonproliferation efforts" and in the process "whet the appetite of other, far less responsible nuclear have-nots, adding impetus to a new, and immensely destabilizing, multilateral arms race."[4] This was one of the major themes of chapter 2, and it stands as an important rationale for additional arms control.

Yet it might be wrong for the United States to reject outright the possibility of threatening to use—or even using—nuclear weapons in regional conflicts *for deterrent and, if necessary, retaliatory purposes.* If Iraq had invaded Kuwait two years later than it did, for example, with the added advantage of a nascent nuclear force, any U.S. response would have had to center on the deterrent effect of U.S. nuclear weapons. Otherwise, U.S. expeditionary forces, as well as U.S. allies such as Saudi Arabia and Egypt, would have been vulnerable to nuclear attack. It may be impossible to claim with complete certainty that U.S. nuclear forces will *never* be used, or their use never threatened, in regional crises or wars.

The question for U.S. planners, then, is straightforward: What threats might justify the use of nuclear weapons in deterrent or combat roles? We will examine three: conventional aggression, chemical or biological attack, and nuclear attack.

Conventional Aggression

There are no conventional threats that we must today deter with nuclear weapons, especially none in the developing world. There were, and are, political reasons that required the West to threaten a nuclear response to conventional aggression in Europe. But similar reasons do not exist in the Third World, in part because the U.S. interests at stake are not as great. A North Korean attack south, an Iranian strike across the Persian Gulf, a widened war in the Balkans—none of these events would call for a nuclear response.

In large measure this is true because there will always be better options in responding to conventional aggression in the developing world than nuclear weapons. Given the range, precision, and destructive power of modern conventional forces, a regional deterrence strategy based on those forces is perfectly sufficient for deterring conventional threats.[5] No regional leader aware of the coalition performance in Desert Storm can doubt the capabilities of modern U.S. and Western military systems. In many cases, moreover—as in, for example, Bosnia—it is difficult to see how the threat or use of nuclear weapons could possibly help.

Only two conventional scenarios might violate this rule. One is an imminent threat to Middle East oil supplies that could not be headed off by conventional means alone. If Iraq, for example, had kept moving south in early August 1991 into Saudi Arabia, and if Saddam Hussein had announced an intention to capture Saudi oil fields as well as those of the Gulf sheikdoms, the world economy would have been teetering on the edge of an abyss. Some in the U.S. government might have called for nuclear first use to halt the Iraqi advance.

Even this case, however, would not require the employment of nuclear weapons. Today there is little threat of such an overwhelming attack; neither Iraq nor Iran has the military infrastructure or power-projection capabilities capable of supporting such a major offensive. If the West is careful, it can prevent them from acquiring such capabilities again; and if it fails at that, it will have numerous conventional options for halting an Iraqi or Iranian advance short of nuclear use. Finally, even in the Gulf War, a nuclear cure (surely the use of nuclear weapons, probably even the explicit threat of their use) would have been worse than the disease. We would have won conventionally, but at much greater political and human cost than in Desert Storm.

The other situation in which the use of nuclear weapons might be discussed is that of an imminent, dire threat to large U.S. military forces. If, for example, the 82nd Airborne Division had arrived in Saudi Arabia only to be surrounded by Iraqi troops, then a terrible dilemma might have arisen in which a nuclear strike appeared to be the only means of saving the beleaguered U.S. unit. Again, however, many alternatives will exist to nuclear use, ranging from conventional military operations to political threats to horizontal escalation with conventional forces. And, in the end, the possible results of nuclear use—international condemnation, the collapse of military coalitions, accelerated proliferation—may constitute a greater evil than the loss of a military unit.

Chemical or Biological Attack

The United States could also use its nuclear arsenal to help deter the use of chemical or biological arms against the territory or military forces of the United States or its allies. Because the United States does not maintain an operational stockpile of chemical weapons, and no stockpile at all of biological munitions, some contend that the only suitable retaliatory weapon in the U.S. inventory would be a nuclear bomb. Advocates of such use of nuclear weapons point to the Persian Gulf War and argue that veiled U.S. threats of nuclear use influenced the thinking of the Iraqi leadership and was instrumental in forestalling Iraqi use of chemical weapons.

At first glance, such a connection between nuclear weapons and their chemical and biological cousins appears logical. All are "weapons of mass destruction," distinct from conventional arms in terms of both the scale of death and destruction they can inflict (at least, for nuclear and biological arms; this is less true of chemical weapons) and the manner in which they do so. The world community has outlawed both biological weapons (in the Biological Weapons Convention, or BWC, of 1975) and, in the new Chemical Weapons Convention (CWC), chemical arms; nuclear weapons seem a perfectly logical hedge against the illegal use of chemical and biological weapons (CBWs).

On closer examination, however, the case for *explicit* threats of nuclear use, or for a U.S. policy of nuclear retaliation against CBW attack, looks less attractive. In fact, such policies are neither advisable nor necessary.

The one recent experience we have is not very instructive on how useful nuclear threats are in deterring chemical attacks. Most U.S. military officers who served in the Gulf War and helped debrief top Iraqi commanders agree that the Iraqis decided not to use chemicals because they were unable to do so, not because they had been deterred. Round-the-clock U.S. air bombardments, the enormous difficulty of moving any supplies overland, and the risk that chemical stocks attacked by the enemy could explode in the midst of Iraqi troops apparently rendered the possibility of a high-level Iraqi decision to use chemical weapons moot. Iraq simply could not get the chemicals into the field at the right time in the battle with the necessary weather. At the same time, it is entirely possible that Saddam Hussein and his top aides did expect a nuclear response if they used chemical weapons, and that this restrained them.

We are left, then, with theory and conjecture to determine what role U.S. nuclear weapons can play in deterring chemical or biological warfare. Any effort to enmesh those three categories of weapons of mass destruction into an inextricable web of deterrence must take account of one sobering fact: if nuclear weapons become an escape clause of sorts for chemical and biological arms control, then the process of *nuclear* arms control will be greatly complicated. Nuclear disarmament would be out of the question if nuclear weapons came to be viewed as a necessary backstop to worldwide bans on CBWs. United States nuclear targeting needs, and hence U.S. warhead requirements, would grow, and the prospect for dramatic arms reductions would dim—as would, almost certainly, the hope for nonproliferation, as other states turned to nuclear weapons for the same purpose.

Any nuclear threats in this context will also face an unavoidable problem of credibility. Aggressors simply might not believe U.S. statements that chemical attacks will be met with nuclear responses, particularly if those statements—as in the Gulf—are highly ambiguous and contradicted by U.S. allies. (In the Gulf, both the British and French explicitly ruled out the use of nuclear weapons.) The experience of extended deterrence, in which U.S. pledges to protect a vital interest (the safety of Western Europe) with nuclear weapons were questioned almost from their inception, suggests that much more pervasive doubt (amounting to disbelief) would arise about a policy of nuclear retaliation for CBW use.

Conventional weapons also provide a perfectly suitable means of threatening massive damage to an aggressor who uses CBWs. Modern conventional warheads and strike systems allow U.S. and allied military forces to do enormous damage to aggressors, particularly those with less-advanced militaries and fragile, developing economies. Once the United States held air superiority, it could do virtually as much damage as it wished with conventional weapons, constrained only by the supply of ammunition and the moral soundness of the strategy. A threat, therefore, to do great damage to the economy and society of a state that uses CBWs would be just as powerful as a threat to use nuclear weapons, and much more believable.

As in the Gulf, conventional weapons can also be used to prevent the use of CBWs once a conflict has begun. A combination of a rigid air cap, an air campaign designed to paralyze enemy movements, and a coordinated effort to destroy CBW delivery vehicles on the ground (including Scud-type missiles and CBW-capable artillery) would dramatically reduce the threat posed by chemical and biological arms. The coalition's success in such an effort in the Gulf is promising in this regard, and the U.S. military is working to fill gaps in its capability, such as the difficulty in locating Scuds.

There are also political alternatives to nuclear deterrence of CBWs. The United States and any coalition partners could, for example, threaten to modify the goals of a war once chemical or biological munitions had been used. Again using the Iraqi case, President George Bush could have announced that any Iraqi use of chemical weapons would have constituted a war crime, the enforcement of which would have required a change of regime in Baghdad. Such threats would be especially persuasive if backed by the international community in the form of UN resolutions. And the UN could take other steps, threatening to impose decade-long embargoes of political recognition and certain industrial goods on nations that use CBWs.

The literature on CBWs sometimes mentions doomsday scenarios in which some terrorist group or adversary state manages to inject large amounts of chemical or biological agents into the U.S. water supply or otherwise find a way to poison millions of Americans. It goes without saying that, in the event of such a horrific act, U.S. leaders might well consider a nuclear retaliation—if it can be proved who launched the attack and if the perpetrators are susceptible to nuclear retaliation (as terrorist groups might not be). But this scenario is so extreme and unlikely that it need not become a basis for stated policy.

In general, therefore, the United States should not and need not explicitly connect nuclear weapons with CBWs. It is in the U.S. interest to develop military and political alternatives to nuclear weapons—both their use and the threat of their use—for deterring chemical and biological warfare. This is not to suggest that the United States must rule out nuclear retaliation, although it may choose to do so. But U.S. defense planners must avoid making that ambiguous threat explicit, and should not plan to retaliate against CBW use with nuclear weapons.

Nuclear Attack

Having ruled out the use of nuclear threats for either conventional or CBW deterrence, we are left with what is almost unanimously viewed as a proper, moral, and nonprovocative role for U.S. nuclear weapons: deterring the use of nuclear weapons against U.S. forces or territory.

Yet many caveats attach to this general rule. First, the proper response to a nuclear attack will not always be a nuclear retaliation. In some cases, the United States may deem it more advisable to absorb a small nuclear strike against its troops in the field than to retaliate in kind. A U.S. policy of merely changing the goals of its military operations and seeking the political destruction of the nuclear aggressor's government might help define the attack as more an act of terrorism than a rational military step, which in turn would reinforce the taboo against the use of nuclear weapons.

United States officials would certainly not want to convey this impression in advance, lest regional nuclear powers come to believe they could use nuclear weapons against U.S. forces without fear of retaliation. It is perfectly reasonable for the United States, while ruling out the first use of nuclear weapons, to state explicitly that it reserves the right to retaliate in kind (or even disproportionately) to any nuclear attack on its territory or military forces. This task is not very difficult, and it does not require especially complex nuclear forces or plans. In short, then, the United States will continue to *threaten* the use of nuclear weapons in retaliation for nuclear use; in the actual event, there may be good reasons for U.S. leaders not to follow through on their threats.

Several implications flow from the preceding analysis. The most prominent has to do with the general U.S. policy toward the use, or nonuse, of nuclear weapons in regional contingencies. Since 1978, the United States has officially rejected the use of nuclear weapons against nonnuclear states not allied with any nuclear powers—a pledge that the Bush administration conspicuously de-emphasized during the Gulf War. *This policy should be reaffirmed, expanded to encompass a blanket promise of no first use of weapons of mass destruction in regional conflicts, and enshrined in a national security directive of the highest order.*

Second, because the policy of retaliating in kind for nuclear attacks is inherently credible, *any deterrent threats, or actual strikes with nuclear weapons, in regional conflicts can be accomplished with strategic weapons.* No persuasive advantage is offered by tactical weapons based in theaters of operation or by new nuclear weapons of small yield. One continuing exception to this rule is in Europe, as noted in chapter 4.

Indeed, there are reasons to believe that eschewing smaller nuclear weapons would augment deterrence. If a regional aggressor knew that the use of weapons of mass destruction would spark a U.S. retaliation, deterrence would be served by making that retaliation necessarily very destructive. As long as such regional powers did not have the ability to hit the United States, the fine-tuned calculations of restraint so popular in analyses of the U.S.-Soviet standoff would not apply. The United States would have nothing to lose, and everything to gain (in a deterrent sense), by being restricted to a devastating retaliation and not being able to launch a minor one.

Therefore, *low-yield nuclear weapons* (the inaptly termed "mininukes" and "micronukes") proposed by some as a necessary augmentation to the U.S. nuclear arsenal for regional conflicts[6] *are unnecessary for deterrence.* An even more pressing reason for avoiding a new class of small nuclear weapons is that such weapons would do much more harm to U.S. interests than good. Building a new set of nuclear weapons would require years of research and development work and many nuclear tests, all of which would undermine efforts to dismantle the nuclear infrastructure accumulated during the cold war and slow progress in U.S.-Russian arms control. Such a program would sow the seeds of mistrust throughout the world: nations like India and North Korea would assume they would be on the target lists of the new mininukes, and nationalists in the Russian military would undoubtedly take it as a sign of continuing U.S. pursuit of nuclear warfighting capabilities. Even if such weapons would add a significant capability to the U.S. arsenal, their costs far outweigh their benefits.

A SUBSTITUTE FOR NUCLEAR WEAPONS: INTERNATIONAL RESPONSE

In the long run, the world community may seek a more permanent solution to the problem of nuclear use in regional conflicts. Even during the initial phase of nuclear arms control, the promise of international sanctions could supplement unilateral deterrent threats. Any first use of nuclear weapons would be regarded as a threat to international peace and security and would trigger automatic punishment, probably under the aegis of the United Nations.

Such an arrangement might require a formal treaty binding all nations of the earth to respond to nuclear first use with political, economic, and possibly even military action.[7] This would supplement the ban on chemical and biological weapons contained in the Chemical and Biological Weapons Conventions. Various sanctions might be threatened in the event of such use:

- *Political sanctions.* The treaty could stipulate, as suggested above, that any first use of weapons of mass destruction is a war crime and that the entire top political and military leadership of any state using such weapons will be held accountable. This provision would constitute the centerpiece of the sanctions regime, providing a justification for other steps. If the state were at war, the world community would seek its total defeat and/or the removal of its leadership. If the nuclear use occurred during a civil war or insurgency or in the closing stages of an interstate conflict, then other nations would break off diplomatic relations and take additional steps to isolate the offending nation.

- *Economic sanctions.* Until the government responsible for nuclear or CBW use had resigned, the treaty could require a complete international embargo of trade with the state, perhaps enforced by military forces from UN countries. It would be difficult to embargo such items as food and medical supplies; a prohibition on purchases of any modern technology would probably suffice. The leaders of the embargoed state—and, more important, its citizens—would know that their economy would constantly deteriorate as long as that government remained in power.

- *Military sanctions.* Such a treaty might also contain language endorsing "all military means necessary" to keep the offending state from winning a military victory in the conflict in which it used nuclear weapons. These means might include providing weapons or other assistance to the nation fighting the offending government, backing insurgent groups seeking its downfall, or, in extreme cases, actually committing UN troops against it.

This much could be accomplished in the next few years. Eventually, this international regime could be strengthened to include more mandatory action. A revised treaty might, for example, *require* the United Nations to send military forces against the nation that used nuclear, chemical, or biological weapons. And eventually, such a treaty could help support complete, or near complete, disarmament. A robust global agreement that provided for crippling political, economic, and military sanctions in the event of nuclear use could in effect take the place of a credible nuclear retaliation in deterring nuclear war. And the treaty might some day be extended to prohibit *any* use of weapons of mass destruction, not merely their first use.

Obviously, such an agreement will depend for its success on the support of the international community. If China or Russia refused to agree to it, as either might well do today, or if they or other states offered lukewarm support for its provisions, then the agreement would not be able to substitute for any national policies. But even a partial agreement would be helpful, providing the legal basis for sanctions against nations that use weapons of mass destruction and establishing the foundation for more comprehensive treaties in later years. And this assumes, of course, that the United States and its NATO allies, which have relied on the threat of nuclear first use in the past, would agree to such a treaty; the analysis in chapter 4 suggests that they might well be willing to do so before long.

A DENUCLEARIZED REGIONAL STRATEGY

This chapter has suggested that the only role for U.S. nuclear forces in regional conflicts is to deter the use of nuclear weapons against U.S. military forces or U.S. territory. While U.S. leaders might not want explicitly to rule out the threat of nuclear use to deter chemical or biological attacks, they would be well advised to avoid the actual use of nuclear weapons in retaliation for such attacks. The United States should reject the use of nuclear weapons to help deter conventional attacks, and it should make this rejection public. It should seek an international treaty banning the first use of weapons of mass destruction and providing for specific sanctions in the event of such use.

NOTES

1. George Questor and Victor Utgoff, "Nuclear Dilemmas," *The Washington Quarterly* 16 (Winter 1993).
2. See Michael J. Mazarr, James A. Blackwell, and Don M. Snider, *Desert Storm: The Gulf War and What We Learned* (Boulder, Colo.: Westview Press, 1993), chapter 7.

3. See McGeorge Bundy, "Nuclear Weapons and the Gulf," *Foreign Affairs* 70 (Fall 1991): 83-94.

4. Ralph Earle II and John B. Rhinelander, "Wrong Way on Nuclear Arms," *Washington Post,* January 21, 1992, p. A19.

5. See Gary L. Guertner, "Conventional Deterrence and U.S. Strategy," *The Washington Quarterly* 16 (Winter 1993).

6. See Thomas W. Dowler and Joseph S. Howard, "Countering the Threat of the Well-Armed Tyrant: A Modest Proposal for Small Nuclear Weapons," *Strategic Review* 19 (Fall 1991): 34-40.

7. Various proposals have been made in the UN Conference on Disarmament to ban any use, or the first use, of nuclear weapons; see Thomas Bernauer, *Nuclear Issues on the Agenda of the Conference on Disarmament* (Geneva and New York: United Nations Institute for Disarmament Research, 1991), pp. 12-14. None of these, however, apparently contains any explicit enforcement provisions.

6

Strategic Defenses

In the wake of the Persian Gulf War and the collapse of the Soviet Union, the focus of the Strategic Defense Initiative (SDI) has shifted from defense against massive missile attacks to defense against much smaller attacks. In his 1991 State of the Union address, President George Bush stated:

> Looking forward, I have directed that the SDI program be refocused on providing protection from limited missile strikes, whatever their source. Let us pursue an SDI program that can deal with any future threat to the United States, to our forces overseas, and to our friends and allies.

The Pentagon's Strategic Defense Initiative Organization (SDIO) quickly enshrined these goals in its "global protection against limited strikes" program, later renamed the Global Protection System (GPS). This system is intended to address two types of threats: the possibility of an accidental or unauthorized missile launch from the former Soviet Union and intentional attacks from Third World nations. The GPS and related proposals for limited missile defenses have received substantial support in Congress.[1] This, combined with the recent agreement between Presidents Bush and Yeltsin to explore the possibility of joint work on a global missile defense, has reinvigorated the debate over limited defenses.[2]

An important consideration in designing a limited defense is that it not upset strategic stability—a goal that is well recognized by Congress and the new Clinton administration.[3] The United States and Russia most likely will want to retain a nuclear deterrent for the foreseeable future; if they did not, the problem of accidental or unauthorized launches would be easy to solve.[4]

A nuclear deterrent force requires a survivable and massively destructive retaliatory capability, and this capability must not be threatened by a limited defense. If a limited defense even *appears* capable of nullifying an opponent's nuclear deterrent under some circumstances, it may hinder or even reverse the ongoing process of reducing strategic arsenals, thereby making us less rather than more secure. These critiques do not necessarily apply to tactical missile defenses, which seek only to defend deployed U.S. and allied military forces against local cruise or ballistic missile attack.

FUTURE DEFENSIVE FORCES

As expressed in the Missile Defense Act of 1991, the goal of a limited defense is to provide "a highly effective defense of the United States against limited ballistic missile threats, including accidental or unauthorized launches or Third World attacks, but below a threshold that would bring into question strategic stability." In addition, a limited defense system should "provide a highly effective theater missile defense to forward-deployed expeditionary elements of the Armed Forces of the United States and to friends and allies of the United States." The act was a bipartisan piece of legislation and, in theory, could help guide U.S. policy on strategic defenses even in a Clinton administration.

Limited Attacks

The design of a limited defense depends on the definition of "limited attack." Accidental attacks are usually thought to involve the launching of a single missile, but it is unclear why accidents, whose nature is entirely speculative, would not involve many more weapons. Unauthorized attacks are more readily defined as the launch of the maximum number of missiles under the direct command of a single individual.[5] In the case of Russia, this might be a regiment of ICBMs (e.g., nine SS-25s each armed with 1 warhead), or all of the missiles on a submarine (e.g., twenty SS-N-20s with 5 warheads each).[6]

Third World attacks are also highly speculative because so few nations have missiles capable of attacking the United States. Indeed, the only Third World nation with such forces is China, which has deployed four liquid-fuel ICBMs and twenty-four short-range SLBMs, each armed with a single warhead, and is in the process of modernizing these forces.[7] Israel and India have a latent ICBM capability, since both have orbited satellites using indigenous space launch vehicles, but neither has plans to develop an ICBM. The gradual diffusion of missile technology and expertise may increase the number of countries capable of fielding ICBMs or SLBMs, but it is highly unlikely that any Third World nation would deploy a force significantly larger or more capable than China's.

Setting aside for the moment missile attacks on allies or U.S. forces overseas, which might involve much larger numbers of short-range missiles, *a reasonable goal for a limited defense would be to intercept up to ten ICBMs, carrying ten warheads, launched simultaneously from any point on land, and up to twenty SLBMs, carrying a total of 100 warheads, launched rapidly from any point in the oceans.* The defense should be "highly effective" against such attacks, meaning that it should provide "high confidence of extremely low or no leakage."[8] Here we will interpret "highly effective" to be an average overall effectiveness of 99 percent; that is, an average of only 1 out of 100 incoming warheads would penetrate the defense.

A less demanding measure of effectiveness, such as the ability to intercept just 90 percent of incoming warheads (or even 75 or 50 percent), would ease the burden on any defensive system and reduce the potential instability it might cause. A less capable system would need fewer interceptors and would therefore be less able to disrupt a retaliatory strike. Yet the purposes of a very limited defense demand near-perfection for its truncated missions. A defense explicitly designed to safeguard U.S. cities against accidental, unauthorized, or Third World strikes that allowed the destruction of even one city would be counted as a failure. If a Russian submarine commander succeeded in launching 100 warheads at the United States, for example, a defense that destroyed 90 of them while allowing the rest to smash New York, Chicago, and Washington and kill millions of people would hardly justify either public confidence or the investment of tens of billions of dollars.

Possible Architectures

A wide range of limited-defense architectures has been proposed, ranging from the 100-interceptor, ground-based defense allowed by the 1972 Anti-Ballistic Missile Treaty (ABM Treaty) to a combination of thousands of space-based and ground-based interceptors and sensors. But as noted, an ABM Treaty-compliant system has no hope of meeting the goals outlined by Congress. One hundred interceptors simply could not be made so effective that they could intercept 100 incoming warheads with anything approaching zero leakage. And in any case, even a perfect system based at the treaty-designated site at Grand Forks, North Dakota, would leave most of the U.S. population unprotected. Radars at Grand Forks would be unable to track a wide range of possible missile trajectories, including ICBM attacks by China or North Korea on San Francisco, or by Libya or Iran on Boston. Interceptors based in Grand Forks would, moreover, have no hope of engaging SLBMs launched against coastal targets.[9]

Expanded ground-based systems involving three to seven sites and up to a thousand interceptors have also been proposed. While such systems offer the prospect of defending all U.S. territory, they are unlikely to meet the ambitious goals set for a limited defense. As argued by the U.S. Department of Defense,[10] a single-layer architecture is inherently vulnerable to catastrophic failure if the attack has unusual and unanticipated characteristics.[11] Even if enough interceptors are available for multiple independent shots at each warhead (which would *not* be possible for short-range SLBM launches), "high confidence of extremely low or no leakage" is unlikely.

Nor would ground-based systems protect friends and allies of the United States against surprise attack.[12] Theater defenses might be able to defend particular targets, but only if enough warning is available to deploy the defense. Indeed, reliance on ground-based systems could actually encourage surprise attacks on allies precisely for this reason.

To provide for a highly effective limited defense, SDIO has proposed a two-layer GPS consisting of space-based interceptors (SBIs) and ground-based interceptors (GBIs).[13] Current schemes envision about 1,000 SBIs, or "brilliant pebbles," orbiting the earth, ready to attack missiles soon after they are launched, and up to 1,000 GBIs based in the United States to destroy the warheads before they reenter the atmosphere. Defense of friends and allies would be accomplished by the same constellation of SBIs combined with rapidly deployable ground-based theater defenses. The system apparently was designed to defend against a simultaneous attack by 200 warheads, which is the largest number of warheads now deployed on a single Russian submarine.

A system consisting of roughly 1,000 SBIs and 500 GBIs would be the smallest deployment capable of meeting the goals of limited defense. This projection is consistent with SDIO estimates.[14] Yet a defensive system of this size would, even at the levels of strategic forces set forth in the Washington summit agreement, threaten the survivable retaliatory capability of both Russia and the United States and could prove destabilizing in several other ways.

STRATEGIC STABILITY

To preserve deterrence, one must convince adversaries that one's nuclear forces can inflict unacceptable damage after withstanding an all-out first strike and after penetrating an adversary's defenses. If both sides are convinced that a first strike by either side would lead to the destruction of the attacker, and that the attacker would not be much better off than the victim, then there should be no incentive to strike first. The lack of incentives to strike first, even when the risk of nuclear war appears high, is known as "crisis stability." The insensitivity of the nuclear balance to changes in the number or character of weapons is known as "arms race stability." The most desirable state is when both sides believe that there are no incentives to strike first under any circumstances and when there is little hope (or worry) that the purchase of additional offensive or defensive weapons by either side would change this situation.

The survivability of nuclear forces is highly sensitive to their alert status, since virtually all nonalert forces can be destroyed by a first strike. Table 6.1, "Alert Rates in Peacetime and Crisis," gives optimistic but reasonable assumptions about the percentage of U.S. and Russian forces that might be on alert during normal peacetime operations and during a serious crisis. These alert rates are consistent with recent operational practices as well as recent agreements between the United States and Russia.[15]

Using the offensive force structures and alert rates given in tables 1.1 and 6.1, table 6.2, "Nuclear Weapons Surviving a First Strike," gives estimates of the U.S. and Russian forces that could be expected to survive a first strike

Table 6.1
Alert Rates in Peacetime and Crisis

	United States		Russia	
	Peacetime	Crisis	Peacetime	Crisis
ICBMs	95%	95%	50%	80%
SSBNs	67%	83%	44%	67%
Bombers	0%	50%	0%	50%

by the other and be delivered in retaliation (see Appendix 1 for details). A Russian first strike could destroy about 80 percent of U.S. ICBMs, all ballistic missile submarines (SSBNs) in port, and all bombers not on alert. A U.S. first strike could destroy all nonalert Russian mobile ICBMs, submarines, and bombers and up to 20 percent of the alert mobile ICBMs. Thus, the outcome mostly depends on the alert status of the forces.

An attack when the alert status of opposing forces is low is often referred to a "surprise attack" or a "bolt from the blue." Most analysts consider a bolt-from-the-blue first strike to be implausible, especially in view of the improved relations between the United States and Russia. They believe that a nuclear attack could come only after an extended crisis.

It is worth noting, however, that alert status might be kept low intentionally even during a crisis or that warning of an impending attack might be ignored. For example, Soviet leader Nikita Khrushchev did not raise the alert status of Soviet forces during the Cuban missile crisis, presumably because he believed that alerting forces would increase the risk of war. Stalin ignored warnings of attack by Germany because he feared that defensive preparations

Table 6.2
Nuclear Weapons Surviving a First Strike
(assuming no strategic defenses are deployed)

Weapon	United States		Russia	
	Peacetime	Crisis	Peacetime	Crisis
ICBMs: warheads	110	110	140	220
EMT (equivalent megatons)	50	50	120	180
SLBMs: warheads	1000	1300	690	1000
EMT	310	390	150	220
Bombers: warheads	0	470	0	300
EMT	0	210	0	120
TOTAL: warheads	1100	1900	830	1600
EMT	370	660	260	530

might anger Hitler and prompt an attack. The United States ignored indications of imminent attack by Japan on Pearl Harbor. Thus, many analysts, while admitting the low probability of a bolt-from-the-blue attack, consider it a reasonable basis for prudent defense planning.

Even after suffering a bolt-from-the-blue first strike, both nations could deliver a devastating retaliation equal to about 300 EMT.[16] A retaliatory strike of this magnitude could kill 60 to 100 million people in either country—a prospect that should be more than sufficient to deter a first strike.[17] A first strike when opposing forces are on crisis alert would lead to a retaliatory attack about twice as large, but not much more fearsome.[18] Thus, the nuclear balance is extremely stable at these force levels.

A limited defense can, however, cast doubt on this fearsome retaliatory capability, possibly undermining crisis and arms race stability. For example, a defensive system designed to intercept the missiles from a single submarine launched by an insane commander obviously could intercept the same missiles launched in retaliation. Indeed, because all SSBNs would not be clustered in one small area, and because the victim of a first strike could not fire its SLBMs precisely in unison, many more SLBMs could be engaged. Even if simultaneous, clustered SLBM launches are possible, reliance on such a strategy might lead to hasty retaliatory decisions that undermine efforts to end the war, as well as making SSBNs more vulnerable to antisubmarine warfare.[19]

It may seem counterintuitive to say that a defense designed to intercept 100 warheads would under different circumstances be capable of intercepting thousands, but there are three important differences between defending against a limited attack and defending against a large retaliatory strike: the spatial extent and temporal extent of the attack and the probability of destroying an individual warhead.

In terms of *spatial extent,* a limited defense would be designed to engage up to twenty missiles launched from a single point on the earth and up to 100 warheads targeted against any region in the United States. The same system could, however, destroy many more missiles if the launches were spread out over Russia and the oceans, because many more SBIs could participate in the defense. For example, a defense designed to intercept a few ICBMs *or* SLBMs could destroy both at the same time, just as it could simultaneously destroy ICBMs launched from eastern *and* western Russia. In fact, about six times as many ICBMs can be engaged in the boost phase if the launches are distributed among current bases across Russia rather than at a single point.

A defense's effectiveness would also be affected by the *temporal extent* of attacks. A limited defense would be designed to engage up to ten ICBMs launched simultaneously, and up to twenty SLBMs launched rapidly. While first strikes and limited attacks could be synchronized precisely, it is unlikely that nations would have the same confidence in a retaliatory strike—especially one that took the victim somewhat by surprise. If all of the ICBMs or SLBMs in a given region do not fire in unison, additional SBI will orbit into view and will be able to participate in the defense. If, for example, a retaliatory launch of all the SLBMs from all the submarines in a typical patrol zone takes two to three times as long as a rapid launch of SLBMs from a single submarine, then four to five times as many missiles could be destroyed in the boost phase.[20] If the SSBNs are distributed among two to three such patrol zones, then the number of retaliatory missiles intercepted could be eight to sixteen times more than the number the system was designed to intercept in a limited attack.

All of this affects the system's *probability of kill*. A limited defense designed to engage 100 warheads with a 99 percent probability of kill could engage many more warheads with a somewhat lower kill probability, destroying considerably more than 100 warheads. For example, a two-layer defense in which each layer could engage 100 warheads with an independent kill probability of 90 percent could on average destroy almost twice as many warheads in a large retaliatory attack as in a limited attack (180 vs. 99). Moreover, if three interceptors (each with a kill probability of 54 percent)

Table 6.3
Warheads Surviving a Limited Defense

Warheads	United States		Russia	
	Peacetime	Crisis	Peacetime	Crisis
Peacetime	3500	3500	3000	3000
After First Strike	1100	1900	800	1600
After SBI	600	1300	260	1000
After GBI	130	900	30	540
RESULTS: EMT	40	300	10	200

Source: See appendix for details.

are required in each layer to achieve an overall kill probability of 90 percent, then nearly twice as many missiles or warheads could be destroyed (320 vs. 180).[21] Thus, in this simple example, one can see how a system designed to destroy 99 warheads (out of 100) would be capable of destroying as many as 320 (out of 600).

Table 6.3, "Warheads Surviving a Limited Defense," gives the number of U.S. and Russian warheads and equivalent megatonnage that would survive a counterforce first strike by the other and penetrate both layers of a GPS defense. As described above, the space-based layer is assumed to be capable of intercepting ten ICBMs launched simultaneously from a small area in the United States or Russia and up to twenty SLBMs launched rapidly from a single submarine anywhere in the oceans. The ground-based layer, which is assumed to be capable of intercepting up to 100 warheads targeted against a given region of the United States or Russia, is composed of 500 interceptors.[22] Both layers are assumed to have independent kill probabilities of 90 percent, for an overall kill probability of 99 percent.[23] Retaliatory ICBMs are assumed to be launched simultaneously from existing bases in the United States and Russia; SLBMs are assumed to be launched from two widely separated million-square-kilometer patrol zones;[24] both are assumed to be launched against targets spread across Russia or the United States.

Note that if its strategic forces are on crisis alert, Russia would be capable of delivering a retaliatory strike of roughly 200 EMT after suffering a first strike and penetrating U.S. defenses; under similar circumstances, the United States could deliver somewhat more. In both cases, limited missile defenses reduce the delivered megatonnage by more than a factor of two, with less than half being delivered by missiles (mostly SLBMs). Even so, retaliatory attacks of this magnitude could kill 50 million to 100 million Americans or Russians[25] and should therefore serve as a powerful deterrent. On the other hand, 200 EMT may be uncomfortably low for military planners who typically use "worst-case" assessments that significantly underestimate the performance of their own weaponry while overestimating that of an opponent.

If, however, a first strike is launched when forces are on peacetime alert, no bombers would survive and Russia would be able to deliver only about 10 EMT in a retaliatory strike—twenty times less than the amount that could be delivered without limited defenses. If targeted against the most densely populated U.S. cities, this would be enough to kill 5 million to 10 million people. A U.S. retaliatory strike under similar circumstances would be limited to 40 EMT.

Clearly, then, strategic defenses on the order contemplated in the GPS program would have devastating implications for strategic stability at a level of 500 to 1,000 warheads. Table 6.3 explains, for example, that of the 1,100 warheads from a peacetime-alert U.S. deterrent force surviving a first strike, only 130 would penetrate a GPS-like defense. For a similar Russian retaliation of 830 warheads, fewer than 30 would penetrate. If both nations had only 1,000 warheads in their whole force, with perhaps several hundred surviving a first strike, the number of warheads that would survive a first strike and a limited defense would be very small—at best a few dozen. At a level of 500 warheads, it is possible that a defense would wipe out the retaliation completely. In short, further reductions in offensive arms and limited strategic defenses are incompatible.

THE DANGERS OF DEFENSE

In addition to instability, another danger is that steps taken to reinforce deterrence could lead to a net loss in security. Russia could, for example, reverse its planned reductions in nuclear weapons and its peacetime alert status, or at least prevent deeper reductions from taking place. Doing so would be detrimental to international security because such reductions play an important role in lowering the risk of accidental or unauthorized use of nuclear weapons. Increasing peacetime alert rates by putting bombers back on quick-reaction alert or increasing the number of SSBNs on patrol forces both sides into a more hair-trigger posture, increases opportunities for accidents and unauthorized use, and contributes to the possibility of misunderstanding and unintended escalation.

Even worse, a nation that believes its retaliatory capability is threatened by defenses may resort to offensive countermeasures, such as decoys, maneuvering reentry vehicles, faster-burning boosters, and depressed-trajectory SLBM launches. This might in turn spawn improvements in the defense to maintain the desired effectiveness against limited attacks. The risk of such a new defense-offense arms race would certainly be reduced given the major-power trust and amity presumed in this report. Like large nuclear forces, however, strategic defenses are not appropriate to a world where no risk of war exists, and continued pursuit of them can therefore produce suspicion and mistrust.

In this connection, it is worth mentioning that effective SBIs necessarily would be highly capable antisatellite (ASAT) weapons, even against attack-warning and communications satellites in high orbits. These and other military satellites are crucial components of the U.S. nuclear deterrent, as well as being invaluable force multipliers in conventional conflict, as shown in the Persian Gulf War.[26] For example, Russia might fear that its satellites would be destroyed in an attack by the United States, leaving it incapable of communicating with its retaliatory forces. Thus, the SBIs' inherent ASAT capability would only exacerbate instabilities in the nuclear balance created by limited defenses.

Another danger is that a nation possessing limited defenses might become enamored with the goal of becoming invulnerable to nuclear threats of all kinds. If effective limited defenses could be built while strategic arsenals are reduced, a nation might convince itself that a near-perfect missile defense was within reach. The temptation to expand "limited" missiles defenses and to complement them with an effective air defense might be irresistible.[27] If rival nations wanted to maintain mutual vulnerability, such a decision would almost certainly trigger an arms race.

Even if neither side is tempted to expand the defense, the possibility of rapid expansion will be an unavoidable characteristic of an effective limited defense. Once the necessary SBIs, GBIs, and tracking sensors are developed, tested, and deployed in large numbers, expanding the system simply would be a matter of producing more interceptors. Indeed, any limited defense would require a ready supply of spare interceptors to replace those that are used in tests or in battle or that fail with age. The "brilliant pebble" SBI is so small and light that 1,000 could be orbited with just a dozen or so Titan IV rockets, making quick expansion of the system a real possibility.[28] Moreover, additional SBIs could be placed in orbits optimized for coverage of Russia, where they would be about twice as effective against Russian ICBMs and SLBMs in northern patrol areas as SBIs in orbits chosen for uniform coverage of the earth.[29]

U.S.-RUSSIAN COOPERATION?

It is often said that the dangers of limited defenses could be managed by close cooperation between the United States and Russia, but such cooperation is highly unlikely and even if it were possible would be irrelevant. Either the United States and Russia will want to maintain the other's vulnerability, or they will not. If either nation wants to maintain the vulnerability of the other, then cooperation on limited defenses would be self-defeating, since limited defenses substantially reduce that vulnerability.[30]

If, on the other hand, both the United States and Russia no longer wished to maintain the vulnerability of the other, then there would be much less expensive and much more effective ways of reducing the likelihood of accidental or unauthorized use. The two nations could, for example, cooperate on installing improved permissive action links; improved command, control, and communications facilities; or systems to destroy errant missiles after launch—provided that all those measures are implemented with the proper safeguards and conditions.[31] In short, there is no role for cooperative defenses against accidental or unauthorized attacks: when cooperative defense is possible, it isn't necessary; when it could be useful, it isn't possible.

At the other end of the spectrum, maintenance of large nuclear arsenals and the development of strategic defenses is sometimes justified as a hedge against renewed conflict with Russia. But unless the United States is very careful, such actions are just as likely to generate suspicion and cause friction between the two countries—a self-fulfilling prophesy of renewed military competition. Moreover, if a new cold war erupts *and* defenses are deployed, an offense-defense arms race is likely, with both sides jockeying to maintain a nuclear deterrent in the face of increasingly sophisticated defenses.

EFFECTS ON OTHER NUCLEAR POWERS

One often-ignored but absolutely critical aspect of strategic defenses is their possible effect on the "middle" nuclear powers. United States allies in Europe, as well as China, are likely to object vehemently to any significant deployment of strategic defenses. Defenses could undermine the security of U.S. allies and spark costly and destabilizing new arms buildups in various regions.

China has opposed SDI since its inception, because even a limited defense would effectively nullify China's modest ICBM and SLBM force. If China decided that maintaining the vulnerability of the nuclear superpowers was vital to its security, it would have little choice but to engage in an expensive program to modernize its nuclear arsenal by building more ICBMs and SLBMs, developing multiple warheads and penetration aids for its missiles, or deploying weapons that are invulnerable to ballistic missile defenses, such as bombers and cruise missiles. When the Soviet Union and the United States were developing first-generation ABM systems in the mid-1960s, China responded with programs to develop a larger ICBM, multiple warheads, penetration aids (electronic countermeasures and light exoatmospheric decoys), and a fractional orbital bombardment system.[32] If China responds to GPS in a similar manner, it could stimulate a wider nuclear arms race in South Asia involving India and Pakistan.

France and the United Kingdom would be in a similar position if Russia deployed a limited defense. As now planned, the survivable strategic forces of both nations are likely to consist of one or two SSBNs on patrol during peacetime. This is deemed a sufficient deterrent in the absence of defenses, but if Russia acquires even a limited nationwide defense, France and the United Kingdom would have little choice but to expand their forces greatly or rely on the United States for deterrence.

CONCLUSIONS

A limited defense that provides a high degree of protection against unauthorized, accidental, or other small attacks, including the launch of all SLBMs from a single submarine, would also be highly effective against a retaliatory strike. The ability to deliver a devastating blow in response to a first strike, which is the sine qua non of deterrence, would be substantially reduced. Indeed, a nation's retaliatory capability after absorbing a bolt-from-the-blue attack would fall well below the 200 EMT commonly assumed to represent a minimum deterrent. A potent retaliatory strike is possible only if the attack comes when nuclear forces are on alert, but most of this would be delivered by bombers, not by missiles, and could be subject to attrition by improved air defenses.

If the United States or Russia faced a limited GPS-type defense, it might well conclude that its nuclear deterrent capabilities were lacking. In response, the country might halt planned reductions in nuclear forces or deploy a variety of countermeasures to defeat the defense, inducing both nations to spend additional money without increasing their security. In the extreme case, limited defenses could trigger the kind of offense-defense arms race that the Anti-Ballistic Missile Treaty was designed to prevent. Close U.S.-Russian cooperation could ameliorate the adverse side effects of limited defenses, but if such close cooperation were possible, there would be easier, cheaper, and more effective ways to reduce the threat of unauthorized or accidental missile launches.

Limited defenses would also have a profound effect on the other nuclear powers, whose more modest strategic arsenals would be effectively nullified by a limited defense. Most worrisome would be the reaction of China, which, unlike France and the United Kingdom, could not count on extended deterrence from one of the nuclear superpowers. If, as in the past, China responds to the prospect of superpower defenses by initiating modernization programs to preserve its deterrent, it could trigger a wider nuclear arms race in South Asia.

Under reasonable assumptions about future force structures and the performance of offensive and defensive systems, therefore, limited defenses can threaten strategic stability. Given the very low probability of unauthorized or accidental launches, and the very small number of countries that will have the capacity to attack the United States with ballistic missiles in the foreseeable future, the benefits of limited strategic defenses are not worth the penalty of decreased stability. And while a more ambitious view of strategic defenses, as a hedge against rearmament in a world of tiny nuclear arsenals, might be attractive to some, this chapter suggests that there is no stable path to that nuclear end state.

Apart from extremely small territorial defenses, the one form of missile defenses that does not threaten stability are tactical systems designed to protect deployed military forces. The U.S. military certainly needs better tactical missile defenses, and it will develop and deploy them; indeed, given the risks of strategic defenses, the bulk of U.S. work on missile defenses should focus on tactical systems. The major challenge in the years ahead may be to prevent the effects of those efforts from spilling over into the strategic nuclear realm and creating unwanted instability.

NOTES

1. For example, the Missile Defense Act of 1991 increased SDI funding by 34 percent and called for development of the required technology to allow the deployment of a limited missile defense by 1996. Earlier in 1991, Senators Warner, Cohen, and Lugar proposed a limited defense system consisting of 700 to 1,200 ground-based interceptors based at five to seven sites.

2. White House, Office of the Press Secretary, "Joint U.S.-Russian Statement on a Global Protection System," June 17, 1992.

3. For background on defenses, see Paul L. Chrzanowski, "The Transition to a Deterrence Posture More Reliant on Strategic Defenses," in Dietrich Schoreer and David Hafemeister, eds., *Nuclear Arms Technologies in the 1990s* (New York: American Institute of Physics, 1988), pp. 220-43; Dean Wilkening and Kenneth Watman, "Strategic Defenses and First-Strike Stability" (Santa Monica, Calif.: RAND, R-3412-FF/RC, November 1986); Glenn A. Kent and David E. Thaler, "First-Strike Stability and Strategic Defenses" (Santa Monica, Calif.: RAND, R-3918-AF, October 1990); and William Kerby, "The Impact of Space Weapons on Strategic Stability and the Prospects for Disarmament: A Quantitative Analysis" (Hamburg: Institut fur Friedensforschung und Sicherheitspolitik, October 1986).

4. If, for example, the two countries had no fears about each other, but wanted nevertheless to maintain (vastly smaller) nuclear arsenals as a deterrent to attacks by other nations, they could engage in a multitude of cooperative measures to reduce the probability of unauthorized and accidental launches, such as joint attack warning, improved security and command and control, or the installation of destruct-after-launch systems. Such measures would be far more reliable and far less expensive than building a defensive system to guard against the launch of each other's missiles. See *Reducing the Dangers of Accidental and Unauthorized Nuclear Launch: Alternatives to a Ballistic Missile Defense System* (Washington, D.C.: International Foundation for the Survival and Development of Humanity, January 1990).

5. *Architecture Integration Study: Interim Report* (Washington, D.C.: Strategic Defense Initiative Organization, U.S. Department of Defense, April 1992), p. 9.

6. We assume that Russia will meet the agreed limit on SLBM warheads by reducing the number of warheads carried by each SLBM, not by reducing the number of submarines (which, while saving the most money, would make the force more vulnerable to antisubmarine warfare) or by reducing the number of SLBMs on each submarine (which would make targeting more difficult). For example, the Typhoon, which now carries twenty missiles and 200 warheads, is assumed to carry the same number of missiles but half the number of warheads. If Russia instead reduces the number of submarines, the maximum number of missiles that could be launched in an unauthorized attack would remain the same, but the number of warheads would double; if it reduces the number of missiles per submarine, the number of warheads would remain the same, but the number of missiles would be halved.

7. John Wilson Lewis and Hua Di, "China's Ballistic Missile Programs: Technologies, Strategies, and Goals," *International Security* 17, no. 2 (Fall 1992): 19, 28. According to Lewis and Di, the current SLBMs will be replaced by a much longer-range and more accurate missile in the mid- to late 1990s, and the ICBMs will be replaced by solid-fuel missiles by 2010.

8. *Report to Congress: Conceptual and Burden Sharing Issues Related to Space-based Ballistic Missile Defense Interceptors* (Washington, D.C.: U.S. Department of Defense, March 1992), p. 7.

9. Lisbeth Gronlund and David C. Wright, "Limits on the Coverage of a Treaty-Compliant ABM System," *Physics and Society* 21, no. 2 (April 1992): 6.

10. See *Conceptual and Burden Sharing Issues,* pp. 9, 18-21.

11. For example, the attacker may employ countermeasures intentionally, such as decoys or chaff, or unintentionally, as happened when Iraqi-launched Scuds tumbled and broke up in the atmosphere.

12. Space-based defenses may also be incapable of destroying short-range missiles, especially if the trajectories are slightly depressed. See David C. Wright and Lisbeth Gronlund, "Underflying Brilliant Pebbles," *Nature* 350 (April 25, 1991): 663.

13. To achieve a 99 percent kill probability with a two-layer system, each layer must have a statistically independent kill probability of 90 percent, which, while highly ambitious, is achievable.

14. The initial GPALS (Global Protection Against Limited Strikes) architecture called for 1,000 SBIs and 750 to 1,000 GBIs based at five to seven sites (depending on whether Alaska and Hawaii are defended). Since the maximum number of warheads aboard a submarine is likely to be cut in half for both the United States and Russia, the number of GBIs required should be reduced by a similar factor. The *Architecture Integration Study* (AIS) has suggested that as few as 500 SBIs and 200 GBIs based at three sites might be sufficient, but this ignores several stressing attack scenarios and depends on highly optimistic estimates of mid-course discrimination and interceptor lethality. Using more realistic assumptions, the AIS concludes that 1000 SBI and 600 GBI are needed. See appendix 1 for more detail.

15. Russian road-mobile ICBMs are assumed to have a lower alert rate than U.S. silo-based ICBMs due to the necessity of maintaining crews ready to drive the missile launchers at a moment's notice (much like bombers). Twelve of the eighteen U.S. SSBNs are assumed to be at sea at peacetime, surging to fifteen during a crisis. During the cold war, the alert rate of the (much larger) Soviet SSBN fleet was only about 20 percent (about twelve of sixty subs); I assume that Russia would maintain the same number of SSBNs at sea during peacetime (twelve of twenty-seven), surging to eighteen during a crisis. (According to press reports, however, the alert status of Russian SSBNs has been very low since the breakup of the Soviet Union.) Russian bombers have never been on quick-reaction alert, and the United States removed its bombers from peacetime alert in 1991. During the crisis, I assume that 50 percent of the bombers (both Russian and U.S.) would be ready to take off in a few minutes after warning of an attack is received.

16. The equivalent megatonnage of a warhead is the yield raised to the two-thirds power, since the area that can be destroyed by blast is proportional to the two-thirds power of the yield. (This scaling law does not apply, however, to the other destructive effects of nuclear weapons, such as fire.) The equivalent megatonnage referred to here is the sum of the EMT for all surviving, deliverable warheads and bombs.

17. Barbara G. Levi, Frank N. von Hippel, and William H. Daugherty, "Civilian Casualties from 'Limited' Nuclear Attacks on the Soviet Union," *International Security* 12, no. 3 (Winter 1987/88): 188. The authors give 90 million to 140 million deaths for a 300-EMT attack on the Soviet Union; since Russia contains only 52 percent of the population of the former Soviet Union (but a high percentage of its military and economic targets), it is reasonable to assume that

casualties from a 300-EMT attack on Russia would be closer to the estimates given
for the United States.

18. The diminishing returns of increasingly large attacks are indicated by the fact that
    increasing the delivered EMT by 33 percent (to 400 EMT) increases the number
    of deaths by 5 to 12 percent.

19. The victim of a first strike could conceivably delay the bulk of the retaliatory
    strike, firing the missiles through the"hole" in the SBI defense created by a small
    initial retaliatory strike. But this strategy depends on the implausible assumptions
    that the victim's space-tracking capabilities survive the first strike, that the
    aggressor cannot rapidly maneuver existing SBIs or deploy new SBIs to plug the
    gap in the defense, that the victim would wait days for the hole to appear above
    his forces (while vulnerable to bomber attack and antisubmarine warfare), or that
    SSBNs could quickly maneuver into position below the hole.

20. See Appendix 1 for details. Assumes SBIs with a maximum speed of 6 kilometers
    per second, an altitude of 460 kilometers, and a reaction time of 60 seconds, and
    SLBMs with a burnout time of 170 seconds an a burnout altitude of 240 kilome-
    ters, and that SSBNs are spread over a million-square-kilometer patrol area.

21. See Appendix 1 for details. If p is the kill probability of an interceptor and n is
    the number of interceptors, then the probability of kill P after n independent shots
    is given by $P = 1 - (1-p)^n$. Solving for p, we have $p = 1 - (1-P)^{1/n}$. Thus, if $P = 0.9$
    and $n = 3$, $p = 0.54$. The total number of incoming warheads that can be destroyed
    in one-on-one engagements is proportional to $n \cdot p$.

22. Although Russia is nearly twice as large as the United States, the northern regions
    of the country contain few cities, and it is unlikely that a negotiated agreement on
    defenses would allow Russia more GBIs or GBI sites than the United States.

23. As described in appendix 1, the SBI calculations are based on the scaling for
    boost-phase intercept. If midcourse intercepts are possible with high probability
    (e.g., 90 percent), then a system designed to destroy ten ICBMs or twenty SLBMs
    would be less effective against a retaliatory strike than indicated here, but accurate
    estimates would require detailed orbital simulations. It is far more likely, however,
    that a high probability of kill will not be possible in midcourse; if several intercept
    attempts are required, this would increase the effectiveness against retaliatory
    strikes, as described above. Moreover, we assume that the system is designed to
    intercept twenty rather twenty-four SLBMs, that a retaliatory SLBM strike is
    launched from just two bastions, that only one shot is required to achieve a 90
    percent kill probability in both layers, and that the SBI constellation is perfectly
    matched against both threats (i.e., that a system designed to intercept twenty
    SLBMs could not intercept more than ten ICBMs and vice versa). Thus, it is
    unlikely that the results given here overestimate the capability of a limited defense
    against a retaliatory strike.

24. Russia reportedly keeps its SSBNs on patrol in the Barents Sea and the Sea of Okhotsk, while U.S. SSBNs roam the Atlantic and Pacific oceans. One might assume, however, that the United States would cluster its SSBNs as a countermeasure to a limited defense without greatly increasing their vulnerability. The estimates given here assume that a fleet of SSBNs could not launch its missiles in less than twice the time required by a single SSBN, which seems reasonable after suffering a first strike.

25. Levi, von Hippel, and Daugherty, "Civilian Casualties," p. 188.

26. See, for example, Steve Fetter, "Protecting Our Military Space Systems," in Edmund S. Muskie, ed., *The U.S. in Space: Issues and Policy Choices for a New Era* (Washington, D.C.: Center for National Policy Press, 1988), pp. 1-25.

27. The United States lost interest in air defense after the Soviet Union deployed ICBMs, because a defense against aircraft would do little good without an accompanying defense against missiles. If effective missile defenses are deployed, however, this would be sure to reopen the debate over air defense. For a discussion of the potential of strategic air defense, see Arthur Charo, *Continental Air Defense: A Neglected Dimension of Strategic Defense* (Cambridge, Mass.: Center for Science and International Affairs, Harvard University, 1990).

28. Assuming each brilliant pebble weighs 100 to 150 kilograms (including garage and station-keeping fuel) and that the Titan IV, which has a payload capacity of 18 tonnes to low-earth orbit, could orbit 10 tonnes of brilliant pebbles.

29. For a boost-phase defense, see Christopher T. Cunningham, "The Space-Based Interceptor," in Dietrich Schroeer and David Hafemeister, eds., *Nuclear Arms Technologies in the 1990s* (New York: American Institute of Physics, 1988), p. 278.

30. It would be logically possible for the United States and Russia to maintain a jointly operated defensive system to guard against unauthorized or accidental launches from either country, which could be disabled by either country during a period of potential conflict between the two countries. In addition to the enormous management problems such a system would create, a limited defense that was disabled during crises would not be very useful, since accidental, unauthorized, or limited attacks would be most likely at these times.

31. See Sherman Frankle, "Aborting Unauthorized Launches of Nuclear-armed Ballistic Missiles through Postlaunch Destruction," *Science and Global Security* 2, no. 1 (1990): 1-20, for a discussion on how this can be done in an absolutely secure manner.

32. Lewis and Di, "China's Ballistic Missile Programs," pp. 17, 21.

7

Nuclear End States

As suggested in the previous chapters, any complete discussion of nuclear arms control needs an ultimate point of reference, a long-term goal toward which arms reductions and operational arms control are working. Current nuclear cuts are taking place in a teleological vacuum; to what end are they being pursued? What is the desired nuclear end state? Because one does not exist, the case for additional reductions lacks force; why go below 3,000 strategic warheads, for example, if not as part of a plan to achieve general disarmament?

Charles Glaser makes the connection well. "Although there appears to be a consensus that arms control should be directed at reducing the size" of U.S. and Russian arsenals, Glaser points out, "few proponents explain why smaller forces are preferable. . . . The appeal of disarmament probably explains much of this interest in reductions."[1] There are other reasons cuts in force size might be valuable on their own merits—the potential for damage limitation, for example, or the connection between U.S.-Russian arms control and nonproliferation. As argued in chapter 2, those reasons are sufficient of themselves to justify further progress. To be fully effective, however, arguments for moving toward very small nuclear forces need at least a provisional long-term goal, some persuasive nuclear end state capable of galvanizing support.

Here arises a problem. There is no consensus, nor any immediate prospect of one, that total and complete disarmament will under almost any circumstances be a feasible option. For most analysts (and probably for most publics as well), the risks of cheating and sudden breakout by rogue states are simply too great. And yet it would be a tragedy if the present momentum toward international cooperation and disarmament passed without some attempt to establish a more robust nuclear end state whose practical effect is virtually to eliminate the risk that nuclear weapons will be used.

This chapter represents a first attempt to begin forging a consensus on the ultimate goal of nuclear arms control. Are we headed to complete disarmament or merely a minimal version of the finite deterrence proposed in chapter 3? Do other options exist?

GOALS AND PURPOSES

It is important to clarify at the outset what advantages might be accrued from a second phase of arms control. Chapter 2 laid out several benefits of further progress in arms control, and two of them are especially relevant to that second phase: damage limitation and nonproliferation.

Any nuclear end state must have something more fundamental than those goods as its basic purpose: eliminating any significant role for nuclear weapons in relations among major powers. In a world of finite deterrence, the risk of nuclear war may be very low; the stability of the nuclear balance might become nearly absolute; and the danger of accidental or unauthorized nuclear launches may be essentially eliminated. None of those factors, therefore, helps mark off the boundaries of a more ambitious phase of arms control. Only the most fundamental of purposes—the elimination of the threat of nuclear war as a tool of international politics—can do that.

As with all aspects of arms control, however, removing nuclear weapons from major power relations is a goal with various degrees, and it does not necessarily require the destruction of all existing nuclear weapons. In the strictest sense, the possibility of a nuclear war will never disappear entirely; even friendly nations could become adversaries, and even if all existing nuclear weapons are destroyed new ones could be built. A nuclear end state would aim at ending, in a practical sense, the ability of nations to use nuclear weapons as implements of war on a day-to-day basis. It would end, for all time, the nuclear arms race and remove the cloud of risk and fear that has hung over the nuclear powers for forty years. In this sense it would have as much of a spiritual as practical benefit.

This goal might demand complete and total disarmament. It might, on the other hand, actually recommend the retention of a very limited nuclear arsenal, either by the international community or by a selected group of nations. If the world community was satisfied that those nations could use their nuclear arsenals only to prevent nuclear war, then many nations might see value in preserving minimal forces capable of deterring rogue states from acquiring and using nuclear arsenals. Everything depends on the status of international relations, as the chapter discusses later.

Second, movement to some form of a nuclear end state would help end the threat of nuclear proliferation. As noted in chapter 2, many states, both those party to the Nonproliferation Treaty and those that have not joined it, have demanded that the declared nuclear-weapons states commit themselves to some form of disarmament as a long-term goal. Answering that request, which appears as article VI of the NPT, would constitute a major step toward meeting the concerns of developing nations and would dramatically improve the chances for nonproliferation.

CHANGING ASSUMPTIONS

Nuclear end states are distinguished from near-term progress in arms control in that they no longer respect the assumptions governing current U.S. nuclear policy (those assumptions are reviewed in table 7.1). The nuclear policies of more ambitious arms control are not meant to *bring about* those changes, but rather to *respond* to them. Major, positive developments in world politics are therefore a prerequisite for nuclear end states.

The key to all of the assumptions is found in assumption 1—the existence of an anarchic state system whose major powers have rivalries and disputes that could lead to war. At its extreme, this international system is characterized by fluid balance-of-power politics in which states jockey for position and maintain large military forces. Even when the resulting competition is muted—either by a rigid bipolar structure, as during the cold war, or by newfound partnerships among the major powers, as today—many analysts and national leaders cling to the belief that nuclear weapons play a critical role in deterring major war by making its consequences unacceptable. And because it is impossible to test this hypothesis, abandoning the nuclear "crystal ball" will be an enormously controversial step as long as this basic condition of world politics persists.[2]

Mitigating assumption 1 will require the pervasive belief, by national leaders and publics alike, that nuclear weapons are no longer necessary to deter major war. As most major powers tend toward representative democracy and as the power of international organizations to mediate disputes and prevent and control conflicts grows, it is conceivable that national leaders would cease to consider force as an alternative for settling disputes. In short, war between major powers would have to be viewed as unthinkable,[3] or at least so unlikely as not to justify operational nuclear arsenals.

Table 7.1

Assumptions of Current U.S. Nuclear Policy

Assumption 1. The international system remains fundamentally anarchic, and a case can be made that nuclear weapons play a critical role in keeping peace between major powers by rendering war unthinkably destructive.

Assumption 2. A full-scale nuclear retaliation would be capable of causing what is generally understood to be "assured destruction."

Assumption 3. A full-scale nuclear retaliation would do enough damage to military installations to fulfill the notion of "military sufficiency."

Assumption 4. United States nuclear forces are capable, in both military and political terms, of extending deterrence to allies; French and British nuclear forces cannot do so, or at least not in any substantial fashion.

Assumption 5. The dominant nuclear balance remains a bipolar one.

Assumption 6. Nuclear forces held by developing-world proliferators do not provide a unique guide for force numbers, nuclear strategy, or procurement.

Assumption 7. Pressure from advocates of strategic defense continues a slow, gradual trend toward the deployment of defenses against tactical ballistic missiles as well as limited, ground-based strategic defenses.

Assumption 8. Spending on nuclear forces will continue to decline.

Assumption 9. Arms reductions have significant effects on the drive for reform and democracy in Russia.

Developments supporting such a trend might include a tightly interlocking web of economic, military, and political treaties and commitments; dispute resolution and crisis management mechanisms; and robust security guarantees, all laid over a foundation of exceedingly friendly relations among the great powers. States must have ample opportunities to settle their claims short of force or threat of force and must face stiff—perhaps even fatal—sanctions for resorting to warfare. And, perhaps most important, all major powers must have faith in this system so that no one attempts to hedge against it with covert military programs or other destabilizing behavior. At that point, major war may have become so unlikely, so implausible, that states are willing to abandon it as a planning guide for their military policy.

There is a distinction here, and one we mean to highlight, between *perception* and *objective conditions*. The theoretical possibility of war between major powers will never disappear entirely. But if the leaders of major powers *believe* that the chance of war between them has vanished—as, say, the heads of state of France and the United States believe is true between them today—then the basic condition for nuclear end states will have been satisfied.

Such a perception has already arisen among the nations of Western Europe. Just fifty years ago, Germany was locked in mortal combat with France and Britain; today the three are close allies, and no one believes there is any risk of war among them. Not all international relations need be as warm as those between France and Germany for a movement to a nuclear end state, but the evolution of partnership among the states of Western Europe provides the best example of the changes in perception required.

A resolution of assumption 1 also obviates assumptions 2 and 3, for neither assured destruction nor military sufficiency would be required in relationships of friendship and trust. To the extent that nuclear weapons had become devalued or drastically reduced, assumption 5, of a bipolar nuclear balance, would be meaningless as well.

By the time these further developments in international politics have occurred and nuclear end states can be implemented, the course of U.S.-Russian denuclearization will basically have run its course, and reform in Russia will be firmly rooted—otherwise the criteria for an end state regime will not have been satisfied. The bilateral nuclear standoff should have been completely eradicated, and the focus of denuclearization will therefore have shifted to a global basis. Together, these developments obviate assumptions 6 and 9. Assumption 4—extended deterrence—would remain relevant only in connection with regional proliferation; assumptions 7 and 8 might or might not be significant issues.

With all of these developments, the context for nuclear weapons would be dramatically altered. A new set of criteria would be required for nuclear force planning and nuclear arms control.

CRITERIA FOR NUCLEAR END STATES

If major war were no longer a threat, virtually all nuclear weapons could be abandoned. The rationale for significant nuclear arsenals would have disappeared, and the only question would be whether any such weapons were required at all.

Nonetheless, even end state forces and policies would be expected to safeguard the national interests of the countries involved, particularly those that are today declared nuclear powers. Enforcing various criteria would help preserve national security in a disarmed or near-disarmed world. Several suggested criteria are spelled out below.

1. To fulfill its basic purpose, *a nuclear end state must eliminate any significant role for nuclear weapons in the relations among major powers, a step that should include banning nuclear weapons or slashing their number to some irreducible minimum.*

2. *A nuclear end state should complete nuclear disarmament by the undeclared nuclear powers.* In addition to promoting drastic reductions in the nuclear arsenals of the five declared nuclear powers, an effective end state would create some of the conditions to allow the undeclared nuclear powers—India, Pakistan, and Israel—to abandon whatever nuclear ambitions they currently have. Movement to a nuclear end state alone will not be enough, but it is certainly part of the answer, especially for India and, thereby, for Pakistan as well.

3. *Nuclear end states must contain guarantees against cheating.* Any of the current nuclear powers could, after some years in a nuclear end state, decide covertly or overtly to violate its provisions. To be effective and persuasive, any end state regime must have both stringent verification measures and provisions for sanctions and deterrence in the event verification fails and one of the parties to the accord suddenly fields a large nuclear arsenal. Put another way, a sound end state will be designed to forestall "strategically significant cheating."[4]

4. *Finally, nuclear end states must protect against new proliferation.* To be secure and appealing, any nuclear end state must guard the international community against rogue proliferators and must avoid creating unique new advantages to covert proliferation. For example, if the community of nations decided to renounce nuclear weapons, North Korea might wonder why it should give up its nascent atomic bomb if that bomb would provide a major military advantage over a disarmed world. A nuclear end state must therefore undermine the value of a covert arsenal. To do so, it must preserve the inescapable certainty of retaliation—conventional, nuclear, or otherwise—for any nuclear use. In short, in a nuclear end state, the possession of a nuclear arsenal by some troublemaker should not confer, either actually or perceptually, military superiority.

Nor should an end state produce new motives to proliferate on the part of countries with severe security concerns. Today, the U.S. nuclear arsenal helps make German, Japanese, Korean, and Taiwanese bombs unnecessary through U.S. security commitments. If those commitments were no longer backed by a credible nuclear guarantee, some nations might renounce the disarmament regime and make provision for their own security with a small, perhaps disassembled, nuclear arsenal.

What is important is that this criterion applies to all weapons of mass destruction, not just nuclear weapons. A nuclear end state must not render covert (or overt) CBW arsenals more attractive to aggressive or defensive states. And it must take into account conventional military balances; where those balances need to be equalized by the deterrent power of nuclear weapons, provisions must be made to replace that deterrent effect.

A natural tension exists between the first criterion and the other three. The most radical disarmament measures, those that most fully eliminate nuclear weapons and thus the risk of nuclear war, will also be those that expose the major powers to the greatest risks of cheating and proliferation. Those nuclear end states that only partially address the nuclear risk, and that represent more of an evolutionary step from current arms control, will, because they retain small, national nuclear arsenals of some form, provide the best hedges against illegal nuclear programs.

ALTERNATIVES

A number of alternatives exist that might allow the world to meet the goals and criteria of an effective nuclear end state. These range from total, complete disarmament to various forms of small nuclear forces. Each is appropriate to a different stage of international politics.

Some will immediately object that our assumptions make our suggestions irrelevant. If the risk of major war has disappeared, why does it matter what happens to the small nuclear forces held by major powers? If they will not go to war with one another, then there is no risk of the weapons being used.

But working to eliminate the risk of *nuclear* war, as distinguished from the risk of any war, still makes sense, for several reasons. First, as noted in chapter 2, large, usable nuclear arsenals are symbols of mistrust. Their existence today threatens to push Russia and the United States into a new hostility; their existence in a world of peaceful, like-minded major powers would perpetuate doubts in each nation about the intentions of the others. Moving toward disarmament or some other nuclear end state would support and solidify the transition to friendly relations among the major powers.

Indeed, it is our belief that without commitment to such long-term goals, the current momentum in arms control could be lost.

Second, as long as nuclear forces remain deployed, the risk of accidental and unauthorized nuclear war will persist. It may be a very small risk, but it would be worth eliminating nonetheless.

Third and finally, a nuclear end state might provide a hedge against the failure of a more stable world order. Even the transition to a world of peaceful major powers and strong international institutions would not be irreversible. If a nuclear end state had been established in the meantime, it is possible that it might survive some level of renewed hostility and help stabilize an international system that had fallen out of the idyllic arrangement assumed in this chapter. In the same way that near-term arms control hedges against a collapse of U.S.-Russian amity, a nuclear end state would guard against the return of the risk of major war.

Nonoperational Nuclear Forces

The least ambitious option for a nuclear end state would be the retention of very small, nonoperational nuclear forces by various nations. Under this arrangement, each nation would keep a small number of nuclear weapons, which would be disassembled and made unready for use on a day-to-day basis. Both because of their small size—perhaps fewer than 100 weapons—and their unreadiness, such arsenals could not support any military missions at all; they would be a symbol, a hedge, a form of national insurance, but not a focus of competition or military planning.

We hesitate to call nonoperational nuclear forces a "minimum deterrent," because traditionally minimum deterrence has presupposed the existence of hostility between major powers and the use of nuclear weapons to mitigate that hostility. Our notion of nonoperational nuclear forces presumes the opposite.

To render nuclear forces nonoperational, various levels of dismantlement, or "degrees of unreadiness," could be imagined. Chapter 3 has already outlined the least stringent of these: removing bombers and ICBMs from alert status, providing for more rapid and reliable early warning, establishing guarantees against the use of submarines in a sneak attack, and so on. On the way to a nuclear end state, these steps could be expanded to make nuclear arsenals unusable without weeks, or even months, of reassembly. The goal is to produce deployments where nuclear weapons cannot be used suddenly in a massive attack, and where that fact can be ensured by reliable verification schemes.

For example, all nuclear powers could agree to separate nuclear warheads from their missiles and store the two separately, perhaps hundreds of miles apart. The nuclear devices themselves could be removed from the warheads and locked away in vaults. Eventually, rapid nuclear delivery vehicles—ICBMs and SLBMs—could be completely destroyed, thus requiring a nation attempting to break out of the agreement to produce a whole new fleet of missiles. Scientists could pull apart the nuclear bombs themselves, necessitating days or weeks of reassembly before a nuclear strike could be conducted.

Various force structures might be appropriate for nonoperational nuclear arsenals. One might include a de facto ban on all ballistic missiles, which might help stability; no state would be subject to nuclear attack within the thirty-minute flight time of ICBMs, and a ban on missiles would "diminish the tempo of crises and conflicts, buying time for diplomacy to resolve them."[5] A more complete step would be to dismantle and destroy all but free-fall gravity bombs, thus establishing a bomber-only nuclear force. Bombers fly more slowly than missiles and can be detected at great range and are thus ineffective first-strike tools. Those who appreciate the survivability of strategic submarines might prefer an SSBN-only force, with the submarines in port and separated from their missiles on a day-to-day basis.

Of course, one indispensable element in any such arrangements would be a verification regime sufficient to convince all major powers that none of the others could covertly reassemble its nuclear force. One way of achieving this, and in some senses the ultimate form of unreadiness, would be the formal transfer of control of nuclear weapons on national soil to an international body. Nuclear powers could agree to collect their fissile materials into central locations that would be monitored by international inspectors from the United Nations or another body. The international inspectors would not prevent the materials from being removed and placed on delivery vehicles, but they would make that step known—and thus give strategic warning to any potential victims of attack.

Various degrees of international control exist, and it is possible that a regime that was rudimentary at first could expand in the direction of full control. For example, at some point the United Nations might begin inspections of national nuclear forces to supplement the verification contained in bilateral or multilateral arms control agreements. Indeed, once arms control becomes a multilateral enterprise, some form of international verification will be required. Gradually the UN mandate might grow to include permanent representatives at nuclear sites, a system of hot lines and crisis-management centers, a dedicated UN early warning system, and other elements. Finally, the nuclear powers might agree to dismantle their nuclear weapons and place the warheads in storage under UN authority.

Nonoperational nuclear forces would meet the criteria for a nuclear end state. By removing nuclear weapons from operational military forces and relegating them to a role as geopolitical insurance, such arsenals would not entail a day-to-day risk of nuclear accident or war. They might promote disarmament by some of the undeclared nuclear powers by eliminating the peacetime nuclear threat to them. Yet, by preserving some weapons in national hands, nonoperational forces would establish a firm guarantee against cheating and would undermine the rationale for new proliferation.

An International Nuclear Force

If the perception of the risk of war among major powers has sufficiently eroded, nations might consider even more ambitious nuclear end states. Some observers have proposed placing an operational nuclear force or static nuclear stockpile under the command of an international body—suggested is the United Nations.[6] The weapons and equipment of the force would be loaned or donated by individual member states; the United Nations would not go into the business of nuclear production.

In fact, it might be better to think of such a force as an outgrowth of an established security organization like NATO rather than an appendage to the United Nations. A NATO nuclear force dedicated to the security of its members would be viewed as much more reliable than a similar UN force. It could be that an international arsenal would evolve from the bottom up—from a European force to a NATO force that eventually extended its purview to the East—rather than from the top down, imposed by the United Nations. The developing world, however, might well perceive an international nuclear force developed from such a process to be imperialistic.

However it was designed, an international nuclear force might offer a number of advantages. First and most important, it would provide for complete disarmament among all nation-states, preserving only a small arsenal under international command. Because a nuclear force could not go to war with itself (unless a portion of it is seized by an outside power), the risk of nuclear war would have been eradicated. International command would also energize nonproliferation efforts and eliminate the risk of a global nuclear holocaust; nuclear weapons would shift from instruments of national power to tools of the international community that exist to prevent aggression. An international nuclear force could also set a dramatic precedent: it could become the first step toward an international organization with a monopoly on the use of force.

In all of these senses, an international force clearly meets the first criterion for nuclear end states. It also meets the third and fourth criteria, establishing a clear and explicit safeguard against the risks of cheating under disarmament and of new proliferation. No cheater or new nuclear state would be able to threaten any other states without threat of nuclear response.

An international nuclear force could also perform extended deterrence. Nations (like Germany and Japan) that have based their security partly on a U.S. nuclear umbrella could continue to do so, only they would rely on a new guarantee from an international body. By preserving the umbrella and promoting nonproliferation, the arrangement would make unnecessary a German or Japanese bomb.

A UN or other world nuclear force would therefore eliminate the risk of nuclear war while preserving a hedge against illegal nuclear powers and guaranteeing the security of those major powers that choose not to acquire a nuclear arsenal.

Complications arise when one considers the decision-making mechanism that would be used to enforce the nuclear guarantees of an international force. Countries with explicit nonnuclear principles such as Japan—and their number might grow in a less nuclear world—might be barred from agreeing to nuclear strikes under any circumstances. If the force were controlled by the UN Security Council with its current mandate, it might be all but useless, because any one of its members could launch an aggression and then veto any nuclear response.[7] In many ways these problems are a subset of the larger difficulties of true collective security: national commitments to binding, automatic treaties in advance often are not reliable.

These barriers are not, however, insuperable. For one thing, our assumption is that, by the time a nuclear end state is implemented, international institutions will have been significantly modified and strengthened. They may begin to acquire decision-making authority of their own. And to whatever extent the United Nations (or other world body entrusted with the nuclear force) can act independently, the nations of the world could agree in advance that any nuclear threat would be met with a UN counterthreat and that any nuclear use would result in an automatic UN retaliation. This would make Security Council votes or other consensus decisions in a crisis unnecessary. And again, if the international force is controlled by an expanded NATO, then it would reside in a reasonably sound decision-making venue.

Under such an arrangement, the loyalty, competence, and responsibility of the international nuclear force commanders would be of the utmost importance. But that is already true with national nuclear forces today, and there is no reason to believe that the United Nations or NATO could not obtain an effective staff of reliable officers.

Some fear that an aggressor could use its conventional forces to attack the bases of the UN nuclear arsenal—its airfields, submarine ports, or missile fields—and seize control of the international nuclear force. (Of course, this objection would not hold if the force belonged to NATO or some other alliance.) Even today, however, negotiations are under way on the creation of a UN army, and in ten or twenty years' time such a force could be large enough to defend a nuclear force against attack. The nuclear force could be based at remote locations to prohibit attack over land or with short warning. United Nations nuclear operators would undoubtedly utilize complex launch codes, without which an attacker would be unable to employ the arsenal even if he seized it. Moreover, one can hardly imagine the world community standing idly by during such an attack, knowing that its fate was at stake; any nation or nations that attempted such a gambit would face immediate retaliation from most other developed powers.

Finally, there is a risk that UN nuclear pledges would not be credible. With little "immediate stake" in some crises, would an international body risk its own survival by using nuclear weapons?[8] In fact an international nuclear force might be the most credible deterrent of all, because an aggressor would have nothing at which to launch a second strike. The United Nations is only a building, and its nuclear forces could be based on some remote island. Against whom would an aggressor hit back? Any random shots aimed, for example, at Security Council members would guarantee their immediate participation in the war. Once the UN has retaliated against nuclear use, further nuclear attacks by the aggressor would be either pointless or suicidal—an effective deterrent situation. An international force would allow major powers to share the risk of nuclear deterrence in a manner that renders each of their separate commitments arguably more credible.

So this alternative satisfies a situation in which major powers are ready to cede the nuclear deterrent mission, but in which there is still some concern about one or more big powers breaking away from the peaceful consensus governing the majority.

Total and Complete Disarmament

Finally, there is the traditional conception of the ultimate nuclear end state: complete disarmament. If the risk of nuclear war is to be fully eradicated, some contend, the weapons that embody that risk must be entirely banned.[9]

Clearly, disarmament meets the first two criteria established above for nuclear end states. Nuclear weapons would be banned from the earth. Disarmament would outlaw nuclear weapons from military arsenals and render them illegal as elements of national power.

Beyond that, everything depends on the assumptions that define the second phase of nuclear arms control. Given our assumptions about that phase—that amicable relations prevail among all the major powers, and the risk of war between them has been all but eradicated—the arguments against complete disarmament become less persuasive. This option is therefore only appropriate to a world in which assumption 1 has truly been turned on its head and there is no risk of war among major powers.

Although complete disarmament is commonly assumed to be unrealistic, it is important to keep in mind that, given the assumptions of a world supportive of a nuclear end state, it may one day be seen as appropriate to the circumstances of international politics. For that to occur, the transformation of the world system would have to be more profound than that envisioned as a context for nonoperational or international nuclear forces. Indeed, there is a real question of whether enough trust and stability will ever exist in international politics to persuade national leaders to support complete disarmament.

Some traditional critiques of disarmament seem less telling if the option is considered in the context of a more stable world. We'll consider three here. Perhaps the most common argument deals with the problem of "putting the genie back in the bottle." Many contend that disarmament would not provide the more positive security guarantees of the second, third, and fourth criteria. The world community would be vulnerable to blackmail, or even outright military domination, by a rogue state that managed secretly to assemble 100 or so atomic weapons. Of course, a disarmament regime would include stringent inspection provisions designed to monitor fissile materials and the technologies of nuclear weapons. One can still imagine, however, ways in which such measures could be circumvented. A nation could build a nuclear infrastructure underground—centrifuges, perhaps, on the Iraqi model, not dependent on a civilian nuclear power industry and its attendant IAEA (International Atomic Energy Agency) safeguards—and quietly manufacture uranium bombs. Large, developed countries with big nuclear power industries could establish large-scale cheating programs designed to siphon off and reprocess plutonium. Lesser-developed countries or terrorists could steal plutonium or uranium.

No verification regime could give complete assurance against these risks. None does so today; the way in which the United States and much of the world preserve their security in the face of such threats is by the threat of retaliation, with nuclear weapons if necessary. Thus deterrence, rather than inspection, provides the ultimate hedge against weapons of mass destruction. Of course, in a disarmed world, deterrence could not be performed by nuclear weapons.

It could, however, be performed by other means. The major powers of the world could agree to international regimes mandating stiff penalties for any nations that build nuclear arsenals or use nuclear weapons in crises or conflicts. As this report has already argued (in chapter 5), conventional weapons and various political options (such as changing the goals of a war) provide a perfectly suitable menu of options for retaliating against a nuclear, chemical, or biological attack.

Second, some opponents of disarmament argue that by disarming, major powers would be abandoning the prestige inherent in a nuclear arsenal. Smaller states might become more willing to challenge major powers, which would threaten U.S. interests and make the world more conflict prone. Even today, however, the primacy of economic elements of national power is such that one hardly imagines the United States obtaining much prestige as a result of its possession of nuclear weapons. Neither Germany nor Japan has them, yet their prestige is very great; Russia has thousands and very little prestige. And further progress toward a stable world order will mitigate this effect even further, creating a firm international consensus against aggression that would do much more than major-power nuclear arsenals to deter regional adventurism.

These facts also answer a third common objection to disarmament—that it will "make the world safe for conventional war." It would not do so if major-power conventional war had come to be viewed as out of the question, which is a central assumption of nuclear end states.

Complete nuclear disarmament, then, should not be ruled out as a long-term option. Once the leaders of the major powers have firmly decided that war among them will not occur, and once a system of strong international sanctions for aggression has developed, the "crystal ball" effect of nuclear weapons may be viewed as anachronistic. We do not expect international relations to evolve that far in the next twenty years and hence do not view complete and total disarmament as a likely end state. But it would certainly be wrong to conclude glibly that it can never happen and plan accordingly.

IMPLICATIONS

In an important sense, none of the alternatives proposed above can be described as the "best." Each is appropriate for a different stage in the evolution of international politics. Nonoperational nuclear forces are a logical next step after first-phase arms control; from there, nuclear powers might allow growing international control until, finally, an international nuclear force was established. Each step has its own advantages and risks.

It is important to note that substantial guarantees against cheating and proliferation, in the form of nuclear forces capable of deterring cheaters or proliferators, will remain until the final step, complete disarmament. A critical support, however, to these guarantees—and a prerequisite for complete disarmament—will be the establishment of international agreements providing for automatic sanctions and perhaps retaliation against nuclear first use. It is in these agreements, and not in the residual nuclear forces that will remain, that the bulk of deterrence will be found in the decades to come.

These conclusions hold several implications for current policy. First, *the United States must lead in the establishment of global treaties and agreements providing specific sanctions for nuclear use.* Such treaties will help set the stage for later, more comprehensive and stringent international deterrence and control of nuclear weapons without necessarily using the threat of a nuclear retaliation. In the short term, such accords will help with the problem of proliferation. This magnifies the importance of the treaty proposed in chapter 5.

Second, *U.S. officials should begin discussing the possibility of a nonoperational nuclear force with their Russian, British, French, and Chinese counterparts.* As suggested in chapter 3, portions of this proposal need not await adoption of a nuclear end state to be implemented.

Third and finally, *the opportunity to move to a nuclear end state should concentrate the attention of U.S. and Russian arms control officials on current policy.* Both sides must be very careful to design arms treaties and initiatives that do not leave a residue of doubt and mistrust that would arise to block later progress. If we are not careful enough about verification provisions, then, when the time comes to move to nonoperational nuclear forces, hard-liners on both sides will object, claiming that the other could have cheated on current agreements and hidden a secret nuclear force. We must take care today to ensure that such objections cannot arise tomorrow.

This chapter has argued that, when considering alternative nuclear end states, everything depends upon one's assumptions about the international system. Various types of nuclear regimes are appropriate for different levels of international harmony. It is history, then, and not so much policy, that will determine what long-term nuclear future the world will obtain. But through wise policies and the immediate commitment to some form of a nuclear end state, the United States can promote an international system conducive to a dramatic resolution of the nuclear danger.

NOTES

1. Charles L. Glaser, *Analyzing Strategic Nuclear Policy* (Princeton, N.J.: Princeton University Press, 1990), pp. 166-167.

2. The Harvard Nuclear Study Group, *Living with Nuclear Weapons* (Cambridge, Mass.: Harvard University Press, 1983), especially pp. 3-68.

3. Some writers argue that the risk has already disappeared; see John Mueller, *Retreat from Doomsday: The Obsolescence of Major War* (New York: Basic Books, 1989).

4. Michael E. Brown, "The End of Nuclear Arms Control," *Arms Control* 14 (Summer 1993).

5. Alton Frye, "Zero Ballistic Missiles," *Foreign Policy* 88 (Fall 1992): p. 3.

6. See the essays by William Epstein, Paul Warnke, and Daniel Ellsberg in *Bulletin of the Atomic Scientists* 48, no. 4 (May 1992): 22-23, 36-38, and 42-44.

7. See Brown,"The End of Nuclear Arms Control."

8. Ibid.

9. See Richard A. Falk, "Nuclear Policy and World Order: Why Denuclearization?" in Burns H. Weston, ed., *Toward Nuclear Disarmament and Global Security: A Search for Alternatives* (Boulder, Colo.: Westview Press, 1984), pp. 463-81; Thomas Bernauer, *Nuclear Issues on the Agenda of the Conference on Disarmament* (New York: United Nations Institute for Disarmament Research, 1991); and Gar Alpovitz and Kai Bird, "Dream of Total Disarmament Could Become Reality," *Los Angeles Times,* January 12, 1992.

APPENDIX 1

FIRST-STRIKE SURVIVABILITY AND DEFENSE PENETRATION

by Steve Fetter

The analysis in chapter 6 is supported by estimates of the number of warheads that would survive a first strike and penetrate a two-layer limited defense. This appendix details the methods used to derive these estimates.

1. First-Strike Survivability

1.1. *Silo-based ICBMs.* The probability that a silo-based ICBM would survive an attack by a single warhead to fire in retaliation is given by

$$P_s = R_1 \cdot A_1 \cdot (1 - P_k) \tag{A-1}$$

where R_1 and A_1 are the reliability and alert rate of the ICBM and P_k is the probability that the attacking warhead would destroy the silo. P_k is given by

$$P_k = R_2 \cdot A_2 \cdot [1 - 2^{-(LR/CEP)}]^2 \tag{A-2}$$

where R_2, A_2, and CEP are the reliability, alert rate, and accuracy of the attacking warhead, and LR, the lethal radius, is maximum distance at which the warhead would destroy the silo. For hardened silos, LR is given approximately by

$$LR \approx 470 \cdot (Y/H)^{1/3} \text{ meters} \tag{A-3}$$

where Y is the yield of the attacking warhead in kilotons and H is the hardness of the silo in psi. Here we assume that the 500 Russian SS-25s are used to attack the 500 U.S. Minuteman-III silos; in this case, $Y \approx 750$ kilotons, $H \approx 2000$ psi, and CEP ≈ 200 meters.[1] Assuming that $A \approx 0.95$ and

$R \approx 0.9$ for both missiles gives $P_s = 0.22$; therefore, only 110 of the 500 Minuteman-III missiles would survive to participate in a retaliatory strike.

The above analysis assumed that the SS-25 force does not suffer attrition from a possible limited U.S. missile defense. If such a system exists, the SBI layer would be saturated with little attrition (about 50 missiles—see next paragraph), and the GBI layer could be exhausted by SLBM warheads arriving in the region earlier. Moreover, surplus SLBM warheads or late-arriving bombers also could be used to attack the silos. Thus, the existence of a limited defense would not guarantee the survival of a substantially greater number of silos.

The above analysis also assumes that the Minuteman missiles ride out the attack. If the missiles were launched at first warning of an attack (assuming that it is physically possible to launch the missiles in 15 or 20 minutes), virtually all of the alert and reliable missiles could "survive" to retaliate. Fortunately, numerous statements by government officials have made it clear that "launch on warning" is not the policy of the United States. Launch on warning is not considered to be an acceptable solution to the problem of ICBM vulnerability because of the possibility that an attack might be ordered in response to a false warning. Even if the warning is accurate, the preprogrammed targets might be inappropriate, and the more-or-less automatic use of ICBMs would make a war more difficult to terminate.

1.2. *Road-mobile ICBMs.* If we assume that alert road-mobile ICBMs dash from their shelters upon warning of an attack (rather than randomly roaming a large deployment area), the probability of kill is given by

$$P_k = n \cdot R_2 \cdot A_2 \cdot (LR/RU)^2 \tag{A-4}$$

where n is the number of attacking warheads per shelter and RU, the maximum distance traveled until detonation of the attacking warheads, is given by

$$RU = v \cdot (t - \tau_r) \tag{A-5}$$

where v is the average launcher speed, t is the missile flight time, and τ_r is the reaction time (i.e., the time to detect the missile launches, notify the missile bases, man the launchers, and scatter from the base). A reasonable speed for the SS-25 launcher is 50 kilometers per hour; missile flight times from close-in SSBNs would be 15 to 18 minutes; reaction times might be about 5 to 8 minutes. Inserting these values into equation A-5 gives a mean value for RU of about 8 kilometers. Assuming a launcher hardness of 5 psi and 100-kiloton attacking SLBM warheads detonated at optimum height of burst, LR ≈ 3.2 kilometers. Assuming two attacking warheads per shelter, missile reliabilities of 0.9, and a peacetime alert rate of 0.5 gives a mean P_s of about 0.28; a crisis alert rate of 0.8 gives a mean P_s of about 0.45. Therefore, the mean number of surviving missiles is about 140 and 220, respectively.

1.3. SLBMs and bombers. We assume that all alert SLBMs and bombers would survive an attack, so the fraction available for retaliation is simply equal to R · A. Seventy-five percent of surviving bombers are assumed to function properly, penetrate air defenses, and deliver their weapons. Bomber fly-out patterns could in principle be barraged with SLBM warheads from close-in SSBNs, but a significant percentage of the bombers could be destroyed only if the bombers were based on the coast and depressed-trajectory SLBM launches were used, both of which are highly unlikely. The existence of limited defenses would not improve the survivability of submarines and bombers, since the number of warheads available for a first strike is much larger than the number of submarine and bomber bases or defensive interceptors.

2. SBI Boost-Phase Defense

I focus on boost-phase defense for two reasons. First, it is analytically simple. Because missiles do not travel far in boost phase, simple analytical approximations can be used. Second, intercepting missiles in the boost phase is probably much easier than intercepting warheads in the midcourse phase. It is much easier to detect, track, and destroy a large, hot, fragile booster than a small, cold, and hard reentry vehicle. Moreover, SLBMs will continue to carry more than one reentry vehicle per missile, and penetration aids (chaff, flares, decoys, and antisimulation techniques) will make it difficult to achieve a high probability of kill in midcourse. Thus, we can get a good idea of the effectiveness of limited defenses against retaliatory strikes simply by using boost-phase scaling.[2]

2.1. Simultaneous point launch. The number of SBI required for boost-phase intercept of N_m missiles launched simultaneously from a single point on the earth is approximately equal to

$$N_i \approx AR \cdot N_m \cdot n \tag{A-6}$$

where n is the number of SBI used per missile and AR, the "absentee ratio," is the total number of SBI divided by the number that can participate in the

Table A1.1

The number of interceptors required to give an overall kill probability of 0.9 as a function of the p_k of the interceptor, and the relative number of missiles that can be destroyed in one-on-one engagements.

Interceptor Kill Probability p_k	Number of Interceptors Required n	$\dfrac{n \cdot p_k}{0.9}$
0.90	1	1.0
0.68	2	1.5
0.54	3	1.8
0.44	4	1.9
0.37	5	2.0

defensive engagement. The probability P_k of destroying a missile with n SBI, each of which has an independent probability of destroying the missile of p_k, is given by

$$P_k = 1 - (1 - p_k)^n \tag{A-7}$$

Assuming that the goal of the SBI defense is to achieve an overall kill probability of $P_k = 0.9$, table A1.1 gives the relationship between the p_k of individual SBI and the number of SBI required per missile. Note that if more than one SBI per missile is required to achieve $P_k = 0.9$, then the system would be capable of destroying considerably more missiles in one-on-one engagements compared to systems using one highly effective SBI per missile. The number of missiles that can be destroyed in one-on-one engagements, which is important in evaluating the effectiveness of a defense against a massive strike, is proportional to $n \cdot p_k$.

The fraction of SBI that can participate in the defense is a function of the maximum range of the SBI and the distribution of the attack in space and time. The maximum range of an SBI during the boost phase[3] is given by

$$D = v_i \cdot (t_b - \tau_i) \tag{A-8}$$

where v_i is the maximum SBI velocity, t_b is the missile burn time, and τ_i is the time it takes to detect the launch and fire the SBI plus half the time it takes to accelerate to the maximum velocity. Brilliant pebbles are reportedly designed for $v_i \approx 6$ km/s,[4] and $\tau_i \approx 60$ s represents a reasonable value for attack warning and acceleration.

If the missile launches occur simultaneously at a point anywhere on the earth's surface, the absentee ratio would be given by

$$AR = \frac{4 \cdot \pi \cdot (R_e + h_o) \cdot (R_e + h_b)}{FP} \tag{A-9}$$

where h_o is the SBI orbital altitude (about 460 km for brilliant pebbles), h_b is the burnout altitude of the missile, and R_e is the radius of the earth (about 6,370 km). Each SBI can intercept missiles launched within a certain area on the surface of the earth; this area is called the "footprint" (FP) of the interceptor:

$$FP = \pi \cdot d^2 \tag{A-10}$$

where the radius d is given by

$$d = [D^2 - (h_o - h_b)^2]^{1/2} \tag{A-11}$$

Table A1.2 give values for t_b and h_b for the Trident II and Minuteman III missiles, and the corresponding values of D and FP given by equations A-8 and A-10.[5]

2.2. *Simultaneous distributed launch.* To estimate the effectiveness of the defense against a retaliatory ICBM strike, we must first estimate the number of SBI that would be within range d of the launch sites. The number of SBI that can participate in a defense, and therefore the number of missiles that can be destroyed in the boost phase, is determined by the ratio of this area to the footprint. In other words, the number of missiles that can be engaged in a retaliatory strike, N_r, is approximately equal to

$$N_r \approx N_m \cdot \frac{DA}{FP} \tag{A-12}$$

where N_m is the number that can be engaged if launched from a single point on the earth (in this case, ten), and DA is the area within range d of the retaliatory launch sites.

Table A1.2
**The burn-out time (t$_b$) and altitude (h$_b$) of the
Minuteman III / SS-25 ICBMs and the
Trident II/SS-N-20 SLBMs, the maximum range
at which a 6-km/s SBI could engage these missiles
in the boost phase, and the corresponding SBI footprint.**

Missile	t$_b$ (s)	h$_b$ (km)	D (km)	FP (10^6 km^2)
Trident-II/SS-N-20	170	240	660	1.22
Minuteman-III/SS-25	190	190	780	1.68

An area of about $7.5 \cdot 10^6$ km^2 lies within 730 km of the seven SS-25 bases in Russia; adding a few more bases to accommodate a total of 500 SS-25s might increase this to about $9 \cdot 10^6$ km^2. Thus, an SBI defense designed to engage ten ICBMs launched from a single point on the earth's surface would be able to engage $10 \cdot (9/1.68) = 54$ simultaneously launched SS-25s, destroying about 50 of them.

Similarly, an area of about $4.3 \cdot 10^6$ km^2 lies within 730 km of the four Minuteman III bases. Thus, a limited SBI defense could engage $10 \cdot (4.3/1.68) = 27$ Minuteman III missiles launched simultaneously from current bases, destroying about 25 of them.

2.3. *Rapid point launch.* An SSBN can launch missiles rapidly but not simultaneously, because the hot rocket exhaust would damage adjacent missiles, and because one must wait for the yaw and pitch of the submarine to stabilize. During the launch sequence, additional SBI will orbit within range of the launch point, increasing the fraction of SBI that can participate in the defense.

Estimating the fraction of SBI that can participate in a extended launch from a single point on the earth is rather complicated, since it depends on the details of the SBI orbits. The easiest case to evaluate is when all SBI orbits intersect at the same point (e.g., polar orbits). The minimum SBI density would then be 90 degrees from the points of intersection, where the orbits would be approximately parallel. In this case, the "footprint" or area within which SBI could participate in a boost-phase defense is approximately

$$FP \approx \pi \cdot d^2 + 2 \cdot d \cdot v_o \cdot \tau_m \qquad (A\text{-}13)$$

where v_0 is the orbital velocity of the SBIs (7.6 km/s) and τ_m is time required to launch all 20 or 24 SLBMs. The first term in equation A-13 presents the instantaneous footprint of equation A-10; the second represents the area swept out by the motion of SBIs toward the launch site during the launch sequence.

Note that the total number of SBIs required for a SLBM boost-phase defense depends on the launch time. Unfortunately, estimates of τ_m are rare in the unclassified literature. It is reported that early U.S. Polaris missiles could be fired at the rate of about one per minute.[6] Later estimates of Soviet capabilities give a rate of one every 15 seconds,[7] and there are reports that the Soviet Union fired two SS-N-20 missiles 20 seconds apart in 1982.[8] One source states that the Trident submarine can launch all of its missiles in six minutes.[9] Thus, a reasonable range of values for τ_m is 5 to 20 minutes.

2.4. *Rapid distributed launch.* Unlike an accidental or unauthorized launch, which would come from a single submarine, a retaliatory SLBM strike would be launched by all SSBNs on patrol. It seems reasonable to assume that the SSBNs will be uniformly distributed over patrol areas of at least a million square kilometers.[10] In addition, it is reasonable to assume that it would take longer for a fleet of SSBNs to launch their missiles in retaliation than for a single SSBN to launch its missiles. Thus, the effective footprint for a retaliatory SLBM strike would be given by

$$FP' \approx \pi \cdot (d + r)^2 + 2 \cdot (d + r) \cdot v_0 \cdot t_m \tag{A-14}$$

where r is the effective radius of the patrol area and t_m is the time period over which the retaliatory launches occur. The ratio of the footprint for launches uniformly distributed over a patrol area of radius r to that for launches from a single SSBN is given approximately by

$$\frac{FP'}{FP} = \frac{\pi \cdot (d+r)^2 + 2 \cdot (d+r) \cdot v_0 \cdot t_m}{\pi \cdot d^2 + 2 \cdot d \cdot v_0 \cdot \tau_m} \tag{A-15}$$

Table A1.3 gives the ratio (FP'/FP) for several values of τ_m and (t_m / τ_m). Note that the footprint ratio depends mostly on (t_m / τ_m), and that it is relatively insensitive to τ_m.

It seems reasonable to assume that a retaliatory strike would take at least twice as long as the launch of all the missiles from a single submarine ($t_m / \tau_m = 2$), so I will assume that (FP'/FP) ≈ 3.8. Thus, an SBI defense sized to

Table A1.3
**The ratio of the footprint for SLBMs launches
distributed over an area of 10^6 km^2 and time t_m,
to that for SLBM launches from a
single submarine over time**
τ_m, for τ_m = 5, 10, and 20 minutes, and for t_m/τ_m = 1, 2, and 3.

τ_m (min)	t_m/τ_m		
	1	2	3
5	2.4	3.8	5.1
10	2.2	3.8	5.4
20	2.1	3.8	5.5

engage 20 SLBMs launched rapidly from a single SSBN would be able to engage 20 · 3.8 = 76 SLBMs launched from each patrol area over a time period twice as long. Assuming that alert SSBNs are deployed in two patrol zones, a total of 136 missiles could be destroyed.

3. GBI Defense

I assume that the GBI defense consists of 500 interceptors deployed at five sites in the United States or Russia, with each interceptor having a probability of kill of 0.9. In estimating the number of warheads destroyed by the defense, we assume that the warheads are evenly divided among the five sites; thus, a maximum of 450 incoming warheads could be destroyed. The offense could, of course, choose to concentrate its attack on one or two regions, thereby saturating the defenses in these regions with more incoming warheads than available interceptors, but it is unlikely that military planners would be comfortable with basing deterrence on such a strategy. Currently, deterrence is based on being able to destroy a broad range of geographically distributed targets.

NOTES

1. The International Institute for Strategic Studies, *The Military Balance, 1991-1992* (London: IISS, 1991), p. 225.
2. Strategic Defense Initiative Organization plans to intercept a substantial fraction of reentry vehicles in midcourse. Unfortunately, estimating the effectiveness of midcourse defenses requires detailed and complicated orbital simulations that are beyond the scope of this work. As noted in this paragraph, I believe that it will not prove possible to achieve a high single-shot probability of kill during mid-course. The use of boost-phase scaling may overestimate the effectiveness against retaliatory strikes somewhat, but several other assumptions in this analysis work in the opposite direction: a very high single-shot SBI kill probability in boost phase (0.9); the precise matching of capabilities against ICBM and SLBM threats (i.e., a SBI constellation designed to intercept ten ICBMs would be able to intercept no more than 20 SLBMs, and vice versa); and that alert SSBNs are clustered in just two patrol zones.
3. Corrections for the rotation of the earth or limitations imposed by the earth's atmosphere can be neglected for boost-phase intercept. See Christopher T. Cunningham, "The Space-Based Interceptor," in Dietrich Schroeer and David Hafemeister, eds., *Nuclear Arms Technologies in the 1990s* (New York: American Institute of Physics, 1988), p. 269.
4. Dr. Lowell Wood of Lawrence Livermore National Laboratory has stated that a brilliant pebble would have enough fuel to leave earth's orbit and go into orbit around Mars, which would require a total delta-v of 6.0 km/s.
5. Assuming a uniform acceleration of $30 \cdot g$, 20 s would be required to accelerate the SBI to 6 km/s, during which time the average velocity would be 3 km/s, so the time lost to acceleration is roughly 10 s. In addition, at least 30 to 40 s would be required for the target missile to rise above the highest clouds at altitudes of 10-15 km, where the hot booster plume could be detected, and tens of seconds would be required to activate and target the SBI. General Abrahamson, former head of SDIO, stated in testimony before the Senate Defense Appropriations Subcommittee on 19 March 1987 that the response time would be 70 s.
6. Herbert Scoville, Jr., "Missile Submarines and National Security," *Scientific American* (June 1972).
7. James W. Winnefeld and Carl H. Builder, "ASW—Now or Never," *United States Naval Institute Proceedings,* Vol. 97 (September 1971), p. 21, quoted in Alton H. Quanbeck and Archie L. Wood, *Modernizing the Strategic Bomber Force: Why and How* (Washington, D.C.: Brookings, 1976), p. 45; and *The START*

Treaty and Beyond (Washington, D.C.: U.S. Congressional Budget Office, October 1991), p. 157.

8. *Aviation Week and Space Technology* (November 25, 1982), p. 82; quoted in Thomas B. Cochran, William M. Arkin, Robert S. Norris, and Jeffrey I. Sands, *Soviet Nuclear Weapons,* vol. IV of *Nuclear Weapons Databook* (Cambridge, Mass.: Ballinger, 1989), p. 150.

9. D. Douglass Dalgleish and Larry Schweikart, *Trident* (Carbondale, Ill.: Southern Illinois University Press, 1984), p. 29.

10. For example, two of Russia's patrol areas, the Sea of Okhotsk and the Barents Sea, each have areas of 1.4 to 1.6 million square kilometers.

APPENDIX 2

MILITARY TARGETS FOR A MINIMUM DETERRENT: AFTER THE COLD WAR, HOW MUCH IS ENOUGH?

by Michael J. Mazarr

With the cold war over, many now believe it is time to sweep away its most terrible legacy. Dozens of analysts outside government have proposed deep reductions in U.S. and Russian nuclear forces, down to a level of just a few thousand warheads and perhaps much less.[1] For the first time since about 1950, the question of "how much is enough" is one with immediate policy relevance. There is, in particular, a renewed interest in minimum deterrence, the practice of deploying only as many nuclear weapons as are required for central deterrence and giving up more ambitious nuclear missions and the "overkill" in capabilities that goes along with them.[2]

Under minimum deterrence the conduct of central deterrence would change radically. No longer could the United States and Russia threaten the devastation offered by thousands of nuclear weapons to help deter war, nor would U.S. or Russian leaders be able to rely on overkill and excess capacity to guarantee a retaliation. Today a Russian attack that destroyed 80 percent of U.S. warheads would be a catastrophe for Moscow—over 2,000 nuclear weapons would be fired back at it. In a minimum deterrent, retaliating warheads would be much smaller. This leads many to conclude that a minimum deterrent would be insufficient for deterrence.

This is not so much true in the area of societal destruction, where little doubt exists that very few warheads could do a vast amount of damage.[3] Indeed, what is striking about the destruction done to society by nuclear weapons is how quickly the "overkill" stage is reached. Just one or two hundred nuclear weapons can destroy the bulk of any modern society, and short of marking out each and every town for destruction, there is little use for a larger arsenal.[4] Specifically, the industrial damage capable of being inflicted with very few weapons is quite impressive, given the centralization and mutual dependency of modern economies.[5] This is not to say that 2,000 warheads would cause no more damage than 200, but the difference *in terms of societal effect* might not be great enough to tempt a national leader to risk war at one level and not at the other.[6]

To look at societal damage, however, is to presuppose a countervalue targeting strategy aimed largely at cities, and it is precisely this assumption that dooms minimum deterrence in the minds of many observers. Two of the most common arguments against minimum deterrence are that it would require countervalue targeting, and thus the immoral and imprudent attacks on innocent civilians; and that it would be capable of very little military effect and would therefore be inadequate for deterrence. Indeed, criticisms of countervalue policies are often accompanied by arguments that the counter-force or military component of a nuclear targeting plan is, and must be, very large. Using Department of Defense references and other sources, one study estimates the basic target base as about 4,000 sites: 330 bomber, SSBN, and mobile ICBM bases; 1,560 other military forces (airbases, naval ports and bases, ground forces, nuclear weapons facilities, and others); 1,000 military manufacturing sites; and 1,080 government and command-and-control locations.[7] Minimum deterrent forces capable of only a fraction of such attacks have not been seen as adequate for deterrence.

A recent study on the future of nuclear strategy prepared for the Department of Defense, for example, is not sanguine about the status of deterrence at very low levels of nuclear weapons. It argues that

> the concept of a minimum deterrent, based upon a few hundred weapons or less, is unrealistic. It is immoral to plan for a war which targets only civilians or cities *per se,* which is inherent in the minimum deterrence concept. Such an inventory also would be self-deterring to a major power. It allows for virtually no options, and is the least credible of all nuclear posture. No nonnuclear industrial power is going to believe security guarantees from a nation with this posture.[8]

This appendix seeks to defend minimum deterrence against these two arguments, and it does so by grounding its analysis in the specifics of nuclear-strike planning. It proposes a targeting strategy and a potential Russian[9] nonnuclear target base that is small, yet adequate for deterrence. By threatening to fire merely 200 warheads at Russian *military* forces and industries, it contends, the United States can achieve all the deterrence it requires *without* countervalue targeting. One of my major arguments is that the concept of overkill, which has been widely understood to apply to countervalue targeting, also applies to the targeting of conventional military forces and military industries. Specifically, there is no persuasive reason why a 1,500-warhead retaliation (produced by a 3,000-warhead START II arsenal) would cause enough military damage for deterrence while a minimum deterrent retaliation of 200 warheads would not.

TARGETING STRATEGY

The first step in outlining the requirements of a minimum deterrent is to develop a targeting strategy. Before we can estimate what a given retaliation would do, we must know where its warheads will strike. In a general sense most targeting strategies fall into one of two primary schools: counterforce, which aims an attack at Russian nuclear and conventional weapons sites, sometimes with an emphasis on the former; and countervalue attacks on urban-industrial targets designed to maximize societal impact. United States nuclear plans reportedly contain a mix of both types of targets with an emphasis on counterforce applications that dates from the 1950s. For various reasons, neither strategy, at least in their extreme versions, can make up the basic targeting doctrine of a minimum deterrent.

Counterforce

A minimum deterrent would not be capable of full counterforce targeting, because the number of weapons on each side would be a fraction of that required for successful attacks. (Although counterforce strategies encompass both nuclear and nonnuclear targets, the term is commonly used to describe war plans whose primary emphasis is Russian nuclear forces. I will use the term *counterpower* to describe strategies aimed at nonnuclear military assets.) Even today, counterforce doctrines are already on the decline.[10] Primarily this is true because

> new generations of weapons—land-mobile missiles, cruise missiles, and perhaps low-observable (stealth) bombers—cannot be effectively targeted. Although pressures to compensate for this development can be expected, only a very limited redress seems possible. Therefore, the situation is driven back to conceptions developed in the 1950s, that is, to seek security in highly survivable or invulnerable weapons that would be reinforced by cooperation between adversaries so that such weapons (second-strike) would not be put at risk. . . .[I]t is hardly likely that the priority for counterforce capability can be sustained.[11]

A minimum deterrence would move even further in that direction, rendering strikes against opposing nuclear forces out of the question. Still, it would be possible to fight against this trend—in part by rejecting minimum deterrence—if counterforce targeting were essential to deterrence.

But it is not. To begin with, it is simply not possible that the major Russian aim in a nuclear exchange would be to end up with a few more warheads than the United States. If tens of millions of Russian citizens were killed, most Russian conventional forces and military industry wiped out, and Russian society crippled, it would matter little how many nuclear weapons they had left. A decision to undertake war on such a basis would be irrational, because the war would not have gained anything. As Bernard Brodie recognized 33 years ago, "the capacity to deter is usually confused with the capacity to win a war," in part because "the potential deterrence value of an admittedly inferior force may be sharply greater than it has ever been before."[12]

The key issues revolve around what Russian leaders would be asking themselves in a crisis. If their questions inquired about Russian ability to strike first, endure an American retaliation and perhaps have nuclear superiority, then perhaps Russian military people could claim that their strategies could achieve that goal. But if the Russians wanted to limit damage to their country and to emerge from the conflict with any semblance of societal order and national power, then there is essentially no chance Russian nuclear forces could achieve that mission today or under a stable minimum deterrent balance.

Even if we could, somehow, hold Russian nuclear reserve forces at risk with a breathtakingly effective counterforce retaliation, and even if this did threaten Russian victory aims, would this prospect establish the key elements of deterrence? Probably not. In fact "nations frequently start wars that they do not really believe that they are likely to win." Misplaced hope in the potential for victory, national honor, fears that crises have escalated to the point of no return, and other motivations can cause nations to initiate hostilities that they have no objective guarantee, or in some cases even hope, of winning. "History is rife with example of nations not deterred from war solely by the clear prospect of military defeat."[13] If this is true, then counterforce policies are certainly bankrupt. Even if the United States were to achieve clear nuclear superiority, when the time came to make the decision the Russians might still be tempted to strike first before the situation becomes even more unfavorable.

Such thoughts would probably be relevant only in times of incredible tension in which both sides truly fear that a war is imminent. Yet it is precisely then that warfighting plans become most dangerous, because they establish the mutual fear that an opponent would attempt a disarming first strike. Ironically, then, warfighting deterrence works to subvert the peace in the only situations in which in might be required to defend it. This suggests why counterforce targeting is destabilizing. If indeed the sort of gradual nuclear exchanges discussed by counterforce proponents could occur, then the U.S. goal must be to limit them and to end the war. This is in fact one of the key elements of declared U.S. policy—to terminate a conflict "on conditions that are satisfactory to the United States."[14] Yet counterforce targeting threatens to ruin such escalation control, because once the United States begins firing at Russian nuclear assets it may feel a need to launch its whole force.

Thus George Quester concludes that to assist war termination "strategic nuclear forces should probably be avoided, for fear of panicking the other side into firing them off in anticipation of preemption."[15] "Disarmament," writes Harold Feiveson, "is a far surer and less catastrophic way to reduce the counterforce capabilities of the nuclear arsenals than counterforce attacks."[16] As Bernard Brodie argued, "Our over-riding interest [in deterrence] is of course the security of our own retaliatory force. But that does not mean that we especially desire the other side's retaliatory force to be insecure. If the opponent feels insecure," then he might be "more trigger-happy."[17]

Moreover, in most cases there would probably be nothing for a counterforce retaliation to hit back at. Many Western analysts have long argued that the Russians possess little faith in the notion of a limited nuclear war[18] and therefore would launch all or nearly all their nuclear force in a first strike. Such a strategy would undermine U.S. counterforce retaliation policies by leaving no nuclear weapons for the United States to retaliate against. In a minimum deterrent, of course, these proclivities would be magnified. Each side, with so few weapons to begin with, would have to launch virtually all to have any hope of success.[19] Even if the Russians did intend to hold back a reserve force from their first strike, however, there is no reason why they would allow that reserve to ride out a U.S. retaliation. It is likely that an attacker would launch its reserve forces on warning of a retaliation.[20]

Counterforce targeting, then, is both infeasible and undesirable. Most important, it is unnecessary for deterrence. A minimum deterrent's inability to target opposing nuclear forces is therefore not a justification for maintaining larger forces.

Countervalue

If counterforce is out of the reach of a minimum deterrent, countervalue targeting may be too easily within it. Critics of very small nuclear forces have argued that the targeteers of a minimum deterrent, with only a few hundred warheads to work with, would have no alternative but to threaten enemy urban centers. To achieve the required deterrent effect, it is said, no other strategy would suffice.

It is indeed true that, for several reasons, retaliating against civilian targets alone is not a promising option.[21] First, aiming nuclear strikes explicitly at innocent civilians is distasteful and often held to be "morally objectionable."[22] This may be especially true now that the Russian people and the citizens of other former Soviet republics have become allies in the quest to mellow Russian policy. Whether one agrees that countervalue targeting is immoral or not, it is probably true that a strategy aimed purely at the Russian people and their cities is not politically sustainable. There is no doubt that an assured destruction strategy will contemplate vast societal damage, and any minimum deterrent targeting strategy will involve some urban-industrial targeting of necessity. If such results can be achieved indirectly through a strategy that is primarily military in nature, however, some moral and political complications would be eased.

Yet millions of Russians would still die in other forms of retaliation, and moral considerations alone may be insufficient to favor other strategies over countervalue targeting. Other reasons are available, however. A second one is that U.S. targeting officials are unlikely to adopt a countervalue-only policy. The legacy of 40 years of counterforce targeting argues strongly against such a radical shift. If a targeting policy is to be persuasive to U.S. military leaders, it must have some military element. Third, one of the most traditional—and still valid—arguments against countervalue targeting is that it makes little provision for escalation control. Retaliating against any attacks with immediate strikes at Russian cities would offer U.S. cities up for destruction.

Indeed, the knowledge of this fact creates a fourth problem with countervalue targeting—self-deterrence. If Russia launched 100 weapons at U.S. military targets and the United States possessed a pure countervalue strategy, American leaders might be hesitant to fire back because they would call down a Russian second strike on their cities. For this reason, countervalue targeting may also lack credibility. United States leaders must possess some option for responding to a limited nuclear attack by another power, including Russia, besides immediately beginning the destruction of Russian society—and U.S. society as well. Especially to the extent that any extended deterrent missions remain in U.S. nuclear strategy, some flexibility in targeting would be desirable.

Fifth and finally, while a war-winning capability is unnecessary for deterrence and might actually undermine it, a more limited military effect might augment deterrence. Presumably, questions of nuclear targeting would only be relevant during great U.S.-Russian tension involving a military standoff. In such a context, it may be important to be able to pledge a military effect of a strike.

Counterpower

What is required, then, is something between counterforce and countervalue, a strategy that aims some retaliation against Soviet military targets yet continues to promise severe societal damage. Strategies known as "counterpower" (or "countercombatant" or "countermilitary"), which aim a retaliation at conventional military forces, military bases and other facilities, defense industry, and other military-related targets, represent just such a doctrine.[23] Counterpower strategies target Soviet conventional forces and the war industries that support them, with the corollary that many industrial cities are targeted as well. Nuclear forces are generally left off counterpower target lists, both because counternuclear targeting is increasingly difficult and because leaving them off may help escalation control—as noted above, holding nuclear forces at risk encourages their early use. Under a minimum deterrent, of course, counternuclear targeting would be essentially impossible.[24]

Counterpower targeting would offer advantages over both counterforce and countervalue strategies. It would avoid the instability created by counterforce, because in a crisis neither side (or no side, if there are more than two) will fear for the safety of its deterrent force. Counterpower sidesteps the moral problems of countervalue by not explicitly targeting civilians solely for the purpose of causing deaths, and it would provide many targeting options besides suicidal ones. On the whole it is less provocative than counterforce and more flexible and powerful than countervalue.

To maintain assured destruction and yet offer some military effect for deterrence, then, a minimum deterrent could use counterpower targeting.[25] This fact alone answers a criticism of minimum deterrence, that it would require a purely countervalue policy; clearly it would not, as a state with a very small nuclear arsenal could threaten to retaliate against a potential opponent's conventional forces rather than its cities. What is left to be determined is what effect a minimum deterrent's counterpower retaliation would have, and whether such a retaliation would be adequate for deterrence.

DEVELOPING A MILITARY TARGET LIST:
GROUND FORCES

The task of determining "enoughness" in a military sense has been immensely complicated by developments in the former Soviet Union. After Moscow's empire collapsed in December 1991, many former Soviet republics achieved independence and probably earned exemption from U.S. target lists. In the 1990s and beyond, the U.S. task will be to target the *Russian* military, not the Soviet one. It is difficult enough to obtain a reliable, unclassified portrait of the former Soviet military's bases, industries, and deployment areas; any attempt to sketch out the Russian military's likely future size and shape would of necessity be speculative. The following analysis, then, uses figures for the former Soviet military as a baseline and subtracts those bases, ports, airfields, or other fixed locations known to be in now independent republics.

Potential counterpower targets include air, naval, and ground bases, command-and-control centers, and military production sites. Russian military basing is in a state of dramatic flux, many bases in Eastern Europe having been lost and others in Russia and other republics being closed down. Ground forces are the hardest to pin down: in many cases ground units are more likely to be dispersed within a given geographic area rather than quartered at a specific base. An unclassified analysis such as this will not be able fully to assess potential Russian targets, moreover, because it lacks access to the most detailed information about them.[26] Nonetheless, a notional set of targets can be constructed that gives some indication of a minimum deterrence's likely military effect.

Of the variety of military targets within Russia—military bases, deployed forces, defense industries, ports, and so on—those with the highest priority are likely to be those that represent forces in being. A tank plant cannot attack or defend, but a tank division can, and to achieve immediate military effect existing military units must be attacked. Let us look first, then, to Russian military bases and deployments.[27] This section will consider ground forces.

The basic unit of measurement of Russian ground forces—the total number of divisions in the Russian inventory (some 188 former Soviet units as of 1991, including 46 tank divisions and 142 motor rifle divisions)[28]—is misleading. For various reasons, the actual number of targets that a nuclear strike might profitably hit would be much smaller. For one thing, Soviet units were in the past deployed in various states of readiness, and only the more complete divisions would be ready for imminent hostilities. United States intelligence sources divide Russian divisions into four categories.[29] Only about 40 former Soviet offensive divisions—17 tank and 23 motor rifle—were estimated to be in category A readiness in 1991. Another 46 divisions, 19 tank and 27 motor rifle, were at category B, and fully 103 divisions were in category C or mobilization status.[30] Destroying or seriously degrading just 30 to 40 former Soviet divisions would therefore have wiped out all the top-line combat power in the Soviet army; destroying 80 divisions would have incapacitated all the units even close to combat readiness.[31]

Ground forces could also be targeted by theater of operation: the U.S. Defense Department's *Soviet Military Power 1990* suggested that there were 57 divisions in the Western theater, 29 in the Southern, and 23 in the Southwestern, the three theaters with most potential for offensive actions against Eastern Europe and the West. Of those 109 divisions, the divisions deployed in outlying republics, if they had been made up largely of conscripts from those republics, could also have been excluded from target lists. Ground troops in the Russian Far East were, and remain, of little concern because of Moscow's lack of amphibious power projection.

Of course, a minimum deterrent would not be targeted at the former Soviet army. The trends as of this writing are running to the dissolution of a central Commonwealth of Independent States armed forces and toward the creation of independent forces in each of the former republics. In February 1992 senior military advisers to President Boris M. Yeltsin confirmed that Russia would indeed field its own military.[32] Although the composition, doctrine, and command system of this force are not at all determined,[33] it is possible to venture a few educated guesses about its scope.

Most evidence today suggests that the eventual size of the Russian military might be in the range of 1.5 to 2 million personnel. Some military reformers in the former Soviet Union had proposed a force level goal of some 3 million. That was for a unified force, however, and other reformers complained that it would still be too large a burden on the economy and should be cut by another half million.[34] One 1990 estimate by Soviet officials for a military from which ethnic nationalities had been purged was 2 million;[35] again, that seems to reflect the perspectives of less radical reformers. Indeed, indications from Russian military officials in March and April 1992 were that Russia would field a military of roughly 1.2 million personnel.[36]

Another means of estimating the size of a Russian military is to compare it with Western European countries. The "big three" European NATO members—France, Germany, and the United Kingdom—have a combined population of 190 million, in the same range as a Russian nation.[37] Their combined armed forces total just over 1 million. For several reasons, we cannot expect Russia to go that low: historically, Moscow has perceived more of a threat around its borders; today the Russian military is an important source of employment, and too-drastic cuts would only add to the unemployment lines; and as long as the right wing in Moscow is looking over Boris Yeltsin's shoulder, his military cuts will be restrained. Still, the size of comparable European nations' militaries supports the argument that a Russian force would be something over 1 million strong, though probably not any larger than 2 million.

How many ground force divisions would Russia field from this force? In the past, Soviet armies have been slightly more than one-third the size of the military as a whole. In 1992, for example, the former Soviet military was reportedly 3.4 million strong, with an army of 1.4 million—40 percent of the total military.[38] This same ratio applied to militaries of 1.5 to 2 million produces ground forces of between 600,000 and 800,000. We might expect Moscow to deploy a force closer to the higher figure, because Russia itself will be a more land-oriented nation than was the former Soviet Union, having lost many connections to the Baltic and Black Seas. NATO's big three in Europe, for example, have armies almost 700,000 strong, well over 60 percent of their militaries as a whole. Let us, then, postulate a Russian army of 800,000 personnel, equipped with the weapons it is permitted by the treaty on Conventional Forces in Europe (CFE): 20,000 main battle tanks, 20,000 armored fighting vehicles of other types, and 13,000 artillery pieces.

One recent analysis has suggested that a Commonwealth-type unified force of 2.5 to 3 million with a CFE-compliant arsenal could have fielded between 40 and 60 divisions.[39] The range depends on the mix of divisions (a higher proportion of motor rifle as opposed to tank divisions increases the number) and their readiness. If Moscow wished to maximize the number of divisions and yet have a fairly ready army, it might field 10 tank and 50 motor rifle divisions for a total of 60. Russian-only armies of 1.5 to 2 million would be one-third smaller, thus producing a total ground force of some 40 divisions. This again stands up to comparisons with NATO's big three, who field roughly 25 divisions, some of them substantially bigger than Russian ones and enjoying better logistical support, from a slightly smaller force.

Not all of the Russian divisions would be of immediate concern to U.S. targeteers. A few might not be at full readiness, or category A in the old terminology. Some will inevitably be deployed in the Far East, and without large-scale amphibious support would not pose a significant threat to American allies in the Pacific. Given that it may be desirable for the United States to threaten attacks on all deployed Russian divisions, I will continue to use the total of 40, but the limitations on Russian forces noted above make clear that this is a very conservative estimate.

With 40 potential targets, U.S. planners would have to determine how many weapons would be required to attack them—in essence, how many ground zeroes a Russian army would comprise. A 1991 National Academy of Sciences study suggested a "point" scheme to estimate the destruction of former Soviet ground forces.[40] By assigning 6 warheads to each division—one for the headquarters and one to each combat brigade—the study concluded that roughly 300 warheads would destroy 50 percent of the former USSR's ground formations. Yet this number seems inflated, based on cold war ideas about nuclear warfighting, radiation tolerances, and so on. Many divisions would be located in single bases, vulnerable to one nuclear detonation. Even if the personnel were not all present, much of the division's equipment would be in storage at a central site. This would be especially true if ground units were massing for an attack; if they were not, inflicting damage on them would be less urgent, and the United States could withhold some warheads until such massing was under way.

Moreover, even if a unit is spread out over a wide area, a single nuclear attack would do terrible damage to a combat division. At 10 kilometers from a one-megaton burst, soldiers would suffer third-degree burns and any flammable material would spontaneously ignite; anyone looking at the explosion up to 50 kilometers away would suffer permanent eye damage; and the radioactive lethal area of a one-megaton explosion, in which an individual would be exposed to 400 rems in one day (sufficient to kill half those exposed), is roughly 1,000 square kilometers. Over 13,000 square kilometers would be uninhabitable for six months after a single one-megaton ground burst; 3,000 square kilometers would remain deadly for a full year.[41] Clearly, a single nuclear explosion, even if it did not kill all or even most of a division's personnel or destroy most of its equipment, would severely disrupt that formation's operation and render it an unreliable fighting force.

Admittedly, all estimates of a Russian conventional force target base, and especially those for ground forces, are sensitive to the state of Russian military mobilization. After a prolonged crisis, a fully mobilized Russian army might contain far more than 30 to 40 complete divisions, and those divisions might have deployed from their peacetime bases into dispersed field locations. But the damage to fixed military installations—major ground force bases, storage sites, and military industry—would remain the same, and the best-trained, most professional ground divisions could still be targeted. It must be presumed, moreover, that if Russian forces are fully mobilized then European and perhaps U.S. forces would be also, thus reducing the premium (from the perspective of deterrence) on damage done to Russian conventional forces.

Besides standing ground forces, a retaliation could include other military and military-related targets as well. Russian military storage areas might provide promising targets. According to the U.S. Department of Defense, as of the mid-1980s these facilities contained over 8,000 reserve tanks and armored personnel carriers, 18,000 reserve artillery and antiaircraft guns, and 10 million metric tons of stockpiled ammunition. The DoD's 1984 edition of *Soviet Military Power* identifies some 11 armor stockpiles, 30 artillery sites, and 60 ammunition dumps. Some of these facilities were located in Eastern Europe, and many others—though the information does not allow a complete analysis of this point—are duplicate, that is, ammunition and tanks and artillery are stored at the same location.[42] Under CFE, much of this equipment will likely be destroyed, and, recently, Russian officers have talked of consolidating supply depots into central locations. In any case, attacking just ten major depots would do enormous damage, destroying virtually all reserve armored vehicles and vast stores of ammunition, artillery, gasoline, and other equipment.[43] A full strike on all reserve sites might entail roughly 50 to 80 separate attacks.

AIR AND NAVAL FORCES

In addition to ground forces, a counterpower strike would also attack air and naval bases and deployed units. These are somewhat easier to target and destroy because they depend more heavily than ground forces on static facilities—airfields and ports. Little has been written about the likely size and shape of a Russian navy or air force, and the calculations below will rely primarily on modified numbers taken from descriptions of the former Soviet military. They are, therefore, by nature conservative estimates.

The *Nuclear Weapons Databook* lists 22 major Soviet bomber and airbases, dispersed throughout the former Soviet Union.[44] Of those two are only test sites, presumably less able to sustain military operations than a full base; this leaves 20 major potential airbase targets. More broadly, one edition of the Department of Defense's *Soviet Military Power* contains a large map with symbols representing major Russian military installations, broken down by theater of operations (TVD). The breakdown of air forces is displayed in table A2.1, "Soviet Air Force Facilities."

Obviously a minimum deterrent could not hit all of these targets; some prioritization is required. The Far Eastern TVD equipment and bases can be

Table A2.1
Soviet Air Force Facilities

Theater	Airbases/Aircraft	
Western	8	27/1,901
Southwestern	2	34/558
Southern	16	34/868
Northwestern	14	20/114
Far Eastern	28	31/896
Total	68	146 bases

Source: Soviet Military Power 1990, pull-out map. Bold numbers to the left of the totals are the numbers of bases thought to be in the Russian republic itself. The map indicates that the symbols are "representative," that they may not reflect the actual numbers of forces. This may be less true of airbases than divisions, however, and in any case the numbers of divisions given and the numbers of symbols on the charts are comparable. Another estimate puts the total number of Russian airbases at 71; see Brian Taylor, "Red Army Blues," MIT Defense and Arms Control Studies Program *Breakthroughs* 2/1 (Spring 1992), p. 3.

eliminated because they pose no immediate threat to Europe and only a marginal threat of invasion of Korea or Japan. The Northwestern TVD is small and lacks a significant offensive capability. Of the remaining three theaters, the Western TVD should probably enjoy top priority, both because its forces were oriented most directly against Germany and the West and because its airbases appear to have a higher concentration of aircraft than the other two, making for better targets. In terms of tactical airbases, then, a minimum deterrent aimed at the former Soviet air force might have targeted about 30: the 20 largest Western TVD airfields and some in the Southern and Southwestern TVDs as well.[45]

As with ground forces, however, U.S. targeteers will look at the various republics in and outside the Commonwealth of Independent States with differing levels of concern. After the coup, as the Baltics have become fully independent and other republics increasingly so, it is clear that target lists can be pared down accordingly. For example, of the 27 Western TVD airbases, 4 are (or were) in Latvia, 3 in Lithuania, 13 in Belarus; only 8 were in the Russian Republic. Of the 34 airbases in the Southwest TVD, only 2 were in Russia—3 were in Belarus and the remainder were in Ukraine or Moldova. Eight of the 34 Southern TVD airbases were in Georgia, 1 in Ukraine, 6 in Azerbaijan, and 3 in other republics besides Russia.[46] As noted in table A2.1, only about 70 of the nearly 150 major airbases of the former Soviet Union appear to be in Russia, and of those only 36 lie in high-priority TVDs from a Western perspective. Only 10 reside in the key Western and Southwestern TVDs.

In the case of Russian air units, those deployed in the Far Eastern theater would be of more concern than ground forces similarly deployed. Air units could attack U.S. or allied forces in Korea or Japan from bases in Russia. Being more intrinsically mobile than ground units, air squadrons or wings could redeploy to the West relatively quickly to replace units destroyed in a U.S. attack.

Still, several arguments support the notion that air units not deployed opposite Europe are of less concern and need not be targeted. For one thing, Korea and Japan possess strong indigenous air defense, bolstered by the presence of U.S. tactical fighter wings in both countries. Using early warning systems such as AWACS and radars deployed on land and supported by American aircraft and aircraft carriers, Korea and Japan should be able to defend themselves. (The same may well be true of Western Europe, but Russia's military power has traditionally been focused more on the West, and table A2.1 reflects such an emphasis.) Nor is the redeployment argument convincing: Russian aircraft could not use the bases that had been hit with nuclear strikes, and would have to shift operations to smaller, less capable bases. Their combat ability would be much reduced, and those bases would of course come under conventional attack as well.

The story is similar for Russian naval forces, which are in a terrible state of disrepair and whose numbers are falling precipitously.[47] The former Soviet navy reportedly possessed some 15 major and 23 minor naval bases.[48] The major bases include the headquarters for all four Russian fleets—Baltic, Northern, Black Sea, and Pacific—as well as the home ports of most major Russian naval combatants.[49] A comparison of *Soviet Military Power 1990, The Nuclear Weapons Databook,* and other sources yields some 25 total ports in Russia: 12 Barents Sea ports (9 on the Kola Peninsula, including Severomorsk and Murmansk, and 3 farther south, just east of St. Petersburg, including Arkhangelsk); 2 Baltic ports north of St. Petersburg; 1 or 2 Black Sea ports on the Russian coast between Ukraine and Georgia; and 9 Pacific ports, including facilities on the Bering Sea and the seas of Japan and Okhotsk, such as Petropavlovsk-Kamchatski and Vladivostock. Note that this includes all major ports, east and west. If the Pacific ports were left off the target list, U.S. targeteers could allocate 2 warheads to every naval base west of the Urals.[50]

It is possible to conclude, then, that attacks on the 30 largest Western-oriented airfields and 30 most important ports within Russia would destroy or render inoperable virtually all of Moscow's conventional air and naval power capable of attacking the West. These numbers would include virtually every airfield in the three westernmost TVDs, and would allow 1 warhead for every naval base in all of Russia with 5 to spare.

DEFENSE INDUSTRY

Finally, there is the potential target base offered by Russian military industry. The Russian defense industrial base is vast, like its U.S. counterpart comprising hundreds of major factories and thousands of subcontractors, and so the industry offers a practically unlimited target base. A counterpower retaliation would include, indeed would be explicitly targeted against, many of these facilities.

Initially it is possible to set aside smaller factories, the thousands of subcontractors whose parts feed into the major production sites. A tank tread or an aircraft tire is useless without the weapon itself. Similarly it is possible to discount the plants that produce support equipment, including radars, trucks, communications gear, and the like; alone such equipment poses no military threat. Excluding those two categories appears to leave roughly 150 major military plants dispersed in a few dozen strategic locations.[51]

The number of those locations is important, for U.S. targeting requirements will be a function of locations and not specific plants (although more than one weapon may be required for certain locations). A thorough reading of several editions of *Soviet Military Power* and other unclassified Department of Defense sources produces an industrial list of some 60 to 70 major plant locations,[52] but again some of these may be located contiguously. Perhaps the best distillation of former Soviet defense industry sites is a chart from *Soviet Military Power 1986* which lists 37 "Key Soviet Military Production Centers," ranging from Leningrad, Minsk, Nikolayev, and Rostov in the west to Komsomolsk and Arsenyev in the east.[53]

Like the former Soviet military, Moscow's defense industry is undergoing wrenching change, and the total of roughly 40 sites may be a great exaggeration today. For one thing, some of these industries are located outside Russia—indeed 13 of the 37 production centers isolated by *Soviet Military*

Power appear to have been outside the Russian Republic—and many of those could be removed from target lists. Various parts of the former Soviet defense industry are being closed down or converted to civilian uses, and this may wipe a few more factories from target lists. Even if a given plant is left standing and unconverted, moreover, if it ceases production it may not be a target of urgent importance. All told, then, a reasonable target list might include about 30 major military production centers.

Again, the question arises of how many warheads must be targeted against each industrial site. A persuasive case can be made that just one warhead per plant would do the job, because significant structural damage, major fires, and severe radiation would render most parts of the plants useless even if they were not knocked down. Theodore Postol has argued for a minimalist conception of targeting requirements: a single one-megaton burst over Washington, he notes, would knock down frame buildings throughout the capital and would send mass fires and radiation well out into Virginia and Maryland, including such potential targets as the Defense Mapping Agency and the Central Intelligence Agency.[54] This one bomb could do all the damage required, he suggests, rather than the six 50-kiloton or four one-megaton warheads that more "official" targeting plans might allocate.

According to Postol, existing targeting plans may "seriously overstate the probable hardness of installations that are to be attacked," and thus exaggerate the damage effects required. Using one warhead for a large area target would mean that

all facilities within this region (except perhaps highly reinforced underground facilities with enclosed air supplies and self-contained power and cooling) would be rendered unusable by the combined effects of blast, fire, and prolonged secondary heating from fire-heated rubble. The assessment that monumental buildings must be reduced to rubble to deny their use to the adversary would therefore result in the commitment of vast numbers of warheads, inflicting damage that is not more meaningful militarily than that achieved by [a] single airburst.[55]

The U.S. military indirectly confirmed Postol's arguments during the 1991 Gulf War. Precision weapons were used to destroy military and civilian facilities, not always by completely knocking them down, but by penetrating them and doing enough damage to render them useless. Military planners seemed satisfied if a target was penetrated, and did not demand that it be flattened. A similar standard applied to nuclear targeting would reduce the need for overkill in military targeting.

Table A2.2
Minimal Russian Military Target Set

Target Type	Warheads Proposed
Tactical Airbases	30
Major Naval Bases	30
Ground Force Sites	40
Military Storage	10
Defense Industry	90
Total	**200**

Nonetheless, given the fact that some plants are undoubtedly very large, and in order to be conservative, I will assign 3 warheads to each of the 30 major production centers. This also allows some flexibility in case the estimate of 30 sites is low, though if anything it might appear inflated for a Russia committed to gradual reductions in military forces and the principle of reasonable sufficiency. In sum, a minimum deterrent might reserve about 90 warheads for Russian military industry.

MINIMUM NUCLEAR FORCES AND DETERRENCE

Table A2.2, ""Minimal Russian Military Target Set," summarizes the military targets outlined so far. Destruction of these locations alone would have a devastating effect: it would smash the Russian Navy, destroy much of the air forces of the key West-facing TVDs, severely degrade its long-range bomber fleet, and annihilate most of the Red Army's combat-ready forces in the western TVDs. All armored vehicles and a significant proportion of the artillery and ammunition in storage would have been destroyed. And the Russian defense industry would have been crippled: as can best be determined from unclassified Department of Defense sources, virtually all production of every major ground, sea, and air weapon system would be ended indefinitely, perhaps permanently from existing industrial plants.[56]

In short, a retaliation composed of roughly 200 nuclear weapons would have catastrophic implications for Russia's ability to defend itself and would render large-scale offensive operations out of the question.[57] Note also that all the categories save one—ground forces—are not extraordinarily sensitive to mobilization levels. Tactical aircraft could be dispersed from major bases and ships sailed from port, but the fixed sites themselves could not be moved. Military industry is an even more static target.

In the context of military effect, it must also be kept in mind that, in a general war, many potential targets of a counterpower strike would be under constant attack by U.S. and allied *conventional* forces. Indeed, a major lesson of the 1991 Gulf War is that the precision of modern weapons can substitute for the brute explosive force of atomic bombs, and that conventional forces can now accomplish many missions traditionally assigned to nuclear forces. This includes attacking such hardened targets as command-and-control nodes, reinforced bunkers, and others. Many military assets not accounted for in a 200-warhead counterpower attack could be assigned to conventional forces—if coherent military operations and thoughts of victory persisted through a nuclear holocaust.

Of course, they might not. The societal effects of even a 200-warhead attack would be devastating. One calculation has suggested that a 100-warhead attack on the United States against military production centers, similar to the 90 this essay suggests have been targeted against Russian defense industries, would kill between 20 and 30 million Americans.[58] No estimate is given for a similar attack on Russia, but given its higher population densities, most models of nuclear war posit higher casualty figures there than in North America. The additional 110 warheads fired at conventional military bases and forces in the field would kill, not only the military personnel against which they were targeted, but also millions more civilians. Any Russian leader contemplating the effects of the roughly 200-warhead retaliation proposed here would have to assume that tens of millions of people would die, perhaps as many as 50 million. It is difficult to believe that the United States would need to threaten more potential devastation than that for deterrence.

More and more analysts outside government support further reduction from START-mandated arsenals to mutual nuclear forces of roughly 3,000 warheads. As noted at the outset, then, my purpose here is partly comparative, to examine a possible START II deterrent and compare it to minimal nuclear forces. Table A2.3, "Comparison of 200 and 1,500 Warhead Attacks," makes such a rough comparison based on the analysis in this appendix and other sources.[59] The key question is what difference would

Table A2.3
**Comparison of 200 and 1,500
Warhead Attacks: Military Effect
(United States Retaliation against Russia)**

	200 Warheads (counterpower attacks)	**1,500 Warheads (counterforce targeting)**
Ground Forces	combat-ready divisioned in western TVDs 75 to 90 percent degraded	all combat-ready and many cadre units destroyed
Naval Forces	all major bases hit; 50 percent + ships destroyed	all major and minor bases hits, virtually all ships destroyed
Air Forces	all major tactical bases in western TVDs destroyed	all major and minor bomber and tactical airbases destroyed
Nuclear Forces[61]	none attacked	many weapons and storage facilities hit
Defense Industry	all major production centers hit	all major and minor sites destroyed

the additional retaliatory weapons—in this comparison, some 1,300 of them—make? In terms of societal damage, very little—the urban-industrial component of a minimum deterrent would kill as many millions of people as a much larger attack—and certainly none of any consequence for the strength of deterrence. A larger attack could go after Russian nuclear forces, but as we have seen, this strategy would have limited effectiveness and be of dubious usefulness.

The only potentially meaningful difference between attacks of 200 and 1,500 warheads would be their effect on former Soviet military industry and conventional forces. The larger attack would do a more complete job of destroying both. Whether this completeness is necessary for deterrence, however, is open to question. If a future Russian leader were contemplating the results of America's minimum deterrent retaliation, he (or she) would know that tens of millions of Russians would be dead; dozens of its largest cities smashed; half or more of its general industry and most of its military industry destroyed or rendered unusable for months or years; all its major naval bases flattened; dozens of its airbases destroyed and most combat-ready ground units wiped out.

Whether, *in addition,* a retaliation could grind even more Russian military industry into dust, or annihilate a few dozen extra airbases, or more completely destroy Russian ground forces, seems beside the point. The former vision of destruction is so catastrophic, so utterly beyond comprehension, that the latter one has only a marginally greater psychological effect.[60] Particularly since the 1986 Chernobyl disaster, Russian leaders and citizens alike have been sensitized to the risks of even a nuclear accident; the prospect of 200 "accidents," each hundreds of times more destructive and radioactive than Chernobyl, must be terrifying, and should be more than sufficient for deterrence.

In the end, all judgments about the likely deterrent effect of various nuclear arsenals must be subjective. We cannot know for certain that an arsenal of 200 or 500 or 5,000 weapons would make war impossible; war *could* occur regardless of how many nuclear weapons are deployed, although as we have seen at a certain level of nuclear armament the likely effects of any major war serve as a powerful disincentive to beginning one. No analysis can "prove" that a given threat of retaliation will deter war.

Nonetheless, it is difficult to escape the impression that a retaliation of roughly 200 warheads issuing, perhaps, from a minimum deterrent of 300 to 500 total weapons would be "enough." The level of social and military destruction it would cause might well have been enough even during the cold war, and it seems more than sufficient for the less rigorous deterrent requirements of the 1990s. Given the lack of likely routes to U.S.-Russian conflict and the changing perceptions of Russian leaders, the prospect of 200 nuclear weapons striking their cities and defense establishment cannot fail to make a strong impression. A larger arsenal of roughly 3,000 warheads would not offer unique effects that are necessary for deterrence or stability, at least in terms of central deterrence. The availability of counterpower targeting, the naturally finite nature of even the former Soviet Union's military power, and the contraction of the worrisome aspects of that power into a much smaller Russian force all suggest that a minimum deterrent could do a much better job of deterrence than is commonly assumed.

NOTES

1. See the National Academy of Sciences, *The Future of the U.S.-Soviet Nuclear Relationship* (Washington, D.C.: National Academy of Sciences, 1991); George Perkovich, "Counting the Costs of the Arms Race," *Foreign Policy* No. 85 (Winter 1991-92); Fred Chernoff, "START or Finish? The Future of Strategic Arms Control and Profound Force Reductions," *Defense Analysis* 6/3 (September 1990); and Harold A. Feiveson and Frank N. von Hippel, "Beyond START: How to Make Much Deeper Cuts," *International Security* 15/1 (Summer 1990).

2. See Carl Kaysen, Robert S. McNamara, and George W. Rathjens, "Nuclear Weapons After the Cold War," *Foreign Affairs* 70/4 (Fall 1991).

3. Princeton scholars William Daugherty, Barbara Levi, and Frank von Hippel examined the consequences of "limited" nuclear attacks on both the United States and Russia. In an attack on the United States, they calculated that just 100 one-megaton Russian weapons would kill between 3 and 66 million Americans, and cause between 10 and 71 million total casualties, depending upon how it was targeted. The best-case attack, a counterforce blow aimed solely at U.S. nuclear weapons and supporting facilities, was calculated to produce at least 3 million prompt deaths and 10 million total casualties. Daugherty, von Hippel, and Levi, "The Consequences of 'Limited' Nuclear Attacks on the United States," *International Security* 10/4 (Spring 1986), p. 5.

   For our purposes, their most interesting 100-warhead targeting scenario was one termed "military-industrial." For this they considered attacks on 100 of the 122 facilities "designated as 'priority one' on a target list assembled in 1984 for the U.S. Department of Defense. These facilities produce 'major end-items and critical components' for the U.S. military." This is very similar to the industrial elements of a counterpower strategy and hence might be an accurate picture of a major portion of targeting policy under a minimum deterrent. Casualties expected from a 100-warhead attack against such targets range between 11 and 29 million for prompt deaths and 23 to 35 million for total casualties. "The Consequences of 'Limited' Nuclear Attacks on the United States," p. 25.

4. The notion of "overkill" becomes plainly apparent when we compare these estimates to predicted casualties from much larger attacks. Daugherty, Levi, and Hippel also examined a 3,000-warhead attack against more than 1,200 counterforce targets in the United States, many of them strategic nuclear weapons or nuclear command-and-control or support centers. According to their calculations, such an attack would produce 13 to 34 million deaths—a strikingly similar range to the one for a 100-warhead attack against military-industrial targets.("The

Consequences of 'Limited' Nuclear Attacks," p. 5) By expending 30 times as many warheads, a Russian attacker might kill just a few million more Americans and might actually do less damage to U.S. military industry, since the larger attack is aimed mostly at nuclear forces. Comparing these two results, a U.S. leader would be hard-pressed to find any added incentive to begin a war with the expectation of the 100-warhead retaliation rather than one many times larger.

Michael May, George Bing, and John Steinbruner, in *Strategic Arms Reductions* (Washington, D.C.: The Brookings Institution, 1988), p. 67, roughly calculate casualties for seven different strike packages of 3,000 to 10,000 warheads. Their estimates range from 11 to 77 million prompt deaths for the United States, and 12 to 106 million deaths for Russia. These are in the same range as the Princeton estimates, and they confirm the impression of greater expected Russian casualties.

5. For example, one estimate suggests that the 30 largest Russian cities alone contain 25 percent of the Russian population as well as 25 to 40 percent of its industrial capacity. Dietrich Schroeer, *Science, Technology, and the Nuclear Arms Race* (New York: John Wiley and Sons, 1984), p. 84. The damage curve in Michael May's remarks in W. Thomas Wander, Elizabeth J. Kirk, and Eric H. Arnett, eds., *Technology and Arms Control in the 1990s* (Washington, D.C.: American Association for the Advancement of Science, 1989), p. 76, similarly suggests that less than 50 aimpoints would destroy 40 percent of "cumulative industrial capacity in the top 300 cities" in the former Soviet Union. Even at this low level, the declining marginal value of more nuclear weapons is evident: expanding the list to 50 cities gives us just 34 percent of the Russian population and barely over 40 percent of its industry.

In a 1987 report, three MIT experts looked at the impact on the U.S. economy of various nuclear attacks that would qualify here as "minimum" ones. In a "counter-energy" attack consisting of some 239 nuclear attacks (but only 110 equivalent megatons) on facilities that refine, store or transport liquid fuels, the United States would lose at least 33 percent of its capacity to produce energy products and 8 percent of its overall manufacturing capability (as well as 20 million civilians immediately after the attack, with probably tens of millions dying later). But the impact in terms of energy and transportation shortfalls would cause a general economic collapse: GNP would drop by two thirds initially, and even after 25 years would only be back to half its preattack levels. The psychological effects of such an attack on the population would probably further reduce productivity, the authors conclude, pushing GNP down to about a quarter of preattack levels for a generation or ending the society as a functioning organization. M. Anjali Sastry, Joseph J. Romm, and Kosta Tsipis, *Nuclear Crash: The U.S. Economy After Small Nuclear Attacks* (Cambridge, Mass.: Massachusetts Institute of Technology, 1986), pp. 93-100.

"The U.S. economy can be severely damaged," these authors conclude, "by small, bottlenecking attacks that consume as little as one percent of the Soviet strategic arsenal." Because of many optimistic assumptions regarding economic activity after the attack, moreover, the authors believed that "economic collapse would probably occur at an even smaller level of attack." Even under such small attacks, "it is far from clear that such a level of activity represents the functioning of a nationally integrated, complex economy as we have come to know it." Their conclusion: even reductions of 95 percent in both sides' strategic arsenals, leaving roughly 500 weapons on each side, would preserve liberal doses of "unacceptable damage." Sastry, Romm, and Tsipis, *Nuclear Crash,* pp. 106-7.

The situation is similar for Russia. Just 18 targets represented 50 percent of the former Soviet Union's production of nickel, magnesium, titanium, lead, copper, and aluminum; 19 more aimpoints would destroy half the steel production, and 35 more would halve the production of petroleum. An additional 75 warheads would increase that rate of destruction to 75 percent for all products except petroleum. Figures cited in Congressional Budget Office, *The Start Treaty and Beyond* (Washington, D.C.: CBO, October 1991), p. 23. Less than 50 warheads would have destroyed some 40 percent of all electric generating capacity in the Soviet Union. Michael May, remarks in Wander, et al., eds., *Technology and Arms Control for the 1990s,* p. 76.

6. Others have made similar analyses. In a U.S. attack on Russia, William Martel and Paul Savage have calculated that dropping 85 warheads on 26 major bomber bases and 4 submarine pens would cause some 14 million casualties. Sixty detonations on command-and-control centers in such cities as Moscow would cause an additional 11.4 million casualties. On the whole, Martel and Savage calculate that a limited U.S. counterforce attack would cause nearly 40 million prompt Soviet casualties.

In Russian attacks on the United States, the numbers are somewhat lower. A 50-warhead strike against command-and-control sites would cause 3.4 million casualties; attacks on ICBM fields would kill or wound 1.6 million more; 50 detonations on bomber bases would add 2.7 million casualties, and 15 bombs dropped on submarine bases would add 2 million more. If the Russian warheads were targeted on cities, the devastation would of course be far greater: "The detonation of roughly 100 one-megaton nuclear weapons," they conclude, " . . . would result in roughly 18 million prompt deaths," and countless millions more injuries and slower, cancer-induced deaths. Martel and Savage, *Strategic Nuclear War: What the Superpowers Target and Why* (New York: Greenwood Press, 1986), pp. 72, 58, 82, 87, 92, and 100.

7. May, Bing, and Steinbruner, *Strategic Arms Reductions,* p. 32.

8. Thomas C. Reed and Michael O. Wheeler, "The Role of Nuclear Weapons in the New World Order," mimeographed report, Washington, D.C., December 1991. For description of the origins and status of the report, see R. Jeffrey Smith, "U.S. Urged to Cut 50 Percent of A-Arms," *Washington Post,* January 6, 1992, p. A1.

9. The enunciation of a target set in Russia causes two problems. First, most information on former Soviet military forces and facilities is of cold war vintage, and in many cases does not distinguish between capabilities in Russia and those in other republics. The analysis and calculations below have attempted to deal with this lack of information as well as possible; where there are gaps in the unclassified literature, the analysis will assume the existence of former Soviet deployments and bases, thus providing an authomatically conservative estimate.

   Second, some will object that targeting Russia is not the U.S. task at all today, that Russia is no longer an adversary of the West. It is important for me to emphasize that I use Russia only as an example. It is the most demanding targeting challenge the United States would have if the United States could have high confidence of deterring any other potential adversaries. The purpose of my argument is to promote cooperation: if the analysis which follows is correct, Washington and Moscow can dismantle most of their respective nuclear arsenals and get on with the business of building a lasting friendship.

10. For more thorough analysis of these arguments and of the counterpower strategy proposed below, see Mazarr, "Beyond Counterforce," *Comparative Strategy* 9/4 (1990); and idem, *START and the Future of Deterrence* (London: Macmillan, 1990), chapter 4.

11. Paul Doty, "Arms Control: 1960, 1990, 2020," *Daedalus* 120/4 (Winter 1991), pp. 48-49.

12. Bernard Brodie, *Strategy in the Missile Age* (Princeton, N.J.: Princeton University Press, 1959), pp. 274-5.

13. Henry Shue, "Having It Both Ways: The Gradual Wrong Turn in American Strategy," in Shue, ed., *Nuclear Deterrence and Moral Restraint: Critical Choices for American Strategy* (New York: Cambridge University Press, 1989), p. 26.

14. General John T. Chain, "Statement" in *Department of Defense Authorization for Appropriations for Fiscal Years 1990 and 1991.* Hearings before the Senate Committee on Armed Services, May 10, 1989, p. 79.

15. George Quester,"The Difficult Logic of Terminating a Nuclear War," in Steven Cimbala, ed., *Strategic War Termination* (New York: Praeger, 1986), p. 71. Richard Betts wonders "whether it is wise to threaten Soviet ICBMs even under the logic of the countervailing strategy. . . . Escalation control might argue against a threat large enough to provoke launch on warning." Betts, *Cruise Missiles and U.S. Policy* (Washington, D.C.: The Brookings Institution, 1982), 18. See also Philip Bobbitt, *Democracy and Deterrence: The History and Future of Nuclear*

Strategy (New York: St. Martin's Press, 1988), p. 174, where he argues that the lack of a countersilo capability might actually help U.S. strategy "because it reduces [U.S.] self-deterrence lest the Soviet Union fear that its control systems are being attacked."

16. Harold A. Feiveson, "Finite Deterrence," in Shue, ed., *Nuclear Deterrence and Moral Restraint*, p. 273.

17. Brodie, *Strategy in the Missile Age*, p. 302.

18. See Andrew Goldberg, "Offense and Defense in the Postnuclear Era," *The Washington Quarterly* 11/2 (Spring 1988), p. 58; Bobbitt, *Democracy and Deterrence*, pp. 147-48; and Robert Jervis, *The Illogic of American Nuclear Strategy* (Ithaca, N.Y.: Cornell University Press, 1984), pp. 106-9.

19. Paradoxically, U.S. counterforce policies may in this sense be the engine of their own irrelevancy: there is no more powerful incentive for the Russians to launch all their weapons in an initial blow than the knowledge that those that stayed behind would be subject to attack. By threatening to destroy a Russian nuclear reserve, the United States provides the former Soviets with a good reason to abandon the idea of one.

20. Michael Nacht, *The Age of Vulnerability: Threats to the Nuclear Stalemate* (Washington, D.C.: The Brookings Institution, 1985), p. 93.

21. A similar point is made in the Congressional Budget Office report, *The START Treaty and Beyond*, p. xvii.

22. Ashton Carter, "Emerging Themes in Nuclear Arms Control," *Daedalus* 120/4 (Winter 1991), p. 241.

23. Counterpower strategies have been examined at length elsewhere. See Jeffrey Richelson, "The Dilemmas of Counterpower Targeting," in Desmond Ball and Richelson, eds., *Strategic Nuclear Targeting* (Ithaca, N.Y.: Cornell University Press, 1985); Bernard Albert, "Constructive Counterpower," *Orbis* 20/3 (Summer 1976); and Bruce Russett, "Assured Destruction of What? A Countercombatant Alternative to Nuclear MADness," *Public Policy* 22/2 (Spring 1974).

24. For an analysis of the minimum deterrence/counterpower connection, see Bruce Russett, "An Acceptable Role for Nuclear Weapons," in Charles W. Kegley and Kenneth L. Schwab, eds., *After the Cold War: Questioning the Morality of Nuclear Deterrence* (Boulder, Colo.: Westview Press, 1991), pp. 136-39.

25. The potential list of Russian conventional force and military industry targets is extremely long of course, and would reasonably support a target base much larger than that contemplated here. The analysis below, however, will suggest that sufficient military damage could be done with just 200 warheads. If the USA makes a specific commitment to minimum deterrence, the military's past insatiable appetite for targets will be overcome.

26. The official Defense Intelligence Agency office for handling Freedom of Information Act requests reported that *Soviet Military Power* is the only unclassified government publication containing information on Soviet military basing and deployments. Correspondence with the author, September 5, 1991.

27. It should be noted that nuclear targets are excluded from these lists. Nuclear weapons are left off because of the nonnuclear targeting strategy outlined above. A ban on all strategic missile and nuclear weapon production is proposed as part of a minimum deterrent, and the abolishment of all nondeployed stocks. Such potential targets would therefore disappear.

   The target lists do include air and naval bases which might harbor strategic bombers or missile-firing submarines, and care must be taken to avoid counternuclear targeting if indeed that is a goal. The risk of keeping counterforce targeting alive is a small one in any case—presumably many bombers would be on alert during a crisis and would not be vulnerable to ICBM strikes on air bases, and few if any SSBNs would be in port.

28. International Institute for Strategic Studies, *The Military Balance 1990-91* (London: IISS, 1991), p. 34.

29. Category A, in which divisions are essentially at full strength; B, where divisions possess only 50 to 75 percent of full manpower; C, 20 to 50 percent of full complement; and mobilization units with less than 5 percent of the active duty troops they would have when at full strength.

30. *The Military Balance 1990-1991*, pp. 38-39. Six Soviet airborne divisions were also in category A, but being light infantry and light armored forces, they could not pose a significant overland offensive threat.

31. If the nuclear strike came at the end of a long crisis, of course, all Soviet reserves may have been mobilized, giving a total of far more than 40 category A divisions. A 40-weapon strike would nonetheless do vast damage to the Soviet army; and presumably European (and perhaps Chinese and Japanese) armies would have been mobilized as well, which would tend to reduce the need to threaten Soviet conventional forces for deterrence.

32. Fred Hiatt, "Russia to Field Armed Forces of Its Own," *The Washington Post*, February 13, 1992, p. A33.

33. See Stephen R. Covington and John Lough, "Russia's Post-Revolution Challenge: Reform of the Soviet Superpower Paradigm," *The Washington Quarterly* 15/1 (Winter 1992).

34. John W. R. Lepingwell, "Towards a Post-Soviet Army," *Orbis* 36/1 (Winter 1992), p. 98.

35. "Analysts See Major Upheavals in Soviet Military," *Defense Daily*, April 13, 1990, p. 79.

36. In March 1992 General Dmitry Volkgonov, military adviser to Russian President Boris Yeltsin, told Russian deputies that the armed forces would "take two years to create and might number between 1.25 and 1.5 million men." Quoted in John Lloyd, "Russia to Form Its Own Army," *Financial Times,* March 17, 1992, p. 1. In April U.S. defense officials revealed that Russian officials had told them the Russian military would be in the range of 1.2 to 1.3 million troops. See "Russia to Make Steep Cuts in Troops, Adopt Defensive Stance," *Washington Post,* April 2, 1991; and Eric Schmitt, "Russia Is Said to Plan for a Smaller Armed Force," *New York Times,* April 2, 1992.

37. Most of these figures are from International Institute for Strategic Studies, *The Military Balance 1991-1992* (London: IISS, Spring 1992).

38. Ibid., pp. 36-45.

39. Lepingwell, "Towards a Post-Soviet Army," pp. 90-91, 99.

40. National Academy of Sciences, *The Future of the U.S.-Soviet Nuclear Relationship,* pp. 56-58.

41. Kosta Tsipis, *Arsenal: Understanding Weapons in the Nuclear Age* (New York: Simon and Schuster, 1983), pp. 48-67.

42. U.S. Department of Defense, *Soviet Military Power 1984* (Washington, D.C.: Government Printing Office, 1984), p. 81.

43. CBO, *The START Treaty and Beyond,* p. 22, lists 10 major supply depots as potential targets.

44. Thomas Cochran, William Arkin, Robert Norris, and Jeffrey Sands, *Soviet Nuclear Weapons,* vol. IV of *Nuclear Weapons Databook* (New York: Harper and Row, 1989), p. 61. These bases include Adler, Alekseyevka, Anadyr, Belaya, Bykhov, Bobruysk, Chernyakhovsk, Dolan, Engel's, Murmansk, Mys Shmidta, Oktyabr'skoye, Olenegorsk, Ramenskoye, Saki, Sol'tsy, Tartu, Tiksi, Ukraina, Vladimirovka, Varkuta, and Voronezh.

45. CBO, *The START Treaty and Beyond,* p. 22, lists 30 to 40 major tactical airfields.

46. These figures come from the 1990 *Soviet Military Power* map, which is one of the few unclassified documents that breaks military bases and deployments down explicitly by republic.

47. Reports indicate that from 1990 to 1992 more than 260 former Soviet naval vessels had been sold for scrap, and dozens of others faced an imminent end to their service life. Many warships under construction will be scrapped. See Gabriel Schoenfeld, "Seasick," Center for Strategic and International Studies, *Post-Soviet Prospects* No. 12 (April 1992), pp. 3-4.

48. *Nuclear Weapons Databook* vol. IV, p. 64. The major bases are Arkhangelsk, Baltiysk, Kaliningrad, Kronshtadt, Liepaja, Murmansk, Petropavlovsk-Kamchatski, Polarnyy, Poti, Sevastopol, Severomorsk, Vladivostok, and Zapadnaya Litsa.

49. The National Academy of Sciences report, *The Future of the U.S.-Soviet Nuclear Relationship*, p. 56, similarly estimates 20 major port targets, against which it would fire 50 warheads; the CBO, in *The Start Treaty and Beyond* p. 24, estimates 25.

50. Taylor, "Red Army Blues," p. 3, cites only nine major naval bases in Russia itself.

51. *Soviet Military Power 1986*, p. 115, refers to a total of 150 major production plants; the *Nuclear Weapons Databook*, p. 77, counts 181, but that number includes several dozen of unknown military application.

52. These include four tank plants—Nizhniy Tagil, Kharkov, Omsk, and Chelyabinsk; seven factories making other armored fighting vehicles; artillery production at Sverdlovsk and Perm; helicopter production at Kazan, Ulan Ude, Arsenyev, Rostov, and other sites; aircraft production at Kuybyshev (BEAR H), Gorkiy (Foxhound), Moscow (Fulcrum), Tbilisi (Frogfoot), Komsomolsk (Flanker), and Tashkent (Candid); surface-to-air missile industries at Leningrad, Kirov, and Kovrov; submarine production at Severodvinsk, Gorkiy, Admiralty, Komsomolsk, and Sudomekh; and facilities of unknown product at Minsk, Zagorsk, Bryansk, Kiev, Dnepropetrovsk, Nikolayev, Zaporozhye, Pavlograd, Voronezh, Ulyanovsk, Volgograd, Vodkinsk, Nizhnyaya Tura, Kurgan, Kemerovo, Novosibirsk, Biysk, Krasnoyarsk, and Irkutsk. Another source estimated that between 46 and 64 percent of this total for the former Soviet Union is in Russia itself; Taylor, "Red Army Blues," p. 2.

53. *Soviet Military Power 1986*, p. 112; and the CIA, Directorate of Intelligence, "The Soviet Weapons Industry: An Overview," unclassified report, September 1986, p. 2.

54. Theodore Postol, "Targeting," in Ashton Carter, John Steinbruner, and Charles Zraket, eds., *Managing Nuclear Operations* (Washington, D.C.: The Brookings Institution, 1987), pp. 377-78, 392-93.

55. Postol, "Targeting," pp. 392-93.

56. Perceptive readers will notice that command-and-control targets are absent from this accumulated list. There are two reasons for this omission. First, I am sympathetic to arguments that general leadership targeting is dangerous because it threatens escalation control and war termination. Second, field commands for the military services are subsumed in the target bases presented. For example, naval headquarters are located at some of the bases targeted; airbases hold air units' commanders. A few specific headquarters could be added to the mix if necessary.

57. For comparative purposes, I present the Congressional Budget Office's example: 600-warhead retaliation would hit 200 "major depots," 50 marshaling yards, 100 tactical airbases, 50 major headquarters, and 200 industrial targets. The general allocation is similar to that proposed here. CBO, *The START Treaty and Beyond*, p. 15.

58. See n. 3.
59. May, Bing, and Steinbruner, *Strategic Arms Reductions,* pp. 48-53, estimate that the retaliation produced by about 3,000 warheads would be between 1,000 and 1,500 warheads. The latter figure has been used for this comparison.
60. The CBO concludes (*The START Treaty and Beyond,* p. xvii): "With 600 warheads the United States could virtually annihilate all major Soviet industries, major transportation nodes, and major fixed military infrastructure in the Soviet Union." With 200, as we have seen, the United States could do a large proportion of that damage.
61. The 1,500 warhead strike would not have to include any nuclear weapons sites. If it did not, the damage done to conventional forces and military industries would rise.

Part II

European Nuclear Forces

8

Britain, Nuclear Weapons, and the Future of Arms Control

by Lawrence Freedman

CONTEXT

The West is no longer dependent upon nuclear arms for its security in the way that NATO claimed itself to be until 1989, nor is it engaged in intense competitive development with the former Soviet Union. In 1990 the alliance explicitly acknowledged that it was "less reliant" upon nuclear weapons than before. All the incentives are to cut the nuclear arsenals as rapidly as possible and sideline them in international affairs. Before a new set of nuclear threats arrives the obvious policy priority is to prevent its appearance through an active nonproliferation policy. There are no obvious contingencies in which the West has any interest in seeing the question of nuclear use raised. In all cases, even against old adversaries, nonnuclear capabilities should be sufficient. The need is to persuade others not to "go nuclear." This makes it very difficult to prescribe or proscribe nuclear policies. A definite adversary can no longer be identified, and the boundaries and internal structure of potential candidates have yet to be settled. Arcane theories of intra-war deterrence, based on overintellectualized searches to find ways to fight a nuclear war in such a way as to avoid mass destruction, are being sent to the archives.

For countries such as Britain this is in many ways a much simpler strategic environment in which to develop a national nuclear policy than the one that it replaced, though in every other respect the current environment is much more complicated. The easiest nuclear doctrine is one geared to the deterrence of another's nuclear use against national territory. This was always difficult for Britain to adopt because of its loyalty to the alliance and the associated strategy of flexible response, which depended on the threat to use nuclear weapons on behalf of allies who could not be defended in the face of a superior conventional force.

Given the small size of its force, it was never clear why Britain would take such a step on its own and, if it would only initiate nuclear war in concert with the United States, exactly what it was adding to the American nuclear clout. However, for the moment, there is no pressing need to worry about deterring conventional threats or worrying about the vulnerabilities of close allies. The residual threat may be remote and defy precise identification, but nuclear strategy has always been geared to remote scenarios and at least the current crop of potential Third World adversaries has the advantage of generally being weaker than Britain and unable to reach British territory with its prospective weapons.

In this chapter I will first describe Britain's nuclear capability and indicate that it is unlikely to grow as much with Trident as is commonly supposed while the substrategic element is shrinking fast. I will then move on to describe the impact of recent changes on rationales for a national nuclear force before moving on to discuss the relevance of this for arms control. The conclusion is that Britain is moving toward a minimum deterrent with a minimum rationale and thus a minimal interest in arms control.

BRITAIN'S CAPABILITIES

One estimate for British nuclear warheads—revealed in 1989—was of 300, of which about 120 were for Polaris/Chevaline and the rest were for the WE-177 "family" of free-fall bombs and depth bombs.[1]

With the Polaris A-3 only 16 targets could be attacked with a shotgun warhead comprised of three 200 KT RVs (kiloton reentry vehicles). The introduction of Chevaline, which began operational service in the summer of 1982,[2] did not commit Britain to an attack on the Moscow area as the only targeting option. However, it may be that it committed Britain to an attack on a few, and possibly no more than one large, target(s). In 1980 it was acknowledged officially that

> There is a concept which Chevaline makes clear, that Governments did not want to have a situation where the adversary could have a sanctuary for his capital and a large area around it.[3]

Whereas with the A-3 warhead all missiles would have to be committed without complete confidence of success, with Chevaline a similar number of missiles would be launched, but with a much greater chance of success. Until Trident becomes operational in late 1994/early 1995, Britain, therefore, will have little flexibility in targeting.[4]

When in 1982 the government decided to opt for the D5 version of the Trident missile instead of the C4 as originally envisaged, it was stated explicitly that Britain would not need extra warheads—that it would stick with a maximum of 8 warheads per missile or 128 on each 16-missile SSBN. With the greater efficiency of the new propulsion units, more submarines could be on station at any given time. A four-boat force would allow at least two and possibly three submarines to be on station simultaneously. A maximum coverage of 384 targets makes a substantial difference from the 32 maximum with Polaris.

In practice it is highly unlikely that the U.K. will have as many as 128 warheads per submarine. There may well be production and special material constraints, even though the capacity of Aldermaston (the U.K.'s nuclear weapons research and engineering facility) has been increased. The most recent formulation is that:

> We have long emphasized that each Trident submarine would carry no more than 128 warheads. This has always been an upper limit, not a specification: the number to be deployed in the mid-1990s onwards will be decided in the light of circumstances at the time.[5]

Presuming that U.S. and Russian cuts continue as planned and that no serious ballistic missile defense is deployed around Moscow, it is possible to speculate that U.K. warheads will be around a third or at most a half of this maximum (which could reflect the American decision to download U.S. Trident D5 missiles to 4 warheads each).

Meanwhile, Britain's "substrategic"[6] capability is in decline. At its most recent peak this capability was as follows:

> The British free-fall nuclear bomb can be delivered by RAF Tornado GR1 and Buccaneer and Royal Navy Sea Harrier aircraft; options to replace it with a tactical air-launched missile are currently being studied. British nuclear depth bombs can be delivered by Royal Navy antisubmarine helicopters; RAF Nimrod maritime patrol aircraft can deliver U.S. nuclear depth bombs. An army artillery regiment equipped with short-range Lance missiles and four regiments of artillery in the Federal Republic of Germany are capable of firing nuclear warheads supplied by the United States.[7]

However, since then this substrategic capability has been cut back significantly; in the future, it will "consist solely of RAF Tornado and until 1994
Buccaneer dual-cable aircraft and the WE 177 free-fall bomb."[8]

Short-range land-based systems (which were dual key) are being abandoned.
These included four batteries of three Lance short-range missiles,[9] plus sixteen
M-110 203mm self-propelled howitzer and 101 M-109 155mm self-propelled
howitzer.[10] In 1987 it was reported that sixteen 203 mm guns would be
withdrawn completely from the nuclear role so that resources could be concen-
trated on the 155 mm gun. Modernization here would involve deployment of the
U.S. W-28 shell.[11] However, following the NATO decision to abandon short-
range nuclear forces in Germany it was announced that 50 Missile Regiment and
56 Special Weapons Battery Royal Artillery will disband by April 1, 1993.

Britain will no longer retain a maritime tactical nuclear weapons capability. Nuclear depth bombs were carried on board the three Invincible-class
light aircraft carriers, even though many frigates were also allowed to carry
them. Only 20 to 30 were produced, and their yield was put at 5 to 10
kilotons.[12] In the future they will not be carried by Royal Navy ships and
aircraft and the weapons designated for this role will be destroyed. Royal Air
Force Nimrod maritime patrol aircraft were able to carry American nuclear
depth charges. These patrols have been terminated.

The only substrategic weapons being maintained are air delivered. Even
here there are to be reductions. There is to be a reduction from 11 Tornado
and 4 Buccaneer squadrons to 4 Tornado GR 1a/1b squadrons based in the
United Kingdom and 4 GR 1 still based in Germany. The number of WE-177
free-fall bombs available for these aircraft is to be cut by half.

The WE-177 is one of "a family of weapons of different characteristics
having come in at different dates," including the Navy's nuclear depth charge
(WE-177C) as well as the RAF's free-fall bomb (WE-177A and B).[13]
Tornados are normally assumed to carry two WE-177 bombs.[14] One source
gives the yield of these weapons at around 20 kilotons:[15] another suggests
a variable nuclear yield between 5 and 200 kilotons.[16] Both IISS and SIPRI
suggest that there is a variant with a yield of 400 kilotons.[17] The yield varies
according to amount and condition of the Tritium in the bomb. In practice
the bombs kept have yields well below 200 kilotons and probably as low as
10 kilotons.[18] The original yield may have been reduced at the request of
SACEUR (Supreme Allied Command, Europe), out of deference to German
concerns over high-yield weapons being used over its territory.

A major question mark now hangs over the question of a possible new
standoff missile to succeed WE-177. Instead of requiring the aircraft to
operate at the limits of their range and penetrating former Soviet air defenses,

an air-launched standoff missile would give the aircraft more space to maneuver, allowing them to avoid the most dense concentrations of air defenses or extend their effective range. As security policy was reassessed in the wake of the December 1987 U.S.-Soviet INF Treaty, interest in a standoff missile revived. This led to a debate in Whitehall over the comparative merits of collaboration with France or the United States.

In May 1988 there were indications that a decision on the WE-177 replacement would be made by the end of 1990, with a planned in-service date for the end of the 1990s. Almost on the last days of 1990, it was reported that a decision had been made that a Tactical Air to Surface Missile (TASM) should be approved, but the question of whether this should be Anglo-American or Anglo-French had yet to be decided. The requirement was believed to be for a weapon with a 400 to 600 kilometer range, with high accuracy and some "stealthy" features. Some 100 to 200 missiles would be built. Estimates of potential costs, especially in collaboration with the French, have reached £3 billion (compared with just over £10 billion for Trident).

When President George Bush canceled the SRAM-T program in September 1991, he removed the cheapest of the three options being considered by the Ministry of Defence for the British TASM. It has been suggested that it was only with U.K. prompting that Bush included a reference in his announcement to the need to "preserve an effective air-delivered nuclear capability in Europe."[19] Internal studies have since looked at other U.S. programs, including the joint Anglo-American Tactical Integrated Rocket Ramjet Missile and the possibility of working with the French to develop their ASLP-D. However, money is becoming much tighter, especially now that it looks like the British may lose their partners in the European Fighter Aircraft (EFA) and must therefore plan to carry the whole program in the RAF's budget. Studies are therefore reported to have turned to the possible substrategic use of Trident warheads.[20] In the July 1992 Defence Estimates there was no specific mention of a standoff missile,[21] and this was generally taken to mean, probably correctly, that the political logic of the situation was to abandon this program. It is understood, however, that a replacement warhead for the WE-177 has been developed by Aldermaston, and tested in the United States, although the program is not yet complete.

RATIONALES

The future of the national nuclear force is not a major issue in Britain. It only tends to get debated around election time. However, with an antinuclear policy blamed for two election defeats, the Labour Party trod exceedingly softly around the issue in April 1992. An election-eve launch of the first of the Trident submarines, HMS *Vanguard,* might have been expected to spark some argument, but in practice it helped explain why the debate was so halfhearted. Much of the investment in the coming generation of submarines and missiles has now been made, and so the economic case for abandoning the deterrent, which was the basis for the Labour challenge in 1983 and 1987, is weak.

The end of the cold war came too late for the nuclear skeptics. If the government had had to make the case for the investment in a new nuclear force in 1990, it would have been hard pressed. Much has changed since those harsh days of the summer of 1980, when the decision to purchase a new generation of submarine-launched missiles from the United States was announced. Then the headlines were of Soviet troops in Afghanistan, arms control on hold, mass demonstrations against cruise missiles, and Ronald Reagan about to obtain the Republican presidential nomination. There was a keen sense of an intensifying cold war. Now the cold war is history, the former Soviet empire is in fragments, and the Warsaw Pact has evaporated. The United States and Russia are engaged in cooperative disarmament, and President Boris Yeltsin has promised not to target British cities anymore.

In these changed circumstances the former official rationale for Trident has become irrelevant. The case was as follows: NATO had determined that it needed the threat of nuclear war to deter Moscow from unleashing the Warsaw Pact's massive conventional armies in a drive to the English Channel. The United States obviously provided the bulk of the deterrent force, but it was important that one European country make a contribution (with France sitting on the sidelines outside the alliance's integrated command). Furthermore, because there were unavoidable doubts over whether the United States would put itself at risk for the sake of Europe, it was helpful if Moscow had to consider the possibility that London would respond even if Washington held back. It may have been hard to think of occasions in which this might happen, but then the great virtue of nuclear deterrence lay in awareness of the large consequences of slight miscalculations.[22]

In one sense the case for a national nuclear force has been strengthened, in that previous justifications always played on doubts over the durability of the U.S. nuclear guarantee. There is now nothing like the old preoccupation with the U.S. umbrella—which is just as well, as many of the old standards set for extended deterrence can no longer be met. In the past it has been assumed that only the stationing of U.S. nuclear systems on allied territory could provide tangible evidence of the nuclear umbrella. Apart from SLBMs in European waters, whose mobility allows for a speedy withdrawal, this will now at most depend on forward deployment of nuclear-capable aircraft. The number of U.S. nuclear warheads in Europe is set to come down to 700—almost 10 percent of those at peak deployment. The target set has obviously changed, but the dramatic reduction in warheads reflects the level of visible commitment now considered adequate both in the United States and Europe, especially now that the most dire contingencies seem remote.[23] Whether or not the numbers would be seen to be sufficient should one of these contingencies actually arise is a difficult question, as is the general credibility of a "reconstitution" policy for a nuclear umbrella. Once the weapons have been marginalized, will it be possible to give them a revived role without aggravating the crisis that occasioned the reappraisal? Bringing weapons out of store, putting others back on alert, and coyness about deployment and targeting plans will appear provocative.

Even though the local presence of U.S. systems may become an untenable basis for extended deterrence, for the moment NATO countries have little option but to accept U.S. declaratory assurances that extended deterrence is still in place. This is unlikely to be formally withdrawn, but it may not be sustained over the years because it will rarely be a high political priority and so will lapse. There may be a break in the U.S. institutional memory and no tangible reminders of the nature of the nuclear commitment.

The uncoupling of the U.S. nuclear arsenal from European security is now a much more serious prospect than it has ever been—but precisely for that reason, the British government does not want to starting talking of American disengagement as a foregone conclusion. In an important recent restatement of British nuclear policy, the secretary of state for defence observed that it was not in Britain's security interest to encourage

> any tendency toward thinking that there could be a major conflict in Europe in which the question of nuclear use arose which did not involve the vital interests of all the allies including the US.[24]

On this basis it is not surprising that he also indicated that the old "second centre of decision making" theory retained "validity."

Nor has there been much support for the view that an alternative guarantee can be based on France and Britain. It has always been assumed that such a guarantee would lack credibility—in part because of French policy, which remains a problem, and in part because of the balance of forces, which may become less of a problem. There has been no indication that other allies see an Anglo-French guarantee as a serious alternative to an American guarantee, so long as the latter is on offer.

There have been discussions in the past over the possibility of collaboration with regard to patrol areas and targeting. The problems with a joint force were summed up in a White Paper from the 1980s:

> If one were considering a fully integrated, jointly controlled Anglo-French nuclear deterrent, significant problems would arise. Our two countries would need to agree on the criteria the force would have to meet, the targets that would be put at risk, the details of complementary refits and patrol cycles and, by no means least, the problems of consultation leading to the launch of a nuclear weapon and the authority for the actual firing of a weapon. And if a jointly controlled force were contemplated, which country would change its defence philosophy? For certainly there would have to be a change. British nuclear forces are committed to NATO, and the Alliance would unquestionably be weakened in military and political terms if they were removed. France, on the other hand, although a member of the Alliance, is not part of the NATO military structure, and her forces are therefore independent of the Alliance.[25]

For their part the French have shown little inclination to abandon France's independence from any military integration. It has been unwilling to join other powers in targeting discussions, to take part in any consultative group such as the Nuclear Planning Group, or in any way to relinquish its exclusive and jealously guarded control of its nuclear arsenal.

To the extent that a cooperative Anglo-French nuclear effort would be seen as symbolic of a broader commitment to a comprehensive European defense entity, it would take on a wider significance. British policymakers will, on occasion, accept that in some way the national nuclear force is kept on trust for its European allies. Unlike the French, for example, they have made their own explicit nuclear commitment to Germany via the Tornado squadrons.

In his September 1992 speech, Secretary of State for Defence Malcolm Rifkind took this a bit further, arguing that the most credible use of national nuclear forces would be in pursuit of vital interests, and that these were inextricably bound up with NATO allies and European partners. He did not suggest that Anglo-French cooperation could be a basis for an alternative nuclear deterrent. Rather he suggested that such cooperation could help the two countries maximize their influence in nuclear matters. He observed that:

> The more closely we can concert our policies, the more weight we shall carry: where we have failed to do so (as, for example, over nuclear testing), the outcome tends to be to our disadvantage.

Thus he proposed in the further development of the European security structure, "more explicit emphasis on the progressive merging of interests between the Western European nuclear powers and their nonnuclear partners and allies."[26]

French ministers have also been rekindling interest in greater cooperation. The French prime minister Pierre Bérégovoy observed that a European deterrence doctrine would need considerable time and work because of the complexity and sensitivity of the issues raised. A "preliminary step," however, would be to bring together British and French views.[27] At the same time, Defense Minister Pierre Joxe was suggesting that France might be ready to become more involved in NATO, though not yet its military command, indicating a possible degree of convergence in security views. Nonetheless, the major project that could symbolize such cooperation—TASM—seems likely to fall by the wayside as a result of budgetary stringency.

There is nothing at the moment available upon which to start building a distinctive European defense entity. The Yugoslav debacle has exposed the fragility of a European security consensus and of the institutions designed to express it, the generally cautious attitude when confronted with a need for decisive action, and the central position of the United States when it comes to the point of serious military action. The failure of the United States to risk involvement in European quagmires of the Yugoslav variety provides reason for the Europeans to enhance their own cooperation, but it unfortunately tends to reinforce the old presumption that only the Americans could galvanize the Europeans into collective action.

For the British these issues are often publicly posed in terms of a wider NATO versus a narrow Western European Union (WEU) as the basis of a security policy, but—as evidenced in recent economic debates—the national inclination toward a "stand alone" policy remains deep-rooted. There has always been a private rationale for the nuclear force that is less convoluted than the "second centre of decision-making," but this rationale is also more nationalistic and so inappropriate for public declaration at NATO gatherings. According to this Gaullist view, a nuclear capability means that Britain still carries international weight, deserving its permanent place on the UN Security Council and at other "top tables." The ability to devastate any potential enemy provides the "ultimate guarantee of security" were the country ever again forced to "stand alone." In a cruel and uncertain world, who knows what threats might emerge in the future?

With the alliance rationales now looking distinctly dated, the rationale for Trident is tending to revert to the private view, which was probably always the most credible to public opinion. Although Rifkind's speech reaffirmed loyalty to concepts of extended deterrence, the latest Statement on Defence Estimates defined the essence of national strategy in much narrower terms:

> Our defence strategy will continue to be underpinned by nuclear forces as the ultimate guarantee of our country's security. Nuclear weapons guard against any attempt by an adversary to gain advantage by threat or coercion. They are also uniquely able to ensure that aggression is not a realistic option, by presenting to a potential aggressor the prospect of a cost that would far outweigh any hoped-for gain.[28]

Rifkind also acknowledged that nuclear use would be credible, justifiable, and proportionate only when "vital national interests were at stake," and that the most vital of interests were narrowly national—"the most obvious hypothesis being a direct homeland threat from an aggressor equipped with weapons of mass destruction."[29]

It is rather difficult to put too much stress on prestige arguments for a nuclear arsenal at a time when Ukraine, Belarus, and Kazakhstan are being told that they have very little to gain by clinging to pieces of the old Soviet arsenal still residing in their territory, and when a major plank of policy toward the Third World is to prevent the further acquisition of weapons of mass destruction. Britain may feel that it is so much more stable and mature, but that does not tend to be an argument that commends itself to potential proliferators.

In fact, the risks of Third World proliferation are now being used to reinforce the case for the British deterrent. This rarely goes further than the rhetorical "what if (whoever happens to be the most menacing dictator at the time—Galtieri, Qadhafi, Saddam) had nuclear weapons and we did not?"[30]

While the tendency toward various forms of proliferation can be exaggerated, it could have disturbing consequences even on a small scale. Small Third World nuclear arsenals will not be backed by the "conventions of crisis management" as developed over the years between the superpowers. Inevitably European attention will focus on the Continent's periphery. A critical factor here is the means of delivery. In most cases there is little direct risk for Britain because the proliferators would lack the range to pose a threat.

Weapons of mass destruction and their means of delivery to unstable and undemocratic countries bordering on NATO's southern flank could become a direct threat to individual European countries, or even to groups of NATO member states. This raises the question of a nuclear guarantee—for example, to Turkey squabbling with Iran over Central Asia. The role of a nuclear capability in future regional crises would be at most to neutralize any threats of mass destruction being made by a rogue country in the course of an

Iraq-type challenge to international law. This is a serious rationale, but it should be noted that it implies a readiness to make nuclear commitments to other countries that go well beyond anything contemplated in recent years.

Trident is not especially well suited to this role. It would make more sense to develop the accurate but low-yield TASM, though as indicated earlier this program now appears to be slipping away. However, if the only substrategic use of nuclear weapons is a warning-shot function, any strategic weapon could be used for this purpose, the "substrategic" nature of the shot being made clear by the choice of target.

On the basis of past practice and international declarations, it will be no part of Western policy to use nuclear weapons to intimidate nonnuclear powers armed with only conventional forces,[31] although it is ambiguous with regard to other terror (i.e., chemical and biological) weapons. The Gulf crisis raised the question of the readiness to use nuclear forces to deter chemical/biological attacks. In this case at least a capacity for severe retaliation with conventional air power (as well as defensive measures) plus a deterrent threat based on the extension of political objectives to threaten the Iraqi regime appeared sufficient. That should be the pattern in the future.

Rifkind has shown little enthusiasm for nuclear threats in such circumstances. If deterrence relies on rationality and caution in an aggressor, would it work with a "tyrant with little regard for the safety and welfare of his own country and people? If he is a gambler or an adventurer? If his judgment is unbalanced or clouded by isolation." He also expressed concern that public opinion would always think nuclear use disproportionate against a "small country, or an economically weak one." Nor would more "usable" low-yield nuclear weapons be effective as a deterrent: "There is a horror associated with nuclear weapons which we should not attempt to mitigate." The hope here must therefore be placed in nonproliferation regimes, plus the use of conventional weapons with precision technologies and also precision intelligence. In addition:

> Pre-emptive conventional strikes against clearly identifiable targets under appropriate international sanction are a conceivable option, given the capability of modern conventional weapons, and given the availability of good intelligence.[32]

Other than this, the critical focus will still be on the former Soviet Union. The CIS will be an unstable region, perhaps for decades to come, where the potential for authoritarian (albeit noncommunist) regimes is considerable. The key state is the Russian Federation. Even taking into account reductions to 3,500 warheads by the early years of the next century, it will still have a capacity to inflict unacceptable damage on Western nations, and its integration into the Western economic and political system is likely to be at best tenuous. Russia will still have a substantial nuclear arsenal well into the next century. Thus Rifkind argued that: "Our strategy makes military recidivism by any future Russian leadership a pointless option for them."[33]

However, with much reduced overall military power there is no obvious dynamic leading toward total war with the West. The dominant strategic issue is now more the fragility of the former Soviet Union than the old fears of brilliantly executed first strikes. There are still grim forebodings of nuclear weapons getting tangled up with chronic political instability. The possibility of a renegade nuclear power emerging out of the wreckage of the Soviet Union should not be overstated, but it is no less fanciful than many others that have sustained nuclear policy over the years.

Moscow may be ruled by someone less benign, while the Americans may allow their past guarantees to European security to lapse. In a harsher security environment the nonnuclear powers of Western Europe, and in particular Germany, may be grateful that Britain and France have held onto their arsenals. In this way nuclear weapons will play the role that they have always played—reminding us of the folly of total war—but in circumstances less demanding than before. It may be at best a marginal rationale for Trident, but with most of the money spent or committed, perhaps that is all it now needs.

ARMS CONTROL

British governments have always been positive with regard to arms control, and in the past justified nuclear status in part because of the presumed consequential influence on negotiations. It is also difficult for Britain to separate itself from the United States: it shares American missiles and facilities. Though this now means less than before, U.K. forces are still assigned to NATO and—as far as I am aware—targeted with U.S. forces at Omaha.

Nonetheless, Britain has never shown much interest in participating in strategic arms talks. Before 1989, this was explained as follows:

> The US and the Soviet Union between them have about 95 percent of the world's nuclear weapons. The clear priority is to get these huge stockpiles reduced. Even when the UK's nuclear deterrent is modernised with Trident, it will remain less than 3% of the Russians' nuclear potential—at the minimum level for effective deterrence. But the British government has never said "never" to including UK nuclear weapons in the negotiations. If Soviet and American strategic arsenals

are very substantially reduced, and if no new significant changes have occurred in Soviet defences against them, we will be ready to consider how the UK can best contribute to arms control talks in that new situation.[34]

Now that substantial reductions in numbers are scheduled for the rest of this century, the government has been forced to be somewhat more candid in its admission that in practice it has little room for maneuver. It must also reinforce its arms control credentials by drawing attention to initiatives outside the strategic arms area, such as chemical weapons and arms transfers.[35] Credit is also claimed for the cuts in substrategic forces, although here the benefit is described in terms of the objective of confidence building rather than "stability" or "balance":

> All these measures to reduce nuclear force levels not only have obvious attraction for tax-payers and for finance ministers: they also reduce, as a matter of simple mathematics, the risk of an error or an accident; and they contribute to the building of greater confidence, facilitating the development of co-operative relations.[36]

If it is accepted that the Trident force—at least its number of submarines—will be at its effective minimum,[37] then there is scant hope for a formal UK role in future strategic arms talks. Britain could not reduce its four SSBNs to two to match a 50 percent superpower cut because that would mean long periods when no boat was on station (because of the pattern of patrol times and the long refits). Four SSBNs really constitute a minimum deterrent, although with the longer periods between long refits with Trident, three boats might just be feasible. The ambiguity in warhead numbers means that its relative contribution to the world's total stockpile—when Trident is in service—is probably calculated at an exaggerated level. In practice Britain lacks a flexible negotiating position:

> We have always made it clear that the United Kingdom would deploy only the minimum deterrent required for our security needs. These are not determined by the scale of the offensive capabilities of the superpowers. We did not seek to match them in the large build-up in their strategic forces in the 1970s and 1980s, and the reductions they have now agreed on—though very welcome in themselves—are not a determinant in sizing our own deterrent.[38]

The government does not expect this to be a problem because it does not expect further U.S.-Russian agreements following the most recent Bush-

Yeltsin accord. It has, however, continued to use the criteria set down in the past to argue that even if there were opportunities for the U.K. to join formal negotiations the time would not yet be ripe.

> The superpowers have now charted a course which, if all goes well, will lead after another seven to eleven years to substantially smaller strategic stockpiles, reflecting a much improved strategic environment. We very much hope that this improvement will continue; but the course of international events cannot be predicted with certainty. At the same time there is increasing interest in the improvement of ballistic missile defences, and their deployment on a limited basis.[39]

The second condition emphasizes Britain's stake in the persistence of the ABM Treaty. Britain has made little secret of its suspicions of the Bush-Yeltsin agreement to cooperate on strategic defenses, though the informed view is that little is likely to come of it. The agreement to accept possible changes in the ABM Treaty in return for access to U.S. defensive technology represented a major shift in Moscow's declaratory policy, though one that was not surprising given the Russian vulnerability to third-country missile forces.

Even a limited GPALS system—a system capable of dealing with 200 incoming warheads has been mentioned—might be assumed to pose some problems to Britain and France with their limited arsenals. These will be more apparent than real as their arsenals will be able to saturate any Russian GPALS. However, Britain does not see why the Americans should be prepared to make its offensive task vis-à-vis Moscow any harder when the future political philosophy of the resident government cannot be assumed to be friendly. Nor is it sympathetic to the philosophy of attempting to engineer a universal shift to the strategic defense. The British view remains that, for European states, GPALS is extremely expensive, especially in the current harsh financial climate, and of doubtful effectiveness. It would prefer to continue to rely on threats to deter third countries with nuclear weapons. In his recent speech, all Malcolm Rifkind would allow is a possible value in defending against risk of chemical or biological attack when nuclear use could not be justified. It would be easier to deploy troops overseas if they were protected than if they appeared vulnerable. However, the basic view of GPALS was contained in the latest in a series of statements from British governments that have been issued ever since SDI was first launched in 1983. The program is damned with faint praise, and any evidence of administration halfheartedness is highlighted:

> The United States Administration has made very clear that it will not take any action which might prejudice the credibility of the European nuclear deterrents, and is proceeding on a sensible step-by-step basis.[40]

Britain has always been more sympathetic to proposals for confidence-building measures that do not impinge directly on force structure. Thus London has its own "hot-line" with Moscow, and there has been considerable sympathy for the American effort to add to the locks and safety catches safeguarding nuclear arsenals by strengthening command-and-control procedures, the end of quick-reaction alerts, dismantling of warheads, and the separation of nuclear weapons from general purpose forces. Measures have been taken to encourage the nuclear successor states to act responsibly by putting their weapons into Russian territory and under Russian control and promising to abide by the strictures of the NPT Treaty (achieved by offering a say in the ratification of START—which is more than the British ever got). Potentially footloose and fancy-free, nuclear scientists have been persuaded that they could be gainfully employed on projects other than a Libyan or Iranian bomb.[41]

General nonproliferation moves have also been fully supported by Britain. It has no distinctive line on this; it is anxious to see the NPT fully backed in 1995 and to see a strengthened IAEA safeguards regime. There is only one area where there is a direct tension—other than the fundamental issue of principle—between this policy and the desire to protect a national nuclear force, and that is the question of a test ban. In principle it has always supported a comprehensive ban. In practice Aldermaston has always been opposed and the Ministry of Defence has been lukewarm for the past decade.

Many years have now passed since a test ban would have been able to stop weapons development in its tracks, although it could still cause problems for would-be proliferators. The importance of a ban would be in providing yet another sign that one stage of the nuclear age is now over. The inability of the nuclear powers to agree to a test ban has been a standard complaint from countries objecting to pressure to submit to the demands of the nuclear Nonproliferation Treaty. It has now become extremely difficult to make a credible case for testing to develop new weapons. Warhead design has become, to say the least, a "mature" technology. In the United States there are very few new warhead projects under way. It is hard to see testing becoming a significant limitation on the or British nuclear arsenals for the foreseeable future. (Britain, lacking its own facility, conducts its tests at the Nevada site). The recent moratorium on U.S. nuclear testing is intended (at least by Congress) to lead to a complete ban by 1996. Britain would be allowed one test per year up to 1996,[42] which is probably just enough to complete the testing for the WE-177 replacement. It would not allow future proof testing, but Britain has never conducted such a test up to now.[43]

CONCLUSION

The British government does not see its nuclear arsenal as being of great relevance to strategic arms control, even assuming that strategic arms control itself has a future. It has moved unilaterally to remove the bulk of its substrategic arsenal, and even what is left of this is unlikely to be modernized significantly in the near future. The argument that if Britain believes that it should be allowed to maintain a nuclear arsenal, why not other countries? will tend to get the riposte that other nuclear arsenals might be tolerable if they were in the hands of mature democracies of honorable intent and if they were kept as no more than insurance policies. The problem with nuclear proliferation, according to this view, is not the spread of the technology *per se* but the purposes for which it is acquired and the unsettled strategic environments of the proliferators.

For Britain, nuclear weapons remain little more than a hedge against an uncertain future. The inclination is to keep them well clear of any conflicts in which Britain is likely to be involved in which the future of Western Europe is not directly at stake. Within Europe, the possibility of a revival of a Russian nuclear threat can be acknowledged even though it remains difficult to describe the circumstances that might bring it about. With a substantial premium having already been paid on this particular insurance policy, it is unlikely to be casually abandoned. With future premiums now put at a minimum level, arms control offers no prospect of reduced costs. As there is no reason to believe that the British nuclear arsenal looms large in the calculations of others, it is unclear what benefits could be expected from putting it on the negotiating table presuming that an appropriate table could be found. For three decades Britain has kept its national nuclear force apart from arms control. There is no reason to expect this policy to change now.

NOTES

1. *Independent,* June 23, 1989. President François Mitterrand of France observed in 1987 that Britain had "90-100 [strategic] weapons." cited in Richard Fieldhouse, Robert Norris, and William Arkin, "Nuclear Weapons Developments and

Unilateral Reductions Initiatives," in Stockholm International Peace Research Institute, *SIPRI Yearbook 1992: World Armaments and Disarmament* (London: Oxford University Press, 1992), p. 80.

2. Secretary of State for Defence, Statement on the Defence Estimates 1983, Vol. 1, Command 8951-1 (London: HMSO, 1983), p. 7.

3. HC 36 of 1980-81, p. 107.

4. The nature of the Chevaline concept is to simultaneously rain a series of warheads and decoys over the target so as to swamp the target area. Its effect does not come from the contents of a single missile but from the combined contents of a number of missiles—probably the complement of one SSBN. It is now difficult to disentangle the system to take on a number of targets at once.

5. Secretary of State for Defence, Statement on the Defence Estimates 1993, Vol. 1, Command 1981-1 (London: HMSO, July 1992), p. 22.

6. *Substrategic* is the preferred British nomenclature to the alternatives—prestrategic or nonstrategic.

7. Secretary of State for Defence, Statement on the Defence Estimates 1990, Vol. 1, Command 1022-1 (London: HMSO, 1990), paragraph 201.

8. *Defence Estimates 1992*, p. 28.

9. Lance has a range of 130 kilometers, and an accuracy of 0.4 to 0.45 kilometers, with a yield ranging from 1 to 100 kilotons.

10. The M-110 launched a shell of 2 kilotons to a distance of 14 kilometers with an accuracy from 0.04 to 0.17 kilometers depending on the range. The M-109 had a comparable accuracy and a slightly longer range with a yield of 2 kilotons.

11. *Financial Times,* July 25, 1987. Official Record, July 23, 1987, column 390.

12. *Independent,* June 23, 1989.

13. The weapon was developed in the early 1960s. The first WE-177s were delivered to the RAF in 1966-67. Thereafter more than 180 were produced up to 1982, of which 20-30 were "C" variants. Production continued at Aldermaston and Burghfield until 1978, when manufacturing lines began to produce warheads for Chevaline. The line was interrupted earlier for Polaris production. *Independent,* May 16, 1988; June 23, 1989.

14. *SIPRI Yearbook 1992*, pp. 79-80.

15. Shaun Gregory, *The Command and Control of British Nuclear Weapons* (University of Bradford School of Peace Studies, Peace Research Report Number 13, December 1986).

16. Duncan Campbell, "Too Few Bombs to Go Round," *New Statesman* 29, November 1985.

17. *SIPRI Yearbook 1992*, p. 80; The International Institute for Strategic Studies, *The Military Balance: 1992-93* (London: Brassey's for the IISS, 1992), p. 232.

18. *Independent,* May 16, 1988.

19. For text see *Arms Control Today* (October 1991), pp. 3-5.

20. *Independent,* June 23, 1992.

21. The RAF will continue to make a major contribution to substrategic forces in support of NATO and to provide a national substrategic capability. It is currently studying possible replacements for the WE-177 free-fall bomb, which will approach the end of its service life around the turn of this century. *Defence Estimates 1992,* p. 22.

22. The old rationale is discussed in Lawrence Freedman, *Britain and Nuclear Weapons* (London: Macmillan, 1980).

23. Thus Secretary of State for Defence Malcolm Rifkind interprets the "reduced reliance" on nuclear weapons in NATO's strategic concept as meaning that one can get away with "very significantly lower levels of forces." Secretary of State for Defence, Retired Honorable Malcolm Rifkind (Intervention in Paris Symposium, [September 30, 1992], p. 6). Interpretations of the meaning of "reduced reliance" vary. In December 1990 the Nuclear Planning Group clearly saw reduced reliance as influencing both "Alliance nuclear force levels and structures." It stressed the promise of "further dramatic reductions in the number of NATO's nuclear weapons retained in Europe," but also that the remaining nuclear forces, for which we seek the lowest and most stable level commensurate with our security requirements, must be sufficiently flexible, effective, survivable, and broadly based if they are to make a credible contribution to NATO's overall strategy for the prevention of war. Britain will develop its future nuclear posture in conjunction with the new strategic concept reflecting the principles and new directions for nuclear forces set out in the London Declaration. Nuclear Planning Group, Final Communiqué (December 7, 1990), paragraph 14.

24. Rifkind speech, p. 17.

25. Secretary of State for Defence, Statement on the Defence Estimate 1987, Vol. 1 (London: EMSO, 1987).

26. Rifkind speech, pp. 18, 20-21.

27. *Independent,* October 2, 1992. President Mitterrand raised the possibility of a European nuclear force in January, although then the idea was linked more to hopes for a common European defense entity.

28. *Defence Estimates 1992,* p. 9.

29. Rifkind speech, p. 14.

30. For example, the Rifkind speech:"The thought of what might have happened had Saddam Hussein been able to build a nuclear weapon before the invasion of Kuwait is a sobering one indeed."

31. In 1978, the head of the U.K. delegation to the UN Special Session on Disarmament made the following statement:

    I accordingly give the following assurances on behalf of my government to nonnuclear weapon states which are parties to the Nonproliferation

Treaty or other internationally binding commitments not to manufacture or acquire nuclear explosive devices: Britain undertakes not to use nuclear weapons against such states except in the case of an attack on the United Kingdom, its dependent territories, its armed forces, or its allies by such a state in association or in alliance with a nuclear weapons state.

Annex Q, The United Nations Special Session on Disarmament, Command 7267 (London: HMSO, 1978).

32. Rifkind speech, pp. 10-12.

33. Ibid., p. 5.

34. Questions on Arms Control, Foreign and Commonwealth Office and Ministry of Defence, February 1988. Cited in John Poole, ed., *Independence and Interdependence: A Reader on British Nuclear Weapons Policy* (London: Brassey's, 1990), p. 261.

35. See statement by Prime Minister John Major after Bush proposals of September 1991, *Guardian,* September 28, 1991.

36. Rifkind speech, p. 7.

37. For a discussion of this issue see the colloquy involving Rear Admiral Ian Pirnie in House of Commons Defence Committee, Fifth Report of session 1991-92. The Progress of the Trident Programme, HC-337 March 1992, Minutes of Evidence, pp. 4-7.

38. *Defence Estimates 1992,* p. 22.

39. Ibid.

40. Rifkind speech, p. 13.

41. Britain sent to Russia 250 special containers and 20 vehicles for the safe transport of nuclear warheads, and offered consultancy assistance in various fields, including nuclear accident response techniques, conversion of fissile material for civil use, environmental restoration, and the implementation of IAEA safeguards.

42. The nuclear testing moratorium was adopted against President Bush's objections as part of the FY1993 Energy and Water Appropriations Bill, a measure otherwise eagerly sought by the president. It provides for a moratorium on testing until July 1993. Testing can thereafter only start again under strict conditions, including a plan for a comprehensive test ban and then there can be no more than five tests a year or 15 over four years. According to one clause:

> The President may authorize the United Kingdom to conduct in the United States within a period covered by an annual report one test of a weapon if the President determines that it is in the national interests of the United States to do so. Such a test shall be considered as one of the maximum number of tests that the United States is permitted to conduct under that period. . . .

Congressional Record, September 18 1992, p. S13949.

43. The British Embassy had lobbied against this proposal and restated when it was adopted that "We oppose a moratorium because we still need to carry our minimum test program for reasons of safety, reliability and effectiveness." *Times,* September 26, 1992. The Ministry of Defence's response to the prospect of a complete ban by 1996 was that it would "use the intervening time to ensure our deterrent is on good order for the 21st century," *Independent,* October 3, 1992. The *Defence Estimates 1992* observed that Britain's underground nuclear test program had been very much smaller than those of other nuclear powers, "with a strictly limited number of tests to enhance safety and to establish the effectiveness of new generations of weapons." There have been only 21 tests since 1963. "We shall continue to conduct only the minimum number of tests necessary and to recognise a comprehensive ban on nuclear tests as a long-term goal," p. 22.

9

French Nuclear Policy: Adapting the Gaullist Legacy to the Post-Cold War World

Edward A. Kolodziej

The Gaullist nuclear legacy has undergone repeated change since the creation of the *force de frappe* in the 1960s.[1] The early emphasis in French doctrine on the strict limitation of the French deterrent to the defense of the Hexagon gradually shifted to a stress on the contribution of French nuclear forces to European deterrence, a position officially recognized by NATO at Ottawa in 1974 and reaffirmed thereafter.[2] The role of French conventional forces, while committed in French doctrinal thinking to testing enemy intentions before nuclear weapons were unleashed, was progressively enlarged in the 1970s to permit their engagement in a forward battle with allied conventional forces. In the 1980s the Socialist government of President François Mitterrand created a Rapid Action Force (FAR) to facilitate timely French cooperation with allied forces, principally those of Germany, in meeting a possible aggression from the East. Prestrategic nuclear forces were then quietly downplayed in deference to German concerns about their possible use against targets in Germany.

The policy of the empty chair in arms control and disarmament negotiations pursued by President Charles de Gaulle gradually eroded. In a major address to the United Nations in 1978, President Valéry Giscard d'Estaing announced France's return to the international arms control and disarmament bargaining tables. Under President Mitterrand, France played a leading role in negotiations under the aegis of the Conference on Security and Cooperation in Europe (CSCE) that resulted in a major reduction of NATO and Warsaw Pact conventional forces. Although French forces had been withdrawn from NATO's multilateral command, Paris was still among the most vocal in urging its European allies, notably Germany, to accept U.S. Pershing II and cruise missiles. Paris and Washington were agreed that NATO long-range theater missiles were needed to counter the Soviet Union's attempt to split the alliance and to restore the nuclear balance in Europe that was perceived to be have been upset by Moscow's deployment of SS-20 missiles.

No less remarkable was the adaptability of the French security community and successive governments to these revisions of Gaullist orthodoxy.[3] In contrast to the public turmoil surrounding nuclear modernization in the United States and the United Kingdom,[4] the French domestic consensus, from Right to Left, remained essentially intact despite major changes in French doctrine, operational strategy, and nuclear diplomacy since de Gaulle's resignation in 1969. The domestic consensus was consolidated and deepened in the late 1970s, culminating in 1981 when the Socialist party, previously opposed to a French nuclear force, embraced the Gaullist legacy.[5]

The consensus has since survived sporadic eruptions of partisan controversy over doctrine, force levels and weapon system acquisition priorities, and spending levels. It persisted through an awkward period of cohabitation in 1986-88 during which the presidency and the National Assembly were split between the Left and the Right.[6] President Mitterrand successfully deflected efforts by the Gaullist prime minister Jacques Chirac to intrude on his constitutional power over defense and nuclear affairs, the so-called *domaine réservé* of the French president.[7] Periodic reports of the imminent dissolution of the French nuclear compact have until now proved premature.[8]

Assaulted today from within and without, the French consensus on nuclear policy is again under stress. A *Le Monde* editorial dismissed the assertions of former Defense Minister Pierre Joxe and Prime Minister Pierre Bérégovoy that the nuclear deterrence was the "keystone" of France's defense policy. "Why pretend to respect a Gaullist heritage which while popular is nevertheless obsolete?"[9] Critics of President Mitterrand's decision to suspend nuclear testing in April 1992 accused him of violating the national consensus on nuclear policy. "By acting that way [unilaterally without broad consultation]," argued Pierre Lellouche, "the socialist government has just dealt a blow to France's security and solidarity with its allies, and perhaps a fatal blow as well to the famous French consensus on defense."[10]

The prospects of continued national consensus on nuclear deterrence and, more broadly, on a full range of security issues facing France have never been more problematic since de Gaulle's departure from office, although, as suggested below, cohabitation has not undermined a united front on nuclear policy, particularly with respect to a nuclear test ban treaty and the French moratorium on nuclear testing. Nuclear weapons are losing the battle of the budget. While public opinion polls taken in the early 1990s continued to indicate public support for nuclear weapons and a strategy of nuclear deterrence, less than half also doubted that the defense of France rested primarily on nuclear weapons.[11] Spending for nuclear systems in 1993 is almost 12 percent below 1992; cuts for nuclear testing and for the French Atomic Energy Commission are even greater, falling 16.3 and 13.4 percent, respectively, in the same period.[12] Strategic nuclear forces are being reduced, short-range systems dismantled or mothballed, and the national commitment to a triad of ground-, air-, and sea-launched systems, mainstays of the Gaullist legacy, was also questioned aloud at the highest levels of the former Socialist government.[13] The right-of-center regime of Edouard Baladur, elected to office in the early spring of 1993, will be hard-pressed to find the funds or marshall the will needed to retain a viable triad.

In the post-cold war environment, hard choices must be made between nuclear and conventional forces and their modernization. France's participation in Desert Storm revealed serious weaknesses in military preparedness. French planners now seek to develop France's space intelligence systems as a force multiplier and crisis management tool, and to increase its capability to project forces abroad even as they are being reduced in size as well as in the quantity and quality of the weapon systems at their disposal.

The geopolitical and doctrinal rationale for these forces is also undergoing serious rethinking, not only behind the scenes within official decision-making channels but also in policy journals,[14] in high-level public seminars sponsored by the prime minister or the Ministry of Defense,[15] and in the pronouncements of governmental officials.[16] Whereas the British reexamination of nuclear policy has assumed a cautious tone and low public profile,[17] French officials have stirred public debate about the need to change strategic thinking, military planning, weapons acquisition, and the modalities of multilateral cooperation. Witness President Mitterrand's violation of a Gaullist taboo by declaring that a European nuclear deterrent in which France would participate would be an essential condition for European unity.[18] The focus on Europe is also accompanied by expressions of greater flexibility on the delicate issue of French military cooperation with its allies within the Atlantic Alliance, the Western European Union, the United Nations, or, bilaterally, with Germany and the United Kingdom.[19] These possibilities were realized in France's participation in Desert Storm, where French forces were essentially placed under U.S. command, and in multilateral operations associated with distributing humanitarian aid in Somalia.

In sum, nuclear weapons are losing their centrality in French strategic thinking, military doctrine, and operational strategy.[20] For the first time since the creation of the *force de dissuasion,* France has nuclear weapons searching for a role. This is not to say, however, that nuclear weapons will be unilaterally abandoned any time soon, nor that France will be keen on negotiating them away. Despite cutbacks, the modernization of French nuclear forces is proceeding. Nuclear capabilities, approximate in size to those of the British, will remain a key feature of French military planning for some time to come. Jealous regard for national control of nuclear weapons will not, moreover, hinder—nor necessarily preclude—France's multilateral cooperation with its Western allies. The East European states and the Russian Federation offer little attraction as alliance partners either to counter the economic and political weight of Germany or the military power of the United States. That traditional alliance option, operative for France since the rise of German power in the late nineteenth century, is simply not viable in the post-cold war era. The East European states and the Russian Federation are weak reeds to lean upon.

Nor can much help be found for French interests by relying on developing states, an expectation of the early Gaullist Republic that has little currency today in political circles.[21] The developing world, particularly the Mediterranean basin, is more of a threat to French security interests than an asset in bargaining among the developed states. Less than a decade ago, France was Iraq's largest Western arms supplier and a bridge to nontraditional Arab states. Whatever privileged political access France might have enjoyed to the Middle East has been appreciably narrowed as a consequence of the cold war's end. The United States is presently the ascendant extra-regional power in the region. Neither France nor Europe's collective weight currently count for much.

French weakness does not imply easy compliance with Washington's wishes. The running battle between Paris and Washington over the formation of rapid-action forces under NATO or WEU aegis is illustrative. While such contretemps are scarcely new between the two capitals, it would also be misleading to exaggerate them. They are part of the political and psychological cost of doing business with the French elite, whatever government is in power. Some proportion is gained if current frictions are viewed against the backdrop of Franco-American relations throughout this century. Since World War II, commencing with the frictions between General de Gaulle and President Franklin D. Roosevelt, perceived French status, prestige, and leverage in bargaining with the United States have been viewed by successive

French leaders, most pointedly President de Gaulle, as a function of resisting U.S. power. On the other hand, France insists that is a staunch ally where the national interests of the two countries coincide. On such critical matters as the Cuban missile and Berlin crises, or the Warsaw Pact invasion of Czechoslovakia in 1968, the two states have stood solidly together. Thus, whether under the Free French or the Fourth and Fifth Republics, France has consistently pursued a double game of "get away closer":[22] that is, to ally with the United States against a common rival while resisting the hegemonic proclivities, real or imagined, of the dominant ally.

The why and how of changes in French nuclear thinking and strategic policies may become clearer if the principal external and internal factors prompting and constraining French responses are first outlined. These pressures continue to challenge strict adherence to the Gaullist legacy. They prompt French leaders to search for ways to transform the consensus on nuclear weapons and doctrine and, more generally, on long-term French security and defense policy in order, paradoxically, to save it. These forces define the context within which French decisions about nuclear weapons, roles and missions, and doctrine must be made. It is only within this framework that the changes now under way in French nuclear policy can be fully understood.

FRENCH NUCLEAR POLICY AND POLICYMAKING: EXTERNAL AND INTERNAL DIMENSIONS

The end of the East-West confrontation in Europe has fundamentally altered the assumptions on which French nuclear policy has rested for a generation. First, the cold war has nullified the Gaullist rationale for nuclear weapons: to deter a Soviet attack and to ensure France's place at the top table in defining Europe's security and Germany's future. The collapse of the Soviet Union and its East European empire and the withdrawal of Russian troops have significantly reduced the threat of a general war in Europe. All but eliminated, too, is the possibility of an attack against French territory emanating from the former members of the Warsaw Pact. Removed, thus, has been the principal justification for the *force de dissuasion* as it was originally conceived in the 1960s. A more diffuse and fuzzy set of threats, more socioeconomic and political than military, have replaced a once clear and present Soviet threat. Appeals to nuclear weapons and deterrence do not readily regulate nor resolve these new threats. Residual concerns persist about proliferation and about the enormous size of the nuclear arsenals still at the disposal of the republics of the former Soviet Union, particularly the Russian Federation, Ukraine, Belarus, and Kazakhstan. These worries have not been sufficient, however, to resist reductions in French nuclear capabilities and operational readiness as France adjusts its military and budgetary priorities to the post-cold war world.

The second and more pressing challenge is German unification and its implications for long-term French foreign and security interests.[23] Despite setbacks in domestic support for the Maastricht Treaty and popular disappointment with European Community trade concessions to the United States at the expense of French farmers, the consensus among most, but by no means all, French elites centers at present on binding Germany to French security interests through political union within the European Community.[24] The initial aim is advancing monetary union and a common European currency. The longer-term objective is still the development of a common foreign and defense policy. Maastricht is dedicated to both goals. Nuclear weapons are not immediately relevant to these concerns, and where they arise as issues, they currently serve more to divide than unite. For significant segments of the ruling French elite, nuclear weapons underscore France's special international status and the singularity of its strategic policy, French appeals for the development of a European nuclear deterrent notwithstanding.

Third, the French also appear convinced, partly as a consequence of their own repeated denigration of the American commitment to European security, that U.S. forces will continue to be sharply cut in Europe and, quite conceivably, withdrawn entirely. Such a possibility would seriously weaken France's adaptation to a new strategic environment in Europe and in the developing world. It would force France to rely increasingly on its own resources and diplomatic wits in solving its security problems. But preserving a U.S. presence to widen its options and expand its base of support exacts a high price. The cost is likely to be in the form of greater French willingness to cooperate with Washington on a wide range of issues by no means restricted to Europe. The price may be too high for a domestic consensus already under strain on other grounds from social policy to agricultural subsidies. Cooperation with Washington is also likely to mean reduced national strategic autonomy and freedom of maneuver, central tenets of the Gaullist legacy and key principles on which the domestic security consensus rests.

Fourth, the Gulf War and the collapse of the moderating influence of the superpowers on regional rivalries expose France to security threats arising from the Mediterranean basin; these then extend eastward to the Persian Gulf and then southward to Francophone Africa.[25] The Iraqi aggression revealed France's impotence in meeting such crises on its own, even if it had a will to do so. Trained, well-equipped forces-in-being, ready for prompt deployment to troubled areas, still count. Except for small police actions, France alone cannot cope with conflicts in the developing world that affect its security and foreign policy interests or that bear on its commitments to other states, especially those in Francophone Africa. In meeting the Libyan threat to its interests in Chad, for example, it was heavily dependent on U.S. logistical assistance. And in those instances where France has intervened, it has been ill prepared to play a role equal to its resources or ambition. In Desert Storm, Great Britain, with fewer men under arms, was able to field a larger, better-equipped, and more battle-ready force in less time than France.

Nuclear weapons, moreover, provide little or no leverage in coping with these southern-tier security problems. Nor are they useful in preventing potential adversaries from acquiring nuclear weapons or other weapons of mass destruction and long-range delivery systems. Again, concerted efforts with allies are advised for such contingencies, yet acting on these promptings is not easily reconciled with Gaullist strictures requiring political autonomy and freedom of maneuver.

These international constraints on French strategic policy are further reinforced by domestic limits confronting French planners and leaders. First, the end of the cold war and the diminished threat of war in Europe reinforces pressures for greater welfare expenditures and further cuts in the defense budgets. The French, no less than their allies, are searching to exploit an elusive peace dividend. Since the May riots of 1968, the French government has been sensitive to demands for greater welfare over defense spending. An informal cap of 4 percent of GNP was initially placed on defense spending.[26] The trend line continued downward. Since 1983, French defense spending has declined as a percentage of GNP each year, reaching a low of 3.36 percent in 1992.[27] There is no reason to believe that this downward slide will be arrested. The reported objective of the newly enacted law program voted in 1992 is 3 percent by 1997.[28] The 1993 defense budget, set at 3.15 percent of GNP, continues the downward descent toward this floor.[29]

These budgetary constraints are reinforced by still other limits on French military preparedness and modernization. Weak economic growth, slower than most of its partners in the Organization for Economic Cooperation and Development (OECD), bode ill for increasing military spending as a function of economic expansion. Over the past five years, French economic growth has been less than 3 percent annually, lower than the United States or even much maligned Great Britain.[30] Meanwhile, the costs of research and development and arms acquisition programs increased faster than the rate of economic growth or inflation. The defense budget is also saddled with high-cost weapons, designed more for the cold war in Europe than for speedy and timely force projections to the developing world. These include the heavy Leclerc tank (1.7 million francs for an AMX-30 tank versus 25 to 30 million francs for Leclerc), the Rafale fighter (342 million francs for the Mirage 2000 versus 460 million francs for the Rafale), and the aircraft carrier *Charles de Gaulle* estimated at 15.6 billion francs.[31] Recently announced changes in French acquisition priorities, favoring surveillance satellites and conventional force projection programs, exacerbate the hard choices that have to be made among competing needs.[32] A decrease in spending for nuclear systems provide some funds for reallocation, but not nearly enough to match French needs and ambitions.[33] Quoting Admiral Jacques Lanxade, French chief of staff, *Armées d'Aujourd'hui* observes: "It is clear that the realization of major armament programs, quite like the resolution of major crises, will not long be within the means of a single European nation. . . . [One can envision] a multilateral division of tasks . . . and a high level of interoperability as much at the level of command, through the utilization of common procedures, as of matériel and support."[34] This candid appraisal of the military strategic choices facing France suggests that the aim, if not the pretense, of an independent national security policy is rapidly losing rhetorical and political force in French planning circles.

Yet the slim French vote in favor of the Maastricht Treaty (51 to 49 percent) and differences over economic policy between France and its European Community partners reveal that popular and political party support for multilateralism is not available on demand. Parliamentary elections in 1993, which discredited Socialist rule, will very likely usher in another period of cohabitation that may be more contentious, principally over domestic economic and social policy, than the first. The dilemma confronting French leaders and military planners is that French defense policy is being renationalized from the bottom up at the very time that French taxpayers are reluctant either to support higher defense spending or to tolerate greater cooperation than currently exists with France's allies to address the country's security needs. Domestic support for multilateralism appears to be declining just as the need for it mounts.[35]

How these internal and external constraints are shaping French defense policy and nuclear thinking and capabilities may become clearer if several key questions are addressed. First, how and why are French nuclear capabilities changing in the near and long term? Second, what are the geopolitical and military doctrinal rationales for these forces and in what ways are they changing and why? Third, in what ways and in what multilateral or bilateral settings is French cooperation likely to be exercised? Fourth, what are current and emerging French regional and global arms control and disarmament policies and the aims and bargaining strategies driving them? Finally, and against the background of responses to these questions, where is French nuclear and strategic policy heading and what can France's allies, and especially the United States, do to encourage French cooperation in meeting the needs of European and international security?

QUESTIONS SEARCHING FOR AN ANSWER TO FRENCH NUCLEAR AND STRATEGIC POLICY

Current and Future Military Capabilities

French strategic forces presently consist of a triad of 18 Mirage IVP bimotor aircraft, 18 IRBMs, and 5 nuclear submarines, each armed with 16 MIRVed missiles.[36] The Mirage IVP, with a range of 1,500 kilometers, is armed with a 300-kiloton TN 80 nuclear warhead capable of being launched 100 to 300 kilometers, depending on the angle of flight, by a medium-range air-to-ground missile (ASMP).[37] The Mirage force, which has been upgraded with new radar and electronic equipment, is scheduled to be in service through the rest of the 1990s. Air-delivered nuclear weapons will then be the responsibility of 45 Mirage 2000N (air force), grouped into three squadrons, and 20 Super-Etendard aircraft (navy), capable of being launched from a French aircraft carrier. The Mirage 2000N has a range of 1,570 kilometers and carries a nuclear charge similar to the Mirage IVP; the Super Etendard is similarly configured but its range is restricted to 650 kilometers.[38] Initially, 50 to 55 Super Etendard aircraft were scheduled to be equipped with ASMPs, but budgetary constraints limited the reconversion to 20. In a parallel budgetary cut, an air force plan for 75 Mirage 2000 in its prestrategic fleet was reduced to 45. The Mirage 2000N will be supplemented by the Mirage 2000D, of which 90 may eventually be procured. All these nuclear carriers are dual capable, delivering both nuclear and conventional weapons. As of September 1, 1991, AN-52 15-kiloton gravity bombs, which had been carried by Jaguar, Mirage IIIE, and Super-Etendard aircraft, were withdrawn from service.[39] Supplementing these capabilities are 18 S3D IRBMs based in hardened silos on the Plateau d'Albion in southeastern France. They are armed with one-megaton TN-61 warheads with a range of 3,000 kilometers.

France's submarine-launched ballistic missiles remain the backbone of the *force de dissuasion*. France currently has five nuclear submarines

(SSBNs) in operation. A sixth submarine, *Le Redoutable,* which was commissioned in the 1970s, was withdrawn from service after 58 patrols.[40] Four of the remaining five SSBNs have been retrofitted with M-4B missiles with a range of 6,000 kilometers. These are MIRVed with six 150-kiloton TN-71 warheads. The fifth SSBM, *Le Foudroyant,* was expected to be refitted in 1993. As late as June 1992, three SSBNs were reportedly on patrol at all times, thanks to the practice of dual crews for each SSBN and tightly scheduled refits while in port.[41] Since then, only two submarines were scheduled to be on patrol part of the time, and alert levels were also lowered for aircraft armed with ASMPs.[42]

Important changes have been announced in the implementation of the 1992-94 law program defining France's arms acquisitions through the end of the decade.[43] A planned force of six SSBNs has been cut to four. The first of a new Triomphant-class SSBN is scheduled for entry into service in 1995, followed by three others at 36-month intervals. These SSBNs will be armed initially with M45 MIRVed missiles, each with 6 warheads equal to the destructive force of the M-4B. In 2005 these SSBNs are to be retrofitted with M5 missiles, which will be able to carry up to 12 warheads. Once these modernization plans are implemented, France is likely to maintain no more than two SSBNs on patrol under normal conditions. It is also not likely that all four will be armed. Instead of a full complement of 384 warheads (4 submarines times 64 missiles times 6 warheads), at most three full SSBNs will be armed at any one time. That would place France's strategic arsenal at around 288 warheads, very likely below the more powerful British Trident force.[44] Under current planning, the M5 missile will also serve as the basis for retrofitting the ground-launched IRBMs, whose S3D missiles are scheduled to be dismantled between 2003 and 2005.[45] Plans to fit these silos with a ground version of the S45 were dropped in 1991. The M-5 poses an arms control issue. Since it can carry up to 12 warheads, it might place France at serous odds with other nuclear powers. As François Heisbourg suggests, such a force would be "well beyond the proclaimed threshold of sufficiency of [France's] nuclear doctrine."[46]

The Rafale in its air force and navy versions will assume a nuclear role and eventually replace the Mirage 2000N, but not until the end of the 1990s. Work will continue on developing a long-range air-to-ground missile, perhaps in cooperation with the United Kingdom, which has a similar requirement for its aircraft-delivered nuclear weapons. Given budgetary restrictions, it is not at all clear whether these nuclear modernization programs can be achieved on time. The Rafale is already at least a year behind schedule. The M5 has yet to be developed; and uncertainty surrounds its future. It may well be eliminated or its development stretched out. The ground version may also prove redundant. If the United States and the former Soviet republics succeed in dramatically cutting their nuclear stocks, it might be used as a bargaining chip by France, which would drop the system as a contribution to a new nuclear regime for Europe based on sharply reduced arsenals. In any event, France would still appear to have ample long-range nuclear striking power in the form of air- and sea-launched missiles as well as prestrategic forces with air-launched capabilities to support its nuclear deterrent requirements in and out of Europe. The vulnerability of France's IRBMs, recognized even by the French as more a target than a deterrent, argues against their modernization since the cost will be high and the gain in deterrent capacity arguable.

The most dramatic change in French nuclear planning concerns the cancellation of the Hades prestrategic ground-to-ground missile program and the demobilization of all Pluton regiments. Between 1974 and 1977, France organized five regiments of nuclear artillery, each with six rechargeable launchers carried on an AMX-30 tank. Upwards of 70 missiles may have been developed for the Pluton system. They had a range of approximately 120 kilometers and a nuclear charge of between 15 to 25 kilotons.[47] The 30 Hades missiles, which have been produced with a range of 480 kilometers and armed with 80-kiloton warheads, will be placed in storage at a nuclear site at S.[48]

Priorities have shifted dramatically toward development of enhanced space capabilities. The principal reason for this change stems from the serious lack of real-time intelligence available to French policymakers and military commanders participating in the Desert Storm operation.[49] French decision-makers were almost totally dependent on U.S. intelligence sources during the early stages of the crisis and throughout the military phase and aftermath of hostilities. This dependency was perceived as severely restricting the political maneuverability of French officials while narrowing the choices available to them and military commanders. To remedy this deficiency, defense spending for military space programs rose from 3 billion francs in 1992 to 3.3 billion francs in 1993.[50]

Only France and Great Britain have autonomous military satellite systems. The French deployed its Syracuse I communications system in 1984 and followed with Syracuse II in 1991.[51] The Hélios observation satellite system, based on the commercial Spot system, is scheduled for launching in 1994 and will provide high-resolution pictures from outer space. Hélios II will provide infrared capabilities. These systems will be supplemented by the Osiris radar reconnaissance satellite and the Zénon electromagnetic signal detection satellite capable of the monitoring of foreign command centers and military installations.[52] In addition, French armed forces will acquire by 1997 enhanced electromagnetic intelligence (Sarigue) and field surveillance capabilities (Horizon).[53]

Many of these initiatives have been cast within a European framework. The Hélios intelligence satellite is partially funded by Italy and Spain (14.1 and 7 percent shares, respectively). A satellite data interpretation center at Torréjon, Spain, will train experts in satellite intelligence under WEU sponsorship. In November 1991 Britain and France proposed to study the development of a European military satellite network with Germany, Holland, Spain, and Italy.[54] If France wishes to decrease its reliance on U.S. satellite intelligence, it must in turn increase its dependence on its European allies, another dimension of its progressively enlarging multilateral security effort.

The Changing Geopolitical Rationale for Nuclear Forces

Paradoxically, the end of the cold war and the collapse of the Soviet Union have together changed nothing with respect to the French geopolitical rationale for nuclear weapons and fundamentally undermined much of the political and strategic justification for these forces. As for the sources of stability underlying the Gaullist legacy, French possession of nuclear weapons does not depend finally on the existence of a clear and present foreign threat. The acquisition of nuclear weapons was portrayed from the start of the Fifth Republic as endowing France with a unique international standing—*grandeur*—and as confirming its status as a victorious power in World War II, its privileged position as a permanent member of the UN Security Council, and its glorious history and accomplishments as a modern, scientific state.[55] These attributes legitimated its implicit special responsibility for assuming a leading role in reconstructing the postwar European security system and, specifically, in defining Germany's future. French nuclear doctrine was actually formulated *after* these weapons were in hand. The aims of national survival, political influence, and strategic autonomy, however much pursued by de Gaulle and his successors, are still quite distinct from the relentless and ceaseless search by successive French governments for special status, privilege, weight, and significance for France in the affairs of states. It is no accident that one of the keenest observers of French presidential behavior should have characterized the Fifth Republic as a "nuclear monarchy."[56] In the absence of complete and total nuclear disarmament, including reliable international verification re-gimes, it is not likely that France and its ruling elites will renounce nuclear weapons as long as other states possess them, most particularly the United States and the Russian Federation. The possibility of proliferation in the developing world will serve only to reinforce French resistance to unilateral nuclear disarmament initiatives.

On the other hand, the end of the cold war and the number and scope of the nuclear arms accords signed by Moscow and Washington will put France's geopolitical rationale for its nuclear weapons in a somewhat parlous state if they are ever implemented. That is a big "if." The presence of over 12,000 strategic offensive warheads among four republics of the former Soviet Union provides provisional justification for French possession and modernization of its forces.[57] The resistance of the four republics to meet their obligations under the START and NPT treaties, and the financial and technical problems associated with dismantling nuclear systems and safe-guarding fissionable materials, relax pressures on France to cut long-range systems sometime soon.[58] Even if the Russian Federation (acting for the CIS states) and the United States meet the ambitious goal set by Presidents George Bush and Boris Yeltsin in June 1992 to reduce their nations' arsenals to 3,000 to 3,500 strategic warheads by 2003, French leaders are not likely to be induced very easily into entering negotiations on arms reductions. France's comparable forces would still be less than 10 percent of those of the United States and the Russian Federation, a level that would appear in principle to be well within the arms control conditions defined by Paris as failing to meet the requirement for France's entry into nuclear arms control and disarmament talks.[59]

Nuclear weapons are also an insurance policy against an uncertain future and a change in the strategic environment that might be threatening to France. It is difficult, however, to specify the circumstances in which nuclear weapons might contribute to French security. There is of course the shadow cast by possible German acquisition of nuclear weapons. Such an eventual-ity, however remote, would upset the European balance and violate Germany's treaty obligations under the WEU and NPT treaties. The possi-bility of a nuclear Germany poses an obvious dilemma for France. It relies on German cooperation for its security while it implicitly depends on nuclear weapons to balance German political and economic power as well as con-ventional military capabilities and to contain the adverse repercussions of German acquisition of these weapons.

Currently, these concerns appear moot. There is no discernible movement within Germany to acquire nuclear weapons or to abandon its pro-European, pro-French policy. Neither the conservative Christian Democratic govern-ment nor a Social Democratic successor can be expected to revise that stance. Conversely, growing German national self-assertiveness, stimulated by the unification process, by widespread fear of political instability and civil war in the Balkans, Eastern Europe, and the CIS republics, as well as by the xenophobic backlash against immigrants in Germany, is a disquieting trend, but scarcely a reason for French rejection of close security cooperation with Bonn, precisely to contain the potentially damaging effects of these perturbations. Nuclear weapons have little or no relevance in addressing the socioeconomic and political factors contributing to this deep sense of psychological uncertainty and political unrest within Germany today.

The real and perceived diminishing relevance of nuclear weapons to France's post-cold war security problems is further underscored by the threats arising from the developing world, particularly from the Mediterranean basin. Nuclear weapons might perhaps serve as an umbrella for nonnuclear forces operating in the region against a local state—say Iraq or Iran—that might possess nuclear weapons. In such cases, French threat or use of nuclear weapons, especially against a nonnuclear power, would confront serious political and moral objections for what might be dubious strategic gains. President Mitterrand's announcement in February 1991 that France would not retaliate with nuclear weapons against Iraqi use of chemical agents suggests the sensitivity of French leaders and military planners to the limits of nuclear weapons in response to security threats arising from the south.[60]

France may also find itself checked by a nuclear state outside of Europe. France's strategy of *faible au fort* (from the weak to the strong) might conceivably be turned against it. This scenario presents something of an intellectual stretch to envision how it might play out. France's nuclear capabilities would appear adequate, and no less so after modernization, to deter such an attack. Less clear is whether a determined opponent in the developing world—another Saddam Hussein—would be intimidated by French nuclear threats. French nuclear forces might well be incapable of launching a successful disarming preemptive strike against a nuclear rival, a case that admits no margin of error.[61] The renewed interest in space surveillance and in antimissile systems would appear to be related to these possible strategic scenarios.[62] These contingencies, however, beg the question of containing or arresting the proliferation of mass-destruction weapons and of long-range delivery systems in the developing world, adverse trends that French possession of nuclear weapons serve more as an unintended model to emulate than as a barrier to halt the spread of these weapons.

In Europe, the tight integration of strategic, prestrategic, and conventional forces, previously stipulated by French nuclear doctrine, has now been essentially rendered moot since the precipitate dissolution of the Soviet Union. Ground-launched prestrategic forces—Pluton or Hades—will all but be eliminated from the French arsenal. These cuts appear to be a response to the demise of the Soviet threat and to German concerns. They are also in step with changes in Eastern Europe, whose nations are embarked on the long road toward democratization and free markets and are hardly suitable targets for short-range French nuclear weapons. These cuts also keep pace with the September 1991 accord between the United States and Russia to eliminate all short-range ground-based nuclear systems, carried by missiles or delivered by artillery in Europe.[63]

Aircraft-launched nuclear systems are the core of France's prestrategic forces. The size of these forces would appear to be larger than any anticipated need for them, whether to deter an adversary or to signal intent of further nuclear escalation. There exists no clear or coherent strategic doctrine to guide their use or how they might be employed to cover conventional forces or manage a crisis. This failing has less to do with French oversight of the problem than the difficulty of defining plausible scenarios in which nuclear weapons would be useful or, conversely, would not be a hindrance—even a net negative factor—in advancing French strategic interests. Plans to develop smaller nuclear warheads to create a wider range of options between using large explosive nuclear charges or inaction have been put on hold by President Mitterrand's declaration of a moratorium on nuclear testing. This decision would appear to give stopping proliferation in the developing world—and vertical proliferation among nuclear states—priority over adding new, slippery rungs to France's deterrent ladder.

One significant shift in French thinking and operations is to position the army and tactical fighter aircraft for prompt intervention abroad. The army is now essentially out of the nuclear business. A reversal in priorities has emerged. In November 1991 the army chief of staff announced the creation of two distinct joint staffs, largely composed of army and air force officers. The first was focused on Europe; the second on possible crises arising in the developing world.[64] Improvements in French planning for conventional operations have not been matched, however, by parallel increases in conventional strength. Just the opposite. The army will be reduced from 280,000 to 230,000 by 1997. These limits are further narrowed by the proscription against using conscript forces outside of France (though volunteers did serve in Desert Storm), by a declining defense budget relative to GNP, and by an overhang of costly procurement programs left over from the cold war era. Given these constraints, it is difficult to see how French conventional forces will be better prepared sometime soon than they were for Desert Storm for conflict and peacekeeping roles in Europe or in the developing world.

Incentives for Multilateral Cooperation

If constraints are many and opportunities for initiative and innovation few, it is not surprising to discover—repeated assertions in official rhetoric of French autonomy and independence to the contrary notwithstanding—that French strategic policy, including nuclear weapons and doctrine, is assuming increasingly multilateral dimensions. The choices facing French planners are not easy or straightforward. The menu of choices covers both the framework for preferred cooperation and the modalities of cooperation to be pursued. Some sense of this complexity is suggested by figure 9.1, "Security in Europe: Membership of International Organizations," which summarizes the multilateral organizations concerned with different dimensions of European security, including NATO and its newly organized North Atlantic Coopera-tion Council (NACC), the European Community, the WEU, and the CSCE. These formal frameworks, while important, should not overshadow the importance that French leaders attach to privileged bilateral relations within (or outside) these multilateral organizations. By far the most important one it has is with Germany. Under varying circumstances the United States (e.g., Desert Storm) or Britain (nuclear policy) may take precedence.

From the early years of the Fifth Republic, formally commencing with the Fouchet Plan, the preferred framework for French security policy has been the European Community, anchored to close Franco-German bilateral cooperation. The reasons are several and long-standing as key elements of the Gaullist legacy. Critical is the assurance that German power would be committed to Europe and to French security interests. Through a united Europe, French influence would be bolstered both to balance the United States and the Soviet Union (now only the United States) and, conversely, to provide a measure of insurance against the possibility of U.S. withdrawal of its conventional forces and nuclear umbrella.[65] Cooperation in the 1970s was primarily fostered through the coproduction of military equipment, notably tactical missiles and the Alpha-Jet.[66] Little or no progress, however, was achieved in military planning and operation until President Mitterrand's creation of the FAR and the organization of a joint French-German brigade. If the fighting ability of FAR was marginal, its existence eased Bonn's concerns about France's commitment to Germany's defense and about the timely engagement of French forces in the event of hostilities with the Warsaw Pact. With Germany firmly fixed within NATO's command struc-ture, the Franco-German force bridged, however tenuously, France to NATO. These ties were furthered in the 1980s through increased French interest and priority assigned to the Western European Union.[67]

Figure 9.1: Security in Europe
Membership of International Organizations [1]

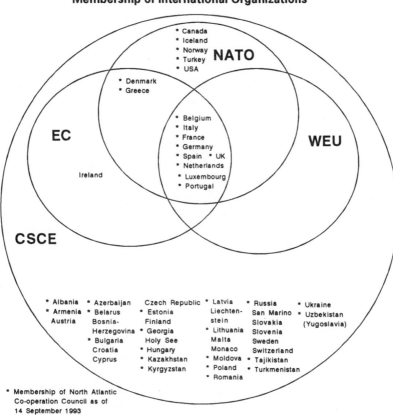

* Canada
* Iceland
* Norway
* Turkey **NATO**
* USA

* Denmark
* Greece

EC

* Belgium
* Italy
* France
* Germany
* Spain * UK
* Netherlands
* Luxembourg
* Portugal

WEU

Ireland

CSCE

* Albania	* Azerbaijan	Czech Republic	* Latvia	* Russia	* Ukraine
* Armenia	* Belarus	* Estonia	Liechten-	San Marino	* Uzbekistan
Austria	Bosnia-	Finland	stein	Slovakia	(Yugoslavia)
	Herzegovina	* Georgia	* Lithuania	Slovenia	
	* Bulgaria	Holy See	Malta	Sweden	
	Croatia	* Hungary	Monaco	Switzerland	
	Cyprus	* Kazakhstan	* Moldova	* Tajikistan	
		* Kyrgyzstan	* Poland	* Turkmenistan	
			* Romania		

* Membership of North Atlantic
Co-operation Council as of
14 September 1993

Source: United Kingdom, Ministry of Defence, *Statement of the Defence Estimates*;
1992 (London: HMSO, 1992). p.17; and *Radio Free Europe/Radio Liberty, Research Report* 2:37 (14 September 1993), p.14.

1. The civil war in Yugoslavia has created at least four states: Bosnia, Herzegovina,
Croatia, and Serbia. The first three are members of CSCE; Serbia is currently not.

These tentative French steps toward greater European defense cooperation were propelled by the success of the Single European Act (SEA), signed in February 1986 and in no small part the product of French initiative. They were given increased urgency and direction by the unanticipated speed of German unification. Activated again were the traditional concerns of the Gaullist legacy about German power and security policy.[68] Europe and the European Community are now central to the multilateralization of French security policy.

The Single European Act broke the taboo blocking EC discussion of foreign and security policy and integrated the process of European Political Cooperation (EPC) into the EC treaty system.[69] Under Article 30, "The High Contracting Parties"—that is, the European Council—is supposed "to formulate and implement a European foreign policy."[70] Ministers for foreign affairs and the commission were charged to meet at least four times a year to discuss foreign policy matters within the framework of the EPC. The member states also pledged their commitment to "closer cooperation on questions of European security" to "contribute in an essential way to the development of a European identity in external policy and economic aspects of security."[71] While the Community itself was precluded under SEA from addressing military questions, it was charged to coordinate its work with the Western European Union and the Atlantic Alliance to ensure that nothing under Title III of the SEA "shall impede closer cooperation in the field of security" between the Community and these organizations.[72]

The Maastricht Treaty went much further in developing the institutional framework for European defense. The treaty no longer prohibits the Community and, specifically, the Council of Ministers, from discussing military and defense problems. In a declaration attached to the treaty, the European Council invites the foreign ministers of the Community to reach a Community policy on the CSCE process, disarmament and arms control in Europe, nuclear nonproliferation, and the economic aspects of security, particularly the transfer of military technology. For the first time, the principle of qualified majority voting is introduced to cover decisions on implementing a previously adopted policy, presumably also including security and defense matters.

The treaty also codifies the informal arrangements developed by the EPC and the WEU on behalf of the Community. The treaty identifies the WEU under Article J.4 as "an integral part the development of the Union."[73] The WEU is at once charged "to elaborate and implement decisions and actions of the union which have defence implications" and to harmonize those initiatives with the obligations of the member states under the Atlantic Alliance.[74] The ambiguity of the Community's role as the European pillar within NATO or as the basis for a separate EC defense policy is deliberately introduced into the treaty and into the Community process. Further precision about roles and missions is left to bargaining and compromise among members. What is significant is that Maastricht consigns debate and bargaining over a common European foreign and defense policy, including the definition of Community and WEU roles, to the process of Community building and union itself.

The Single European Act and Maastricht have established a formal process for the development of a "Common Foreign and Security Policy" (CFSP). A division of labor has been gradually recognized between the EC, as a civil and economic agency, and the WEU, as the principal vehicle for expanding the Community's reach over security and defense issues. The WEU has several advantages.[75] Member states do not suffer from the same reflex opposition to the WEU's treatment of security questions as they do when these same states are acting within the Community process. Changing organizational hats makes a difference. The internal organization and powers of the WEU do not raise the issue of an integrated or federal body as EC processes do. The WEU, unlike the EC, also narrows the gap between France's refusal to return to NATO and the interest of France's EC partners, particularly Germany, to draw a willing Paris into consultations on European security and defense.[76] EC members that are not members of the WEU—Ireland, Denmark, and Greece—are also less of a drag on progress by their absence.

French determination to make the EC-WEU the central pillar of European security and defense coordination, resting on close Franco-German cooperation, runs counter, of course, to the preferences of many NATO-EC states, especially Great Britain, the Netherlands, Denmark, Italy, and Portugal. They worry about weakening NATO as the primary guarantor of European security. They also raise objections about duplication of effort, confusion in command structures, the prospects of Franco-German domination, and the potentially negative effects of a European-centered security policy on the U.S. commitment to Europe.[77] The compromises reached in shaping the security and defense clauses of the Maastricht Treaty between the Franco-German and British-Italian positions, reflect this ongoing struggle. No less do the deliberate temporizings of these concerns in the declaration of NATO ministers in November 1991, which blurred the differences between the EC-WEU vs. NATO frameworks and the discord among alliance members over which framework to use in developing post-cold war security policies for Europe.[78]

The successive decisions of NATO ministers in May and of Paris and Bonn in October 1991, respectively, to create separate rapid-action forces have transformed the sometimes theological debate over European security into questions of military planning and operational readiness. NATO's proposal to create Immediate Reaction Forces (IRF) and larger Rapid Reaction Forces (RRF) under British command met initially with stiff French opposition. Foreign Minister Roland Dumas and Defense Minister Pierre Joxe alternated in attacking the NATO plan as an effort to undermine European cooperation, to implicitly reintegrate French forces into NATO by isolating France. According to Paris, all this had no clear purpose since the NATO force was being formed before a new strategic concept rationalizing its creation was articulated. This was a point well taken but hardly decisive since there was little prospect in the haze of the post-cold war security environment in Europe—witness Yugoslavia—that the Western states would soon agree on a common strategy.[79]

The Franco-German proposals for reinforcing the foreign and security policymaking functions of the Community and WEU as well as for creating a Eurocorps came under no less U.S.-British criticism for all the usual reasons.[80] In May 1992, the Paris-Bonn proposal crystallized in the form of a 35,000 to 40,000 joint force to be built on the Franco-German brigade. Other states of the WEU were invited to join. Three missions were specified for the corps: European defense, peacekeeping missions in Eastern Europe, and humanitarian and environmental protection.[81] The Franco-German accord established corps headquarters at Strasbourg and defined the legal status for the stationing of troops of both countries in their respective countries.

The differences among member states within NATO and the WEU over the Eurocorps and its competition with the IRF and RRF, while real, can be exaggerated. The Eurocorps is presently more a political gesture than an effective military force. Even when organized and operational, it will have limited capability and will be hindered by differences of language, training, doctrine, and equipment.[82] There are also problems associated with the use of French conscripts abroad and of German reluctance to send forces out of NATO areas, an impediment that may be gradually overcome if the dispatch of German forces to support the UN relief mission in Somalia is any indication. What is perhaps of more long-run significance is that the French have gradually softened their stiff stance against double or triple hatting their forces without formally breaking with Gaullist strictures against reintegrating French forces in NATO.[83] In December 1992, Paris and Bonn circulated a memorandum to their NATO allies assuring them that the Eurocorps would be placed under the "operational command" of the Atlantic Alliance in case of threat to European security.[84]

If greater flexibility can be expected from Paris in cooperating with NATO, especially through Bonn, it does not follow that France will return to NATO. While France clearly wishes to keep the United States in Europe, it has no interest, nor feels much compelling reason, to increase U.S. influence by widening the political or geographic scope of the alliance. France resists extending the scope of the alliance beyond Europe. Even in Europe, it would essentially confine the alliance to the territories of its members. It is a reluctant member of the North Atlantic Cooperation Council (NACC) that links NATO and former Warsaw Pact states. It is skeptical of the NACC's effectiveness and wonders what the organization is supposed to do since the Bush administration essentially ruled out NATO's extension to Eastern Europe. Meanwhile, the NACC's membership approaches that of the CSCE. Not only does it appear redundant, but it is a competitor to the CSCE.

Paris prefers to rely on the CSCE to be the vehicle for extending security assurances to Eastern Europe. The CSCE is seen as more inclusive, comprising the neutral states, which are not members of the NACC. With Bonn, Paris also favors gradual development of CSCE institutions—the Conflict Prevention Center (Vienna), the Center for Free Elections (Warsaw), and Secretariat (Prague)—as well as their reinforcement by codifying the legal authority of the CSCE and by creating a court of arbitration and conciliation to resolve differences before they arise. The Eurocorps might also assist in peacekeeping functions under the CSCE aegis. Some support for the French view can also be found within the WEU,[85] but not enough to forestall the NATO accord of December 1992 with former states of the Warsaw Pact to cooperate in possible peacekeeping roles. France acceded to the accord despite its challenge to the French alternative that envisioned assignment of such roles to the Eurocorps acting under WEU-Community aegis within the context of the CSCE.

France's support for the CSCE may be viewed as a part of a larger French strategy to reinforce the United Nations and its position within that body as a Permanent Member of the Security Council. The priority extended to the UN by President Mitterrand is not new. It is part of an evolving process initiated as early as 1978 when President Giscard d'Estaing upgraded the UN in French arms control and disarmament thinking and strategy.[86] Absent from public pronouncements by French officials is Gaullist skepticism about that body's capacity for peacekeeping and peacemaking. French military and diplomatic resources are now actively engaged in U.N. operations in the Middle East, Yugoslavia, Cambodia, and Somalia; its global arms control and disarmament initiatives are centered on the United Nations. Contrast this change with de Gaulle's characterization of the UN Geneva talks of the 1960s on disarmament as a "chorus of old men and women in an ancient tragedy: 'Insoluble difficulty! How to find a way out?' "[87]

Despite reservations, France has supported UN resolutions authorizing military intervention in Iraq, and it took the lead in creating a UN relief mission and so-called safe havens to protect the Kurdish minority in northern Iraq and Shi'ites in the south of the country. Sizable French military units participated in Desert Storm and in the humanitarian effort in Somalia. Meanwhile, some 4,000 French troops were sent under UN command as a peacekeeping force in Yugoslavia. And departing clearly from previous Gaullist practice, the government of Pierre Bérégovoy proposed in September 1992 to permanently earmark 1,000 French troops for the UN's peacekeeping roles. They would be available upon the determination of a state of emergency threatening to peace.[88] What is remarkable about this offer—its immediate practical effect is doubtless limited—is the relaxation of the Gaullist principle that insists on France's direction of its forces and, conversely, on a prohibition against assigning them to a foreign command (i.e., a UN peacekeeping mission). This French shift also contrasts, not without irony, with the U.S. view that opposes such a loss of control over its own contingents,[89] a position reflected in the command arrangements governing the Desert Storm and Somalia operations.

The final remaining option for increased French cooperation in security policymaking is Britain, principally in nuclear affairs.[90] Such a development, which has been pondered since the inception of both programs over a generation ago, would realize President Mitterrand's call for examining the possibility of a European nuclear deterrent. Under any guise, such a deterrent would necessarily have to rely on Franco-British forces. Incentives for cooperation purportedly arise from several sources. There would be specific advantages in principle in coordinating patrols, targeting, intelligence, and communications. Both nations also have a common operational requirement for a long-range air-to-ground missile for their nuclear delivery aircraft—the British Tornadoes and the French Rafale.[91] While the French are planning to develop such a missile alone, if necessary, they would profit from British financial and technical support.

If progress were made on these fronts, Britain would then be France's nuclear bridge to NATO and to the United States, given the close working relations between London and Washington and the dependency of the British deterrent on U.S. technical and financial support. Such cooperation would underwrite reliance on nuclear weapons for Europe's security when the need and legitimacy for such weapons are again being questioned throughout Europe. Cooperation might also conceivably lead to the creation of a Nuclear Planning Group within the WEU, much like its counterpart in NATO, that might blur the distinction within the Community and WEU between nuclear and nonnuclear states.[92] Other benefits might include joint Franco-British and European coordination of efforts to slow or stop proliferation.

The prospects of overcoming the obstacles to Franco-British cooperation are not bright. Since the inception of both independent nuclear deterrents, the option of increased cooperation has been much discussed but little forward progress has been registered. There is likely to be little, if any, advance in the near future, notwithstanding an entirely different international environment from that which prompted the nuclearization of both countries. Neither country, as Lawrence Freedman suggests, has the same targets, patrol schedules, command-and-control systems, or standard operating procedures for the use of these forces. British forces are committed to NATO and those of France are pointedly kept outside of NATO control.[93] United States permission would have to be sought for almost every important facet of anticipated Franco-British cooperation as a consequence of British obligations incurred in securing U.S. nuclear assistance to build and arm the Trident system. There is little likelihood that Washington will relax these strictures to permit even greater information exchange between London and Paris than exists now, although there is precedent, largely hidden from public notice, for some loosening of U.S. restrictions.[94] Finally, a French-British deterrent lacks both urgency and credibility. The threat of a military attack from the East has diminished; the U.S. deterrent is still more credible than a Franco-British force; and Franco-British geopolitical and strategic nuclear thinking and policies remain fundamentally at odds.[95]

In sum, French governmental and elite opinion appears to accept that Gaullist legacy should be retained in its outward trappings: national independence and strategic autonomy, particularly with respect to nuclear weapons; no reintegration into NATO's military command structure (although closer cooperation with the Atlantic Alliance's political institutions is conceivable); and continued pursuit of Gaullist intergovernmental notions of greater cooperation in security and defense policy in Europe. Germany remains the favored partner. The Franco-German partnership is also the core of Paris's conception of European union and of a common foreign and security policy, much as it was under the Fourth and Fifth Republics, however much the modalities of this partnership have changed over the years. What cannot be assured is France's ability to can channel the power of its allies, especially Germany, to do its bidding and to gain allied acceptance of France's singular strategic position and its claimed leadership within the Community and WEU, where it is the weaker partner. It is not a dominant power in any of the European security organizations depicted in figure 9.1. France cannot match U.S. or German power. Nuclear weapons offer little tangible or discernible leverage against German political and economic power; they played no role in modulating or slowing German unification. The dilemmas confronting Paris are acute. Paris cannot dictate the direction of the Community or the WEU, much less that of the Atlantic Alliance, but it must increasingly rely on both to promote its security and foreign policy aims and interests.

French Arms Control and Disarmament Policy

France is pursuing an essentially dual strategy in nuclear and conventional arms control and disarmament talks. In Europe, it shows little disposition to enter into nuclear arms talks that might lead to a negotiated reduction of its forces. In the improbable event that a European nuclear deterrent might be created, this would not necessarily impede or preclude current French nuclear modernization plans. The projected cutback in French strategic nuclear forces, the withdrawal of ground-launched systems from service, and decreases in spending for nuclear forces parallel the de-emphasis on nuclear weapons in Washington and Moscow. They also anticipate pressures, should they again arise, to draw France into nuclear arms reduction talks.

French governing circles see little, if any, benefit from such negotiations. The French would be bargaining away what they perceive to be their principal means of defining Europe's security framework in the post-cold war environment. There is a concern that in possessing modest nuclear bargaining chips relative to the United States and Russia—with few delivery vehicles and with about 400 warheads from all sources[96]—France might have to concede more in national nuclear capabilities than it would receive in return in reliable international security guarantees. There is also the perceived danger that once a nuclear arms accord had been reached, reasserting the importance of nuclear deterrence and national independence in using or threatening them will become difficult, even impossible, either because of external pressures or domestic opposition or both.[97] France risks granting other states a *droit de regard* over its nuclear forces, a cardinal sin in Gaullist nuclear theology.

The three conditions defined by President Mitterrand in 1983 before the United Nations as prerequisites for French participation in global nuclear arms talks remain official policy. These require (1) U.S. and CIS nuclear reductions "comparable to those of the other nuclear powers"; (2) "the elimination of existing asymmetries in conventional forces in Europe, as well as the outlawing of chemical and biological weapon manufacturing and storage"; and (3) "an end to the 'unbridled arms race' in the fields of ballistic missile defences, antisubmarine warfare and antisatellite weapons."[98]

The strategic and domestic political supports on which these conditions rest have progressively eroded since their initial pronouncement. If the United States and Russia reduce their arsenals to the levels of the Bush-Yeltsin accord of spring 1992 (i.e., 3,000 to 3,500 warheads), the French would be under international pressure to make a proportional contribution to nuclear force reductions. As suggested above, it might be able to withstand these demands, noting the unilateral cuts that it has initiated and that even if Moscow and Washington reduce their strategic warheads to 3,000 to 3,500, that level would still be seven to eight times the size of the current French arsenal. This line of argument is hardly supported by invoking the second reservation. It would appear to be essentially fulfilled: the Warsaw Pact is dissolved; Russia has withdrawn most of its forces from Eastern Europe; those in Poland return home in September 1993; those in Germany will depart in 1994; offensive forces have been sharply cut in pursuit of the CFE treaty and of overall domestic, economic, and political reform; and what remains of Russian military forces will pose no threat to Western Europe sometime soon. Indeed, the strategic problem facing Paris is retaining, not cutting, U.S. troops in Europe in light of this diminishing threat. The third condition concerning antimissile systems remains official policy, although it is apparently under serious review. There appears to be some sentiment, still much below the surface of discussions of those within the security community, of French interest in developing such systems in cooperation with France's allies.[99] At least one close adviser to Jacques Chirac, leader of the Gaullist majority in the ruling coalition supporting the Balladur government, has openly advocated French-American cooperation in developing an ABM capacity. Such a shift in policy would essentially nullify an important condition for French entry into nuclear arms control and disarmament talks in Europe.[100] This discernible shift in the debate, by no means welcomed by all participants, responds to the prospects of increased proliferation as a consequence of the breakup of the Soviet Union, the progress of Iraqi nuclear development, which exceeded expert projections, and the prospects of continued horizontal and vertical proliferation in other volatile regions of the developing world.[101] Whether an effective ABM system at an acceptable cost can be developed against these diffuse threats remains problematic.

If France is reticent about either reducing its nuclear forces through international negotiations—preferring unilateral, nationally directed moves—it has assumed an entirely different posture about out-of-Europe arms control and disarmament talks. Outside of Europe, it is keen on multilateral accords covering all states, i.e., international regimes with clear enforcement and verification mechanisms. The empty chair of the de Gaulle era has been replaced by what might be characterized as the policy of musical chairs, but where the music never stops, as French negotiators shuttle between different arms control and disarmament forums, some organized by the French themselves, to address an ever-expanding agenda of security problems. In an address to the United Nations on June 3, 1991, President Mitterrand pledged French cooperation to limit nuclear proliferation; to prohibit chemical and biological weapons; to ban the transfer of long-range delivery systems and technology under the Missile Technology Control Regime (MTCR); to strengthen international control of the transfer of conventional arms; to share satellite information to improve international crisis control and assure regional rivals through increased transparency; and to bolster the UN's role in arms and disarmament discussions and regional security.[102] Even before the June 1991 statement, France had played a major role in the CFE conventional arms talks that culminated in the CFE treaty signed in Paris in November 1990. Paris was also the seat of the international conference on the control of chemical weapons in 1989 and the signature by 127 countries of a treaty in January 1993 to ban chemical weapons.

Subsequent to the announcement of this ambitious arms control and disarmament agenda, France signed the Nonproliferation Treaty, whose provisions it had observed since the late 1960s as a matter of national interest rather than as a treaty obligation. Like Washington, Paris appears keen on blocking regional nuclear proliferation in the developing world. In a surprise move Prime Minister Bérégovoy announced in April 1992 the suspension of French nuclear tests for the remainder of the year. Although the suspension did not please some elements of the RPR-UDF coalition, which swept the March elections in March 1993, the French president, in accord with the Balladur government, announced on July 4 that France would continue to observe the moratorium. (On nuclear policy, cohabitation met its first test.) The reaffirmation of nontesting was taken in response to President Clinton's decision on July 3 to suspend U.S. testing until September 1994. The French presidency noted "that it would favor a complete test ban treaty provided it is global and verifiable."[103] A combination of international factors—widespread opposition to testing, particularly from states near the Muroroa test site, and U.S. and allied pressure to negotiate a test ban treaty—are strong inducements for continuation of the moratorium. If the U.S. continues its suspension of tests under the Clinton administration, it will be harder for any French government to abandon the moratorium, even if China resumes testing, the likely trigger to French resumption of testing. France may well be pressured in the future to sign a partial or comprehensive test ban treaty.

If the French president (who is still principally responsible for defining French nuclear policy) and the Balladur government were to accede to outside pressures, France would be opting for a policy of placing greater reliance on international guarantees over national nuclear modernization and strategic singularity in pursuing its security interests. Such a choice might be squared with the constraints under which French security policy may have to adapt to eventually, but such a change in orientation could not be easily reconciled with the Gaullist legacy and its unilateralist strictures. France will not be able to pursue both national and multilateral policies with equal vigor in the absence of outside assistance, particularly the kind of technical aid enjoyed by Britain, such as access to data from U.S. tests and U.S. conduct of nuclear tests on behalf of the United Kingdom. While there is some precedent for such assistance to France, prospects of U.S. cooperation are not good given congressional and Pentagon resistance to such proposals, not to mention widespread popular opposition to horizontal proliferation, even within the Atlantic Alliance.[104]

It is hard to say at this writing where France might be headed on the test ban issue. French critics of the moratorium are quick to argue that nuclear modernization should come before staunching proliferation. They cite a need to develop smaller, more selective nuclear weapons to bolster the French deterrent and the role of nuclear weapons in the post-cold war era. Jacques Isnard summarized the specific concerns of those opposed to the test moratorium: "Experimental detonations . . . make possible further miniaturization of the explosive charge, the safest possible ignition control system, improvements in cost-effectiveness of designs, enhancement of certain ground effects over others, adjustment of the mix of ingredients, and the development of 'stealth' technology to help the missile avoid premature detection."[105] The conditions attached by President Mitterrand to a test ban—globality and verifiability—provide a way out for France if a comprehensive test ban treaty cannot be negotiated with all real or would-be nuclear powers. The French president openly criticized the North Korean nuclear program during his tour of Asia in summer 1993, but other looming nuclear states, like Iran, Pakistan, or India, may undermine a strategy of international accords on arresting nuclear testing and prompt French decision-makers to again go it alone by resuming testing and accelerating France's nuclear modernization.

These views must contend with countervailing arguments supporting continuance of the test moratorium. Threatening large-scale demographic destruction is so final and formidable that even partisans of nuclear deterrence do not believe that it is credible except under the most dire circumstances. It appears particularly suspect to rely on nuclear weapons to protect French forces operating abroad or to a foster a particular French interest, particularly under circumstances in which France itself is not directly under threat of attack. Domestic and international opinion would certainly limit French recourse to the high explosive yield weapons, which currently comprise the bulk of the French arsenal, ill adapted—if at all—to the kinds of threats emanating from the developing world. If proliferation can be halted in the developing world, the French need for a nuclear deterrent—at least one of the size and sophistication now contemplated for the twenty-first century—will lose much of its strategic logic and justification.

FRENCH NUCLEAR AND SECURITY POLICY: IMPLICATIONS FOR THE UNITED STATES AND THE WESTERN ALLIANCE

Several trends appear to be emerging in post-cold war French security policy. First, nuclear weapons and deterrence are losing their centrality. Expenditures for nuclear systems and modernization are down, and the rate of spending is slowing; the future nuclear arsenal is being reduced; prestrategic forces are being limited to air-launched systems; and the army has all but lost its nuclear role. Arms control and disarmament policy have upgraded nonproliferation of mass destructive weapons as a priority as well as French cooperation with the United Nations in promoting regional stability. France's signature of the Chemical Weapons Convention (CWC), adherence to the NPT, and the 1992 moratorium on nuclear testing underscore the greater significance attached by French strategic planners to arms control and disarmament considerations over nuclear strategic modernization and operational readiness. These are major departures from classical Gaullism. Nuclear weapons are now only one, albeit critical, component of an expanding conception of strategic policy within which conventional forces and arms control and disarmament are vital elements.

These trends do not imply in any way that the French consensus is moving to eliminate nuclear weapons sometime soon. The diminution of the French nuclear forces can be explained on several grounds other than a zero option: a declining threat from Eastern Europe, needed cost reductions, and the perceived diminishing marginal return on investment on deterrence from nuclear weapons in meeting France's strategic needs. Modernization plans, if contemplated, will yield a qualitatively superior long-range striking force. The Triomphant-class submarine and S45 and, later, M5 missiles, will be longer range and more accurate. The Rafale will upgrade the air-launched segment of the nuclear deterrent. Cooperation with allies, principally Britain and, conceivably, the United States, could improve the French arsenal without resort to nuclear testing or to large expenditures for nuclear weapon systems.

Conventional force modernization and aerospace capabilities along a wide front are now central priorities of French defense planning. Shifting spending and armed force organizational priorities in these directions will not be easy, nor will they necessarily be crowned with success. Internal constraints are formidable: expensive procurement projects in the pipeline, caps on the percentage of GNP devoted to defense under conditions of lagging economic growth, no clear doctrine or strategic plan to guide new procurement choices,

French commitment to a *levée en masse* (more responsive to the shared historical values of the French security culture than to current external imperatives), and a rapidly diminishing arms industrial base on which to maintain a nationally independent weapons acquisition policy. External constraints are no less real *and* understood by French security elites: the diminishing utility of nuclear weapons, the urgent but slipping prospects of European unity, the need to preserve U.S. presence, and the gap between enlarging French security interests and diminishing national means, which can be narrowed, if not necessarily closed, by international cooperation, but almost certainly at the expense of further compromise of the Gaullist legacy.[106]

In an ideal world, French security policy might be represented as a series of concentric circles. A tight Franco-German alliance occupies the first ring; the second is composed of the European Community and the WEU as expected outgrowths of the Paris-Bonn axis leading to political union and a common foreign and security policy; in the third ring is a Europe from Vladivostok to Vancouver, covering the states of the CSCE, including the United States and Russia; and in the final ring is the United Nations in which France occupies privileged position as a member of the Security Council. Implicitly bolstering this set of concentric and symmetrical rings is NATO and U.S. nuclear and conventional power, accessible directly by Paris or through its partners, principally Germany.

There is less than meets the eye, however, in characterizing French security policy as the harmonious integration of several reinforcing concentric circles. Lost from sight is the hard fact that on several fronts France has had to modify its preferences to suit those of its stronger allies, principally the United States and Germany. The command structure of Eurocorps will be implicitly incorporated into NATO planning. The corps' peacekeeping roles in Europe are likely to be subordinated to NATO's rapid-action forces. The NACC may well be the principal means of developing NATO-Eastern European consensus on a new European security regime, in which case the CSCE would then be placed in the position of ratifying *faits accomplis* achieved elsewhere. Lost from view, too, are hard choices over weapon systems, doctrine to guide choices and planning, multilateral frameworks within which to work France's will, the modalities of French cooperation, and the in- and out-of-Europe conflicts in which French power will be engaged. Under the best of circumstances these choices would be daunting.

The very range and complexity of these choices, whose implications can only be dimly perceived, strain the domestic consensus on strategic policy even if goodwill and selfless interest were assumed on the part of all competitors within the French security policymaking process. Cohabitation will hardly reinforce consensus. The security consensus survived the last period of cohabitation in 1986-88, but not without strain both to the security consensus itself and to French institutions, principally in the sharing of power over defense and foreign policy between the president and a prime minister from rival parties.[107] The permeability of domestic and foreign policy makes it increasingly more difficult to insulate security and foreign policy problems from the domestic struggle for power or from other policy issues concerned with social welfare or economic development. Witness the controversy over agricultural policy within the European Community, the linkage between monetary union and the prospects of a European identity in defense, and the social tensions across the Community occasioned by immigration.

All the news is not bad. The cold war is over and a general war in Europe has never appeared more distant in this century. Nor is French security policy fundamentally at odds with the larger interests and aims of the United States or with those of other democratic, market-oriented states of the developed world. France remains one of the few states of the developed world where the domestic consensus, however strained at present, is still committed to a strong national defense. The debate in France is over its modes and costs, not over whether France should assume a less active role in creating a new world order. What the Western states have created, notwithstanding profound differences among them, is the clear outline of a security community that stretches from the Pacific Ocean to the Oder-Neisse, no small achievement against the background of four hundred years of internecine warfare in Europe.[108] That the contentious peoples and states of this vast region, with Washington, London, Paris, and Bonn as key centers of decision, should differ over the structure, governance, and processes of bargaining and negotiations of this security regime should not be surprising. Like Samuel Johnson's talking dog, it is remarkable that the dog talks at all, not that it talks badly. The object to be preserved and promoted, then, is this security community, not this form of intervention force or another. From this wider perspective, French power is a source of strength, not weakness, a point that falls on deaf ears in Washington.

Second, the Gaullist legacy has been adapted to the constraints under which it must operate. Remember that de Gaulle himself renounced empire when its costs abroad and divisions at home proved to be impediments to the maximization of French power and influence in world affairs. Under proper coaxing and self-restraint by France's allies, the Gaullist legacy can be expected to be adapted once again to external and internal imperatives. Gaullism should not to be identified with its modalities, say, the refusal of French forces to be integrated into NATO. The essence of the Gaullist legacy is really twofold.

Gaullism, first of all, asserts national independence and autonomy in disposing of France's military power as suits the real and perceived interests of the French state and people. On this score there is little difference between France's behavior and that of its alliance partners. Other member states are as free as France to withdraw their forces; the United States has not been hampered in tapping its NATO assets to meet out-of-area needs in Southeast Asia, the Middle East, or the Persian Gulf or to use NATO bases for support of its forces (and not always with the knowledge or consent of its allies).

Gaullism also makes a more galling claim that France enjoys a special status and a privileged position to define the security order of Europe and the world community. There is little indication that French elites—or the French people—are ready to abandon that latter claim, however much they may otherwise be divided or Delphic in asserting the Gaullist legacy. Resistance to its relinquishment will not be made any easier by the obvious fact that France lacks the power to unilaterally define its special international role and privileged status. It must instead assume the role of *demandeur* while pretending otherwise.

Allies can help to relax the potentially adverse effects of this psychological and political impasse by focusing more on the substance of French policy than on its inevitable atmospherics and tedious stylistics. That requires the United States to welcome French willingness to cooperate in "multiple hatting" its forces for national, European, NATO, and UN roles. Command, communications, and coordination mechanisms will be awkward but not insurmountable if greater interoperability can be achieved. What is important is maintaining the bond between France's national will and French forces. Insisting on canons, however tested and proved, of military efficiency under NATO or U.S. auspices are likely to meet with resistance. The December 1992 communiqué of the NATO Defense Planning Committee that "welcomed the initiative of France and Germany to establish a European Corps" appears to be a step in the right direction.[109]

The security community of the Western states remains a coalition in which all alliance commitments are fundamentally conditional. Under these circumstances, allies, and particularly the United States, can ease the impediments of Gaullist intransigence, most pronounced when French weakness is evident. This can be done by stressing the convergence of allied policies on nuclear arms, on the heightened priority being assigned to conventional forces where the Western alliance states hold a clear technological and military advantage, on closer cooperation in arms acquisition, on coordination of global and regional arms control and disarmament efforts, and on operational readiness and planning for the projection of military forces in European conflicts (the former Yugoslavia) or elsewhere (the Middle East or Africa) where the Western security community faces common, if differentially impacted, dangers. None of these steps will be easy for American policymakers who sometimes exhibit some of Gaullism's less redeeming qualities of Olympian self-assurance and omnipotence. But absent progress along these dimensions of cooperation, including a major role for France, there is the real and palpable danger that the Western states, having won the cold war, will lose the peace.

NOTES

I should like to thank Philip Gordon and David S. Yost for their help in composing this chapter.

1. Several works trace the evolution of French nuclear policy. In chronological order these include Wilfrid Kohl, *French Nuclear Diplomacy* (Princeton: Princeton University Press, 1971); Edward A. Kolodziej, *French International Policy under de Gaulle and Pompidou: The Politics of Grandeur* (Ithaca: Cornell University Press, 1974), esp. 69-175; Michael Harrison, *The Reluctant Ally: France and Atlantic Security* (Baltimore: Johns Hopkins University Press, 1981); and David S. Yost, *France's Deterrent Posture and Security in Europe, Part I: Capabilities and Doctrine,* Adelphi Paper No. 194 (London: International Institute for Strategic Studies [IISS], 1985), and *Part 2: Strategic Arms Control Implications* (London: IISS, 1985); and Diego A. Ruiz Palmer, *French Strategic Options in the 1990s,* Adelphi Paper No. 260 (London: IISS, 1991).
2. NATO Press Service, "The Alliance's New Strategic Concept," agreed to at the meeting of the North Atlantic Council, Rome, November 7-8, 1991, p. 15.
3. What is or is not Gaullist orthodoxy is subject to a wide number of often conflicting opinions. For a recent, notable effort to define this legacy through time, see Philip H. Gordon, *A Certain Idea of France: French Security Policy and the Gaullist Legacy* (Princeton: Princeton University Press, forthcoming).
4. These nuclear policy processes are compared by Edward A. Kolodziej in "Nuclear Weapons and Policy Stability," in *Do Institutions Matter?,* ed. Bert Rockman and Kent Weaver (Washington, D.C.: Brookings Institution, 1993).
5. John G. Mason, "Mitterrand, the Socialists, and French Nuclear Policy," in *French Security Policy in a Disarming World,* ed. Philippe G. Le Prestre (Boulder, Colo.: Lynne Rienner, 1989), pp. 49-84; Harrison, *Reluctant Ally*; and Gordon, *A Certain Idea.*
6. Philippe G. Le Prestre, "The Lessons of Cohabitation," in *French Security Policy,* ed. Mason, pp. 15-48.

7. Jolyon Howoth, "François Mitterrand the 'Domaine Réservé': From Cohabitation to the Gulf War," *French Politics and Society* 10:1 (Winter 1992): 43-58.

8. Pierre Hassner, "Un chef-d'oeuvre en péril: Le consensus français sur la défense," *Esprit,* no. 136 (March 1988), pp. 71-82.

9. Foreign Broadcast Information Service (FBIS), *Western Europe,* April 27, 1992, p. 26.

10. Ibid., p. 28, reprinted from *Le Figaro,* April 16, 1992. See also the critical remarks of Jacques Baurnel, ibid., pp. 28-29, which also appeared in *Le Figaro* on April 21, 1992.

11. Heuré Delcher, "L'opinion publique française et les problèmes de défense en 1991," *Arès* 13:5 (1991-1992): 83.

12. *Le Monde,* October 14, 1992. Estimates are those of Jacques Isnard. See the remarks of Defense Minister Pierre Joxe, FBIS, Western Europe, June 7, 1991, p. 20. Joxe has since returned to a policy keyed to the preservation of the triad. *Le Monde,* September 17, 1992.

14. See, for example, François Heisbourg, "Défense Française: La Quadrature du Cercle," *Politique Internationale,* no. 53 (Fall 1991); Frédéric Bozo, "La France, l'OTAN et l'avenir de la dissuasion en Europe," *Politique Etrangére* 56:2 (1991); Pierre Joxe, "Défense et Renseignement," *Défense Nationale* 47 (July 1991); and the symposium on strategy in *Stratégique: La Stratégie Francaise,* 1/92, no. 53.

15. *Le Monde,* April 4, 1991, and colloquium on "Un nouveau débat stratégique," Paris, September 29, 1992, speech of Defense Minister Pierre Joxe, text supplied by the French Consulate, New York.

16. Speech of Prime Minister Pierre Bérégovoy, before the Institut des Hautes Etudes de Défense Nationale (IHEDN), September 1992, text supplied by the French Consulate, New York. 17. See Lawrence Freedman, "Britain, Nuclear Weapons and the Future of Arms Control," chapter 8 in this volume.

17. See Lawrence Freedman, "Britain, Nuclear Weapons and the Future of Arms Control," chap.8 in this volume.

18. *Le Monde,* January 12-13 and 24, 1992. President Mitterrand echoed sentiments already expressed by a close political ally, Jacques Delors, European Community president, in "European Integration and Security," *Survival* 33 (March-April 1991).

19. See the remarks of Joxe and Bérégovoy in nn. 13 and 14.

20. The role of the developing states in Gaullist international policy is sketched in Kolodziej, *French International Policy,* pp. 447-598.

21. One recent attempt to revive interest in nuclear weapons appears in the symposium sponsored by the journal *Défense Nationale.* See the views of several nuclear proponents described in Paul-Marie de la Gorce, "Dossier: Le Nucléaire militaire," *Défense Nationale* (March 1993).

22. Few observers and almost no American policymakers throughout World War II and through the cold war—with the exception perhaps of President Richard Nixon—have grasped these essential elements of French strategy, rooted in shared elite assumptions in France, across the political spectrum, about France's role in world politics and its purportedly privileged role in defining a new world order. For an exception, see David S. Yost, "France and West European Defence Identity," *Survival* 33:4 (July-August 1991).

23. The implications of German unification for French security, economic, and foreign policy interests have spawned a wealth of articles and commentary in France. See, for example, the symposium on the subject in *Politique Etrangére,* no. 4 (Winter 1991).

24. Important segments of the Gaullist party, joined by Communist deputies and a scattering of support from the UDF and followers of the right-wing nationalist party of Jean-Marie Le Pen, the National Front, were opposed to the treaty. See the debates over constitutional revision pereparatory to the September referendum and the remarks of Marie-France Garaud and Philippe Séguin, Gaullist partisans. Both rejected the treaty as an "unacceptable abandonment of sovereignty in essential areas." *Le Monde,* April 15 and May 7, 1992. There is something of a false debate between Gaullist notions of intergovernmental cooperation and federalism as the basis for European union. There appears general consensus that union will have to develop more on intergovernmental lines than along federal principles. Maastricht actually strengthens the role of heads of government and states and does little to develop the powers of the European Parliament or the institutional ties of its members with their constituents. David S. Yost and Ronald Tiersky discuss French options toward Europe in the following articles: David S. Yost, "France in the New Europe," *Foreign Affairs* 69:5 (Winter 1990-91); Ronald Tiersky, "France in the New Europe," *Foreign Affairs* 71:2 (Spring 1992).

25. Superpower mediation is traced and analyzed in Roger E. Kanet and Edward A. Kolodziej, eds., *The Cold War as Cooperation* (Baltimore: Johns Hopkins University Press, 1991).

26. These budgetary constraints and their implications for French military acquisitions policy and arms sales are developed in Edward A. Kolodziej, *Making and Marketing Arms: The French Experience and Its Implications for the International System* (Princeton: Princeton University Press, 1987).

27. An overview of French military spending is found in Hervé Coutau-Bégarie, "La Politique de Défense de la France," *Stratégique: La Stratégie Francaise,* 1/92, no. 53.

28. Ibid., p. 23.

29. OECD, *Economic Surveys: France* (Paris: OECD, 1992), p. 157ff.

30. Patrice Buffotot, "Force politique et défence en France," *Arès* 13:5 (1991-1992): 35.

31. Maurice Faive, "Les Armements nouveaus, arrivent," *Défense Nationale* (March 1992).

32. Memorandum on "Les Choix pour l'Equipement de Forces," furnished by the French Embassy, Washington, D.C., September 1992.

33. A spirited critique of these spending priorities is found in the analysis of Admiral Antoine Sanguinetti in *Le Monde Diplomatique,* FBIS, *Western Europe,* July 10-11, 1992, pp. 16-20 in a symposium of the journal, *Armées d'Aujourd'hui,* reported in *Le Monde,* September 17, 1992.

34. Ibid.

35. This lament of what is characterized as a somewhat "bankrupt" commitment to Europe underlies recent thinking about future French strategic policy. See Foundation pour les Etudes de Défense Nationale (FEDN), *Stratégique: La Stratégie Francaise,* no. 53 1/92, especially the remarks of Hervé Coutau-Bégaire, "La Politique de Défense de la France," pp. 23-25.

36. References include IISS, *The Military Balance: 1992-1993* (London: Brassey's, 1992), 233-34; Stockholm International Peace Research Institute, *SIPRI Yearbook 1992: World Armament and Disarmament* (Oxford: Oxford University Press, 1992), pp. 80-84; and Ruiz, *French Strategic Options,* pp. 6-8. IISS lists 15 Mirage IVP, with 13 in storage (p. 233); SIPRI notes 18 (p. 80) as the total available.

37. ASMP refers to *air-sol-moyenne portée.*

38. *Le Monde,* April 1, 1992. A fourth Mirage 2000 squadron of 15 planes is dual-capable and is not counted in the totals of nuclear-configured aircraft.

39. Note that Ruiz Palmer also cites 75 Mirage IIIE aircraft as nuclear capable, *French Strategic Options,* p. 8, though these are being phased out of service.

40. SIPRI, *Yearbook,* 1992, p. 80. The *Redoutable* was capable of carrying 16 M-20 missiles (SLBMs), each with a one megaton warhead over a range of 3,000 kilometers.

41. *Le Monde,* October 20, 1991.

42. FBIS, *Western Europe,* July 9, 1992, pp. 21-26.

43. Agence France-Presse, Juin 9, 1992.

44. Estimates for Britain are based on the assumption that only three of the four submarines will be armed. Thus, three submarines would be armed with 16 missiles, each with 8 warheads, for a total of 384 warheads.

45. Memorandum, "Choix pour l'Equipment," p. 4.

46. Quoted in David S. Yost, "France," in *The Allies and Arms Control,* ed. Fen Osler Hampson et al. (Baltimore: Johns Hopkins University Press, 1992), p. 184.

47. See SIPRI, *Yearbook 1992,* 80, and the review of prestrategic forces by Jacques Isnard, *Le Monde,* April 1, 1992.

48. France, Assemblée Nationale, Commission de la Défense Nationale et des Forces Armées, *Avis sur le projet de loi de finances pour 1993,* no. 2931, October 1992,

cited in David S. Yost, *Western Europe and Nuclear Weapons* (Livermore, Calif.: Lawrence Livermore Laboratory, Center for Security and Technological Studies, November 17-18, 1992). For lower estimates, see FBIS, *Western Europe,* August 14, 1992, p. 23. These figures are derived from an article appearing in *L'Usine Nouvelle,* July 9, 1992. See also FBIS, ibid., June 8, 1992, pp. 25-26.

49. Joxe, "Défense et Renseignement."

50. Michel Paul, "L'Effort de défense et de securité de la France en 1992," *Arès* 13:5 (1991-1992): 67.

51. Philip H. Gordon, *French Security Policy after the Cold War* (Santa Monica: Rand, 1992), pp. 40-41, and Memorandum, "Choix pour l'Equipment," p. 2.

52. Ibid.

53. Paul, "L'Effort de defense," p. 67.

54. Gordon, *French Security Policy,* p. 41.

55. This is the overall message of the works cited in n. 1. See also Robert Gilpin, *France and the Rise of the Scientific State* (Princeton, N.J.: Princeton University Press, 1968).

56. Samy Cohen, *La monarchie nucléaire: Les coulisse de la politique etrangére sous la Ve République* (Paris: Hachette, 1986).

57. These figures are derived from the July-August and November issues of *The Bulletin of the Atomic Scientists:* "Estimated Soviet Nuclear Stockpile," July-August, p. 48, and "Where the Weapons Are," November 1991, p. 49. Strategic nuclear warheads are distributed as follows: Russia (9,650); Ukraine (1,300); Kazakhstan (1,150); and Belarus (100). This number excludes an additional 15,000 warheads of various kinds—strategic defensive and land- and sea-based nonstrategic weapons—dispersed among the nations of the Commonwealth of Independent States (CIS). The nuclear warheads of the CIS are estimated to be carried by 31 delivery systems. Ibid.

58. *New York Times,* October 15, 1992, reports that a number of snags in implementing the cuts agreed to in START and between Presidents Bush and Yeltsin have arisen.

59. See below for a discussion of French arms control and disarmament policy.

60. *Washington Post,* February 8, 1991.

61. Ruiz Palmer, *French Strategic Options,* p. 55.

62. See the report on French changing attitudes in Assembly of Western European Union, *Anti-Ballistic Missile Defence* (Paris: November 1992), pp. 13-14.

63. See Thomas A. Wuchte, "Non-Strategic Nuclear Weapons in the Former Soviet Union: A Case for Alarm?" *Military Review* (forthcoming, 1993).

64. Gordon, *French Security Policy,* p. 37.

65. See Gordon, *A Certain Idea.*

66. Kolodziej, *Making and Marketing Arms,* pp. 156-158.

67. For a brief review of the WEU's revitalization, see Alfred Cahen, *The Western European Union and NATO* (London: Brassey's, 1989).

68. France's emphasis on European security and the critical role assigned to Germany is sketched in Gordon, *French Security Policy,* 9-33, and in *A Certain Idea.* See also Yost, "France in a New Europe"; and Tiersky, "France in a New Europe"; Yost, "France and West European Defence Identity."

69. Juliet Lodge, "European Community Security Policy: Rhetoric or Reality?" in *European Security—toward 2000,* ed. Michael C. Pugh (Manchester, Eng.: Manchester University Press, 1992).

70. *Single European Act,* Title III.

71. Ibid., Title III, Article 6(a).

72. Ibid., Article 6(c).

73. European Report, *European Union Treaty,* Article J.4.

74. Ibid.

75. For a useful summary of the pros and cons of the NATO, the WEU and the EC, and the CSCE, consult Adrian G. V. Hyde-Price, *European Security Beyond the Cold War* (Newbury, Eng.: Sage, 1991), esp. pp. 189-262.

76. Lodge, "EC Security Policy," pp. 62-63.

77. Gordon, *French Security Policy,* pp. 22-23.

78. NATO, Press Service, "The Alliance's New Strategic Concept." See also the report on the conference in *Le Figaro,* November 8, 1991.

79. Gordon, *French Security Policy,* pp. 18-19. See also the report of Claire Tréon, *Le Monde,* May 4, 1991. Most of the French objections to NATO rapid-action forces are summarized in André Dumoulin, "Les Force Multinationales," *Défense Nationale* (August-September 1991).

80. See Mitterrand-Kohl announcement, *Le Monde,* October 17, 1991, and *New York Times,* October 17, 1991; and the concerns of Dutch Foreign Minister Hans van den Broek, *Le Monde,* October 18, 1991.

81. *Le Monde,* May 21, 1992, and *International Herald Tribune,* May 19, 1992.

82. A brief comparison between the RRF and the Eurocorps can be found in United Kingdom, House of Commons, International Affairs and Defence Section, *Research Note: Europe the Next Phase: New European Community Structures for Foreign Affairs and Defence,* May 15, 1992.

83. See statement of Pierre Joxe, *Le Monde,* December 4, 1991, and Joxe, FBIS, June 7, 1991, and "Défense et Renseignement."

84. *New York Times,* December 1, 1992.

85. WEU, Assembly of the WEU, *A New Security Order in Europe,* Document 1309 (Paris: May 13, 1992).

86. French Ministry of Foreign Affairs, *La politique étrangère de la France, textes et documents* (Paris: Documentation francaise, 2ième trimestre, 1978), p. 66.

87. *L'Année Politique,* 1960, p. 497.

88. *Le Monde,* September 25, 1992.

89. Ibid.

90. For example, see Bernard de Bressy, "La Coopération franco-britannique dans la nouvelle donnée stratégique," *Défense Nationale* (April 1992), esp. 81-90. For background, see François Heisbourg, "The British and French Nuclear Forces," *Survival* 31:4 (July-August 1989).

91. These talks have been on and off again for some time. In 1989, for example, talks broke off and then resumed, but no accord has yet been found to develop a missile jointly. See *Le Monde,* May 3, 1989.

92. Most of these purported benefits are ably evaluated by Frédéric Bozo, "Une doctrine nucléaire européen pour quoi faire et comment?" *Politique Etrangère* 57:2 (1992).

93. See Lawrence Freedman, "Britain, Nuclear Weapons, and the Future of Arms Control," Chap. 8 in this volume.

94. Richard Ullmann, "The Covert French Connection," *Foreign Policy,* no. 75 (Summer 1989).

95. Bozo, "Une doctrine nucléaire."

96. If Pluton and Hades nuclear munitions are excluded, and if one assumes 288 warheads eventually for the Triomphant-class submarine force, France would appear to have between 400 (on the low side) to a maximum of 500 warheads and bombs. IISS, *Military Balance: 1992-1993* (London: Brassey's, 1992), pp. 231-32. Villars also notes 400, though these estimates are based on somewhat different methods of accounting. Only 15 Mirage IVP and 45 Mirage 2000N and 20 Super-Etendards are included in my total. Villars, "Désarmement nucléaire les options françaises," *Commentaire* 13:52 (1990-91): 691.

97. These concerns are summarized in Villars, "Désarmement nucléaire," pp. 687-693.

98. Quoted in Ruiz Palmer, *French Strategic Options,* p. 30.

99. See the *Le Monde* editorial analyzing France's decision to declare a moratorium on nuclear testing, April 10, 1992. One of the panels of the symposium on security policy organized by the Ministry of Defense in September, 1992, was devoted to an examination of antimissile systems as a possible strategic priority. Also see Heisbourg, "Défense française," p. 263.

100. Pierre Lellouche, "France in Search of Security," *Foreign Affairs* 72:2 (Spring 1993): 127.

101. Bozo, "Une doctrine nucleaire," pp. 419-21, is particularly critical of the GPAL system proposed by the United States.

102. The text is found in *Le Monde,* June 4, 1991.

103. French Embassy, *News from France,* July 16, 1993.

104. *New York Times,* April 9, 1992. Both parties have since formed an alliance for the March elections. French Embassy, *News from France,* December 4, 1992. Their votes could be important to the Socialist party in runoff elections.

105. FBIS, *Western Europe,* April 27, 1992, p. 26, based on an article, appearing in *Le Monde,* April 10, 1992.

106. See the remarks of Jean-Michel Coucheron, chairman of the Defense Committee of the French National Assembly. FBIS, *Western Europe,* January 17, 1992, pp. 16-17.

107. See Jolyon Howoth, *French Politics and Society,* pp. 43-51; for a current review of party opinion, consult Gordon, *French Security Policy,* pp. 43-51.

108. Karl Deutsch et al., *Political Community and the North Atlantic Area* (Princeton: Princeton University Press, 1957).

109. NATO, Press Service, Communiqué of the Defense Planning Committee, December 11, 1992.

10

Russian Views of Nuclear Weapons

Sergei Rogov

In discussing the view in Moscow of nuclear weapons today, I will speak about three subjects. First, I will give a picture of the current thinking in the Russian military about nuclear weapons. Second, I will briefly comment on the European dimension, the relevance of British and French forces to Russian nuclear views. And third, I will make my own suggestions concerning the future of Russian-American nuclear cooperation.

In the present confusion that exists in the former Soviet Union, where the great military machine that the Soviet Union built turned out to be an army without a state, the Russian military today operates without much political-civilian control. The present debate on Russian defense policy, precisely because it is being conducted almost totally without any political guidance from the leadership of the government, provides a very unusual glimpse on Russian military thinking. Many things which in the past were never said in public about nuclear weapons and nuclear strategy are now being openly proclaimed by the Russian military.

ASPECTS OF NUCLEAR STRATEGY

It seems to me that it is possible to distinguish seven major points made by the Russian military today. The first, and the starting point for all defense thinking, is the recognition that Russia has lost, and lost forever, the conventional superiority it once held. In Europe, for instance, Russian conventional assets, such as tanks, have been reduced radically. If three years ago the former Soviet Union had superiority over all of Europe, now by the CFE Treaty and the Tashkent arrangement of the Soviet CFE quota, the ratio of conventional forces in Europe changed to the following: Russia one, former Soviet republics in Europe one, Eastern Europe one, and NATO three. And when you look at other conventional threats—like being the country which has the largest border with China—clearly there is very little desire on the part of the Russian military to give up reliance on nuclear weapons. At the end of the cold war, because of its faltering economy, the Soviet Union was said to be an Upper Volta with missiles; and there is now no desire on the part of Russia to become an Upper Volta without missiles.

As a result of this fall from conventional predominance—and this is the second point—there have been certain changes in the Russian military understanding of the notion of parity. Some Russian military leaders, including Defense Minister Pavel Grachev, have claimed that Russia has actually given up the notion of parity, which is of course not true. But there is a shift in the understanding of the term. Parity used to be understood as encompassing virtually the whole world; Russia was thought to require parity with the United States, Europe, China, and Japan. Now the definition of parity is more or less limited to parity with the United States, and parity in the strategic field.

Deterrence and Its Definition

The third development is an open recognition of deterrence as the foundation of Russian military strategy. Remember that deterrence was never openly accepted by the Soviet military, which would only go as far as admitting the deterring role of the strategic missile forces. Deterrence was a very bad word in Soviet military thinking; only imperialists would conduct a strategy of deterrence. For its part, the former Soviet military planned for the victory of socialism, and thus created worries and doubts in the West that led to its own nuclear warfighting and counterforce strategies. Now deterrence is proclaimed openly as the foundation of Russian defense strategy.

Yet many Russian military thinkers are urging that deterrence be conducted in a very provocative manner. It is linked with the notion of immediate response to aggression, which in English terms means "launch on warning." There is quite an open debate today whether it is possible to give up launch on warning and take a purely retaliatory posture. Amazingly, in the midst of this unprecedented U.S.-Russian warming of relations, the Russian military and military industry began only a few months ago to make public arguments in defense of launch on warning. A few even called for a preemptive posture by Russia.

The question of targeting is also important to deterrence, and is related to what kind of force structure is needed. The major argument of the Russian military today is that it continues to need counterforce targeting; its vision of a nuclear war remains one of a nuclear exchange with the entire range of military targets to be covered by Russian strategic forces. This argument goes hand in hand with President Yeltsin's declaration last January that Russian missiles no longer target U.S. cities. Later on, Marshal Yevgeniy Shaposhnikov explained that while nontargeting was a nice goal, it would take a long time to implement; but just recently Defense Minister Grachev, who now controls the Russian nuclear button, again said that Russian missiles are not targeting U.S. cities. Nobody explained how this miracle happened.

Another aspect to deterrence is the much greater attention being given to the problems of command, control, communications, and intelligence (C^3I) and early warning. Russian weakness in C^3I is openly recognized, and actually it seems that policy efforts continue to improve command, control, and communications capabilities. There is an understanding that the destruction of the Krasnoyarsk radar—a shoe factory now occupies the site—created quite a substantial gap in the early warning system that the Soviet Union possessed. To make matters worse, most of the early warning stations in the European part of the former Soviet Union are now outside Russia. On July 6, an agreement was signed between the Russian defense ministry and the defense ministries of the other republics providing for cooperation between the independent states in operating early warning and space facilities. Article 1 of this agreement says that all facilities on the territory of each former Soviet republic are the property of that republic—thus removing them from Russian control.

It seems to me that this agreement creates a problem. We know that Ukraine, Kazakhstan, and Belarus became parties to the START agreement. With the spread of early warning capabilities, I wonder, how many parties are there now to the ABM Treaty? The ABM-regulated facilities are now outside Russian territory and they belong to foreign states. So would that mean that there has been a formal violation of the ABM Treaty? Or are Ukraine and a number of other republics entitled to become parties to it?

Tactical Nuclear Weapons and Rationales for Nuclear Use

The fourth overall issue in Russian nuclear thinking involves tactical nuclear weapons. It was rather fashionable a couple of years ago to argue for a complete ban on tactical nuclear weapons. Very few people in Russia do it now. To some extent this change is related to the Chinese problem. While relations with China today are pretty good, a military conflict with China has been and will always be a nightmare for Russian military planners. Concerns about whether Russia is capable of fighting a conventional war with China lead to an emphasis in Russian military circles on the need to keep some tactical nuclear weapons. This decision, of course, relates not only to the Russian posture in Asia but also to its posture in Europe.

The fifth issue is the conventional threat to Russian strategic forces and targets. It is now claimed that the United States and NATO can eliminate most Russian strategic assets, including strategic missiles and bombers, with conventional means. It is not accidental that, in the draft military doctrine published last May, a conventional attack on Russian strategic forces is listed among the possible causes of the use of nuclear weapons.

Western conventional weapons are also held up as a threat to nuclear power stations, chemical plants, and other environmentally hazardous installations. The Russian military drew some lessons in this regard from the Gulf War, where U.S. precision weapons displayed an incredible potential to destroy a nation's economic infrastructure. Again, the new Russian military doctrine says that an attack on these facilities would be seen as the beginning of a nuclear attack on Russia, and would therefore justify a Russian nuclear retaliation.

These various concerns have also led to growing criticism of the Russian commitment to no first use of nuclear weapons. The mission of Russian nuclear forces is being reformulated to encompass not only deterrence of nuclear war, but also deterrence of any aggression against Russia. Guided by this consideration, Russian military leaders openly express their unhappiness about the no first use commitment and claim that conventional attacks against strategic nuclear installations, or some economic targets, may force Russia to use nuclear weapons first.

Strategic Defenses and Force Structure

Sixth is the issue of strategic defenses. Strategic ballistic missile defenses have become popular within Russia, and it is clear that quite powerful pressure groups both within the military industry and the military establishment, which were for a long time supporting strategic defense, favor a Russian-style Strategic Defense Initiative (SDI). This impulse was rather strictly controlled in the Gorbachev period. Today, however, such control is absent, and Russia is negotiating with the United States on problems of strategic defense, including possible changes to the ABM Treaty.

I would not say, though, that this attitude is held by all military or industrial leaders. There are many counterarguments against strategic ballistic missile defenses, or, as the United States now phrases the program, Global Protection Against Limited Strikes (GPALS). Much concern remains that deployment of strategic defenses by the United States will severely curtail guaranteed retaliation by Russia, especially under the conditions of deep reductions of strategic offensive forces. Another counterargument—which, by the way, I share—is that it is not clear against which third-party threat GPALS, or Russian-American GPALS, or even Russian GPALS can be directed. For the United States, such third-party threats as, for example, Saddam Hussein or Kim Il Sung are limited and hypothetical. But for Russia, Great Britain, France, and China they are not hypothetical but real. So if limited ballistic missile defenses have the purpose of preventing of accidental launch or intercepting a launch of a few missiles or a few dozen missiles, then it is possible that there are other ways to deal with such problems, which do not necessarily mean deploying something like GPALS. And there is also a problem of stability, for if GPALS is extended enough to protect Russia against ballistic missile attack, let's say from China, then it is going to be a pretty broad and thick ballistic missile defense. Actually, what it then becomes is territorial ballistic missile defense, something capable of upsetting the strategic balance. The question is, what limits limited ballistic missile defense of Russia?

The seventh and last issue is the force structure of the Russian strategic nuclear forces after the reduction and reorganization of those forces required by START and the Bush-Yeltsin Washington summit agreement obligations. Those proposed changes are meeting with a great deal of criticism among the Russian military, which basically has no enthusiasm about reducing the existing force structure. While understanding that something has to be reduced, it wants to keep the bulk of forces the way they are.

The Russian military makes several arguments against the Bush-Yeltsin agreement. They point to the costs of the reorganization, arguing that those costs—of a new ICBM, or modernized bombers and submarines—are prohibitive, and that Russia is not able to pay for such a structural change. By banning multiple-warhead ICBMs, the agreement will make Russia more dependent on submarine-launched ballistic missiles (SLBMs), and the Russian military believes that the geostrategic position of Russia and the tremendous U.S. lead in antisubmarine technologies makes such reliance very dangerous. Meanwhile the airborne leg of the Russian triad has declined to the point of meaninglessness: Russia has stopped production of Blackjack and Bear H bombers; Ukraine nationalized two divisions of heavy bombers, and Russia now has only two Blackjack bombers in its possession; Ukraine also nationalized a division of naval aviation with Backfire bombers; and there is the eventual possibility of the nationalization of another 40 heavy bombers by Kazakhstan. All of these developments leave Russia with about 80 mostly obsolete bombers, which are seen by many as incapable of reaching the Western Hemisphere.

Finally, there are land-based missiles. The Washington summit agreement would leave Russia with fewer than 300 modern single-warhead missiles. Most of them are in a road-mobile configuration, but the present political instability and problems of command and control have diminished enthusiasm for road mobility, and there is a growing argument that single-warhead missiles have to be deployed in silos. And in this case, to save money, instead of building new SS-25s and putting them in silos, it is suggested that Russia should download some of its SS-18s and SS-19s to single warheads. This is also seen as a guarantee against a sudden breakout by the United States, because with the downloading of the D-5 SLBM from 8 to 4 warheads, the United States potentially has an option to add very quickly an additional 1,750 warheads to its SLBM force. Because the D-5 is a weapon that is alleged to possess counterforce capabilities and can be used in a depressed-trajectory mode with low flight time, in the worst-case scenario it could be used to destroy Russian silos. This is a scenario of disarming first strike which, some in Russia believe the United States will be capable of conducting within the Washington summit agreement.

Russian nationalists and military men are using these arguments to push the Yeltsin government to retreat from the commitment that President Yeltsin made last June. In my view, that would mean a disaster in Russian-American relations. There is no way Russia can succeed in violating the obligations that have been made by President Yeltsin in Washington. My own feeling is that the people who are pushing for such a step know that, and that their real goal is a new cold war between Russia and the United States. This is an important element in the present offensive by the right-wingers, consisting of the diehard Communists and Great Russian nationalists.

EUROPEAN NUCLEAR FORCES

So much for current views of nuclear issues within Russian military circles. What of the European dimension? Quite simply, it does not play an important role. Perhaps as a legacy of the superpower mentality, British and French nuclear forces are not seen as a serious threat. There is much greater concern about the stability of Germany in the future, especially if the United States drastically reduces its military presence in Europe. In this sense I think there is now very little opposition to the presence of U.S. tactical nuclear weapons in Europe. A limited number of those weapons is not seen as a threat to Russia, and is viewed as a stabilizing factor at least during the transition period in Europe. British and French and Chinese nuclear weapons are generally mentioned only in discussions of minimum nuclear deterrence; the combined number of nuclear weapons held by all other nations, it is claimed, represents the lowest ceiling to which Russia or the United States can reduce their strategic forces.

In fact, in the discussion about nuclear weapons in Europe, we must give more serious attention to a serious danger about which I have heard little debate: the possibility of a complete sea change as a result of Ukraine going nuclear. The probability of this, in my view, is very high, and it would have a drastic impact on the entire balance of forces in Europe. We should not forget that Ukraine already is the largest military power in Europe after Russia. A nuclear Ukraine—and possibly a nuclear Kazakhstan as well—might lead to changes in attitudes about nuclear weapons in Germany and perhaps even Japan.

This problem was created because Russia totally mishandled the issue, and Russian policy toward Ukraine was absolutely misguided, raising fears of new Russian territorial claims and other elements of hostility. Moscow's actions produced an image of Russia as the greatest threat to the independence of Ukraine—and I think the image has a basis in reality, because Russia is the only country which can threaten the existence of Ukraine. At the same time, the Russian government—and more specifically, the Russian navy—managed to stage the silly dispute over the Black Sea fleet without any political guidance from the government, and provoked a crisis in Russian-Ukrainian relations. Meanwhile Russia almost ignored the inevitable Ukrainian claims for the ownership of nuclear weapons, with the result that about 3,000 strategic warheads remain in Ukraine and Kazakhstan, which do not belong to any state.

It is clear that Ukraine is not going to admit that those weapons are Russian property. Kazakhstan seems to be wavering between the Belarusan position and the Ukrainian position. Belarus has also not admitted that the nuclear weapons on its soil were Russian property, although it is acting as though they are and seems ready to return them to Moscow. And in responding to these decisions, the United States also committed very serious blunders, choosing to accept at face value vague commitments by Ukraine and Kazakhstan to join the Nonproliferation Treaty (NPT) as nonnuclear states. In the Lisbon Protocol last May, the Ukraine succeeded in selling that very same commitment to the United States again.

The U.S. acceptance of these pledges was a blunder because these apparent commitments are in fact not commitments at all. The Lisbon Protocol and Ukrainian President Leonid Kravchuk's letter to President George Bush do not represent an unequivocal promise to give up nuclear weapons; they actually speak to something else. The Lisbon Protocol made Ukraine, Kazakhstan, and Belarus totally equal with Russia as successors to the Soviet obligations under the START Treaty. Each of them is supposed to implement all the obligations independently. They are supposed to decide between themselves which weapons have to be destroyed, and then they are allowed to deal independently with the United States on all matters concerning the implementation of START. So, from their perspective, these new states have become fully equal partners in the nuclear arms control business.

Then there is Article 5 of the Protocol, in which the former republics pledge to join the NPT as nonnuclear states. Only one thing is missing: when. In the five months since the Lisbon Protocol was signed, Ukraine and other republics did nothing to even begin the process of joining the NPT. President Kravchuk's letter to President Bush that accompanied the Protocol includes a commitment to eliminate nuclear weapons in Ukraine by the year 2000, but this is not a very solid commitment. It is, first of all, a unilateral violation of Ukraine's earlier promise in Alma Ata last December, where it signed an agreement to eliminate all nuclear weapons by the year 1994. How can one be a nonnuclear member of the NPT and keep nuclear weapons?

Kravchuk's letter also makes very clever conditions for the implementation of this seven-year obligation. It mentions "highest national security considerations" as reasons to abandon the promise; and the conflict over the Crimea and other problems between Russia and Ukraine can very comfortably be cited as such excuses. Kravchuk also argues that the nuclear weapons in Ukraine should be destroyed there, a return to his earlier demand last March that all tactical nuclear weapons be disposed of there. Destruction of nuclear weapons in Ukraine would require building a dismantling factory; but there are no such things as dismantling factories, because nuclear warheads are disassembled at production factories. So this demand actually means that Ukraine wants to build a nuclear production site.

Furthermore, the letter claims that nuclear warheads should be destroyed under international control. But nuclear warhead destruction within the START arrangement does not occur under international control; indeed there is no elimination, nor any control over the elimination, of warheads or actual nuclear bombs at all under START. This demand by Ukraine, therefore, actually means that Russia should accept international control over its warheads; yet Russia can do it only if the United States will accept international control, which I think most would agree is quite impossible. So Ukraine's demands in this matter are unreasonable and, it seems, calculated to produce a stalemate.

Finally, Kravchuk says that plutonium and other fissionable materials should be returned to Ukraine and not be used for the production of nuclear weapons by other states. This means that the plutonium in the former Soviet weapons is Ukrainian property; and, by extension, that means that the warheads themselves are Ukrainian property. In this way Ukraine has laid a firm claim to those nuclear weapons.

It seems clear that time is on Ukraine's side. As it gradually becomes a truly independent state, Ukraine will be able—and will wish—to fill the gap in military capability that exists in the nuclear area, and particularly in the realm of nuclear infrastructure. Today, Ukraine can neither control nor produce nuclear weapons; it does not have the expertise or capability to do either. But it can bridge that gap in two or three years, and in my view is currently determined to do exactly that.

RUSSIAN-AMERICAN RELATIONS

The last issue that I will discuss is the Russian-American strategic relationship. During the cold war, the then-Soviet Union and the United States built strategic forces that were planned around mutual nuclear deterrence. Today, this relationship is challenged by a simple question: Deter whom? Deterring what kind of threat? In my view, in either a conventional or nuclear sense, Russia is not going to threaten Europe, and it will not threaten the United States. Yet Russia's change of intention does not mean it has lost the capability to threaten either of its former adversaries. So the question that faces Russia today is, when we recognize that neither side has hostile intentions, but when both sides still possess the capabilities to destroy each other, is there a way out of the mutual hostage relationship?

It is possible to foresee a very major transformation of the Russian-American strategic relationship, something more than a mere continuation of mutual deterrence at lower levels. The major factors that drove the Russian-American conflict have now disappeared. There is no ideological conflict between Russia and the United States, the economic and geopolitical interests of the two countries are in almost total harmony, and there are many interests that the two countries share.

What does this mean in terms of mutual deterrence? It is possible to envision a two-stage evolution of the strategic relationship. In the first stage, which will last probably until the end of this decade, both sides will remain within the model of mutual nuclear deterrence, though the essence of deterrence, the character of deterrence, will substantially change. For one thing, notions of escalation control and fine-tuned nuclear war will lose their meaning. Even if one could imagine a conflict between Russia and the United States with the potential for escalation, the withdrawal of U.S. tactical nuclear weapons from Europe and the elimination of most strategic weapons leave very little room at all for traditional notions of horizontal or vertical escalation control. The decline of escalation control theories will lead to a more basic form of deterrence, and not the highly complicated deterrence aimed at escalation control and nuclear warfighting that existed during the cold war.

During this same period, changes in targeting strategies will also create the potential for a more cooperative Russian-American interaction. The trend is toward the reduction of counterforce capabilities, and without them there is not much substance to the discussion of targeting. By definition this requires a greater focus on countervalue targets, which again returns deterrence to a more basic, more fundamental level.

Russia and the United States can also cooperate in creating a joint early warning system, which may include some jointly run, space-based capabilities. The two sides could also agree to station radars or other sensors at each other's missile fields, sensors capable of registering only one thing: the launch of a missile. That would be a very cheap and reliable early warning system, because even if the existing arrays of radars failed, each side would have a nearly foolproof early warning system in place. And with Russian concerns about early warning today, such a system would help reassure Russian military leaders about the soundness of deterrence. Greater cooperation may also develop in the field of destroying nuclear weapons—in warhead dismantlement and the disposal of weapons-grade materials; and in this sense the plans to sell Russian weapons-grade uranium to the United States can be seen as an important factor in this new relationship.

By the end of this first stage—that is, by the end of the decade—it will be possible to think of going beyond deterrence. The British and French nuclear forces provide an example of a relationship between two nations that, despite disagreements and the ever-present capability to destroy each other, is not one of mutual deterrence. It is something else. It is a relationship in which neither side feels threatened by nuclear weapons in the hands of the other; in which nuclear arsenals are not targeted on one another; in which a military mobilization by one would not lead to reactions by the other; and in which nuclear forces and doctrines are not developed in competition. That, it seems to me, ought to be our goal in the second phase of Russian-American nuclear relations, which will begin at the outset of the twenty-first century. And in this way, it is possible to envision that Russia and the United States will be able to transcend deterrence.

ABOUT THE AUTHORS

PART I: U.S. NUCLEAR POLICY

This section is the product of a small but diverse Study Group drawn from universities, think tanks, and advocacy groups in the Washington, D.C., area. Three study group members—Bill Arkin, Ivo Daalder, and Steve Fetter— prepared outstanding first drafts of study chapters. The Senior Advisory Committee worked independently to improve the report, reading drafts and providing suggestions. CSIS is delighted to acknowledge the financial support provided for the study by the W. Alton Jones Foundation.

It is important to note that, for both the Study Group and the Senior Advisory Committee, affiliation with this report does not signify agreement with every one of its conclusions. Study members reserve the right to differ with the report on individual points of emphasis or policy recommendations.

Senior Advisory Committee to the Study Group

HAROLD BROWN, U.S. secretary of defense under the administration of Jimmy Carter, is a Counselor at CSIS.

ZBIGNIEW BRZEZINSKI is a former U.S. national security adviser and is a counselor at CSIS.

THOMAS SCHELLING is professor of economics and public policy at the University of Maryland, College Park.

Nuclear Strategy Study Group

MICHAEL J. MAZARR was a senior fellow in international security studies at CSIS while directing this study. He has since become legislative assistant for foreign policy and defense in the office of Representative Dave McCurdy (Oklahoma). His affiliation reflects his personal views and his work as a member of the CSIS staff. Appendix 2 is reprinted from Dr. Mazarr's article by the same title in *The Journal of Strategic Studies* (vol. 15, no. 2), June 1992.

WILLIAM ARKIN is director of military research at Greenpeace International.

HANS BINNENDIJK was director of the Institute for the Study of Diplomacy at Georgetown University during the course of this study. He has since become principal deputy director of the Policy Planning Staff of the U.S. Department of State. Mr. Binnendijk's participation in the research and writing of this report occurred before he joined the Department of State. The appearance of his name here does not imply the approval of the U.S. Government.

IVO DAALDER is Director of Studies at the Center for International Security Studies at Maryland and an assistant professor at the School of Public Affairs of the University of Maryland, College Park.

DANIEL ELLSBERG is an analyst with Physicians for Social Responsibility in Washington, D.C.

STEVE FETTER is an assistant professor at the University of Maryland School of Public Affairs. During the academic year 1992-93, he served as a Council on Foreign Relations fellow in the departments of State and Defense.

MICHAEL NACHT is dean of the School of Public Affairs at the University of Maryland, College Park.

DON SNIDER is director of Political-Military Studies, CSIS.

PART II: EUROPEAN NUCLEAR FORCES

LAWRENCE FREEDMAN is Professor of War Studies at King's College, London.

EDWARD KOLODZIEJ is a research professor in the Department of Political Science at the University of Illinois at Urbana-Champaign.

SERGEI ROGOV is deputy director of the Institute for the Study of USA and Canada in Moscow. He is also the founding director of a new independent institute on arms control. His article is a transcript of an oral presentation delivered at CSIS, and not a formal prepared paper.

ABOUT THE EDITORS

MICHAEL J. MAZARR was a senior fellow in international security studies at CSIS while editing this book. He has since become legislative assistant for foreign policy and defense in the office of Representative Dave McCurdy (D-Okla.). His affiliation reflects his personal views and his work as a member of the CSIS staff.

ALEXANDER T. LENNON is a research assistant in Political-Military Studies at CSIS.

INDEX